LEGENDARY LOCALS

OF

NEWTON

MASSACHUSETTS

GAIL SPECTOR

LEGENDARY LOCALS

ISBN 978-1-4671-0146-2

Legendary Locals is an imprint of Arcadia Publishing
Charleston, South Carolina

Printed in the United States of America

Library of Congress Control Number: 2013955142

For all general information, please contact Arcadia Publishing:
Telephone 843-853-2070
Fax 843-853-0044
E-mail sales@arcadiapublishing.com
For customer service and orders:
Toll-Free 1-888-313-2665

Visit us on the Internet at www.arcadiapublishing.com

Dedication
To all of Newton's legends whose stories I was unable to share; I wish I could have included you all.

On the Front Cover: Clockwise from top left:
Jim Koch, founder of Boston Beer Company (Courtesy of Boston Beer Company; see page 50), Louise Bruyn, Vietnam War protestor (Courtesy of Louise Bruyn; see page 25), Ted Williams, Red Sox batting champion (Courtesy of the Boston Red Sox; see page 91), Tenley Albright, Olympic gold medalist (Courtesy of US Figure Skating; see page 93), Ted Mann campaign (Courtesy of the Mann family; see pages 38, 39), James Hyde, first mayor of Newton (Courtesy of Historic Newton; see page 10), Edmund Kelley, founder of Myrtle Baptist Church (Courtesy of Myrtle Baptist Church; see page 70), Leonard Zakim, civil rights activist (Courtesy of Joyce Zakim; see pages 18, 19), Shirley Lewis, gospel and blues singer (Courtesy of Angela Warner; see page 102).

On the Back Cover: From left to right:
Frank Avruch, first nationally syndicated Bozo the clown (Courtesy of Frank Avruch; see page 112), opening of Myrtle Baptist Church (Courtesy of the Myrtle Baptist Church; see page 70).

LEGENDARY LOCALS

OF

NEWTON

MASSACHUSETTS

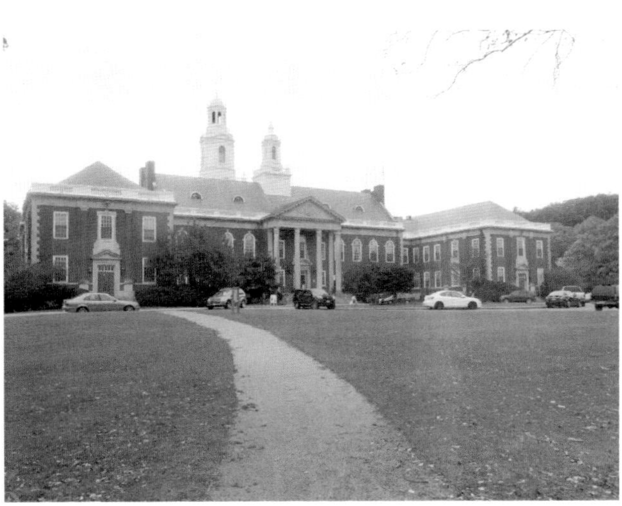

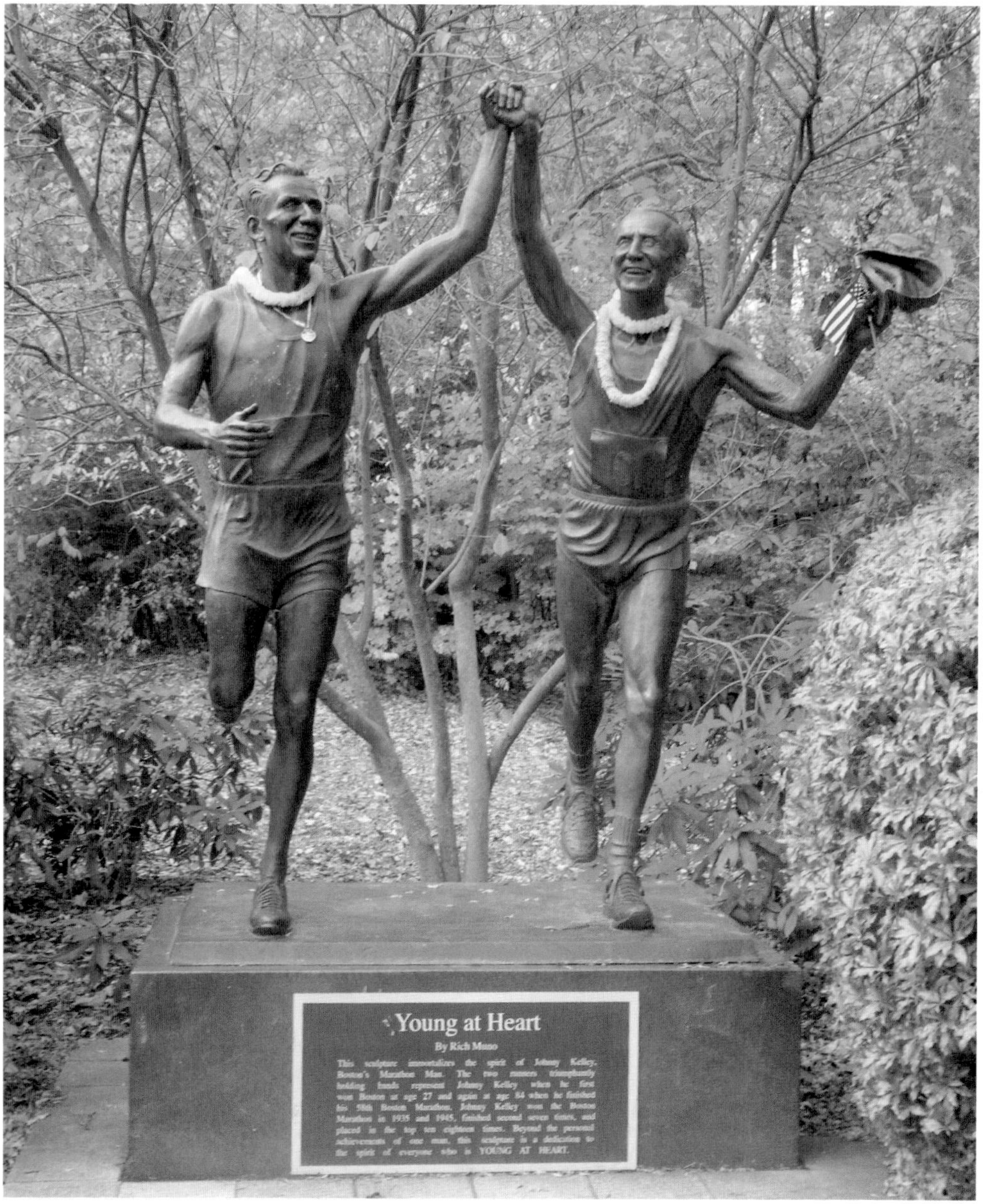

Statue on Boston Marathon Route
This bronze statue, *Young at Heart*, represents Johnny Kelley both winning the Boston Marathon at age 27 and finishing it at age 84. It stands at mile 19 of the marathon route, across from Newton City Hall, and about a mile before the infamous Heartbreak Hill. (Photograph by Gail Spector.)

Page 1: Newton City Hall
Newton City Hall was built between 1931 and 1932 during the administration of Mayor Sinclair Weeks. The architect of the Georgian Revival–style building was the firm Allen & Collens, and the landscaping was designed by the Olmsted Brothers. (Photograph by Gail Spector.)

CONTENTS

Acknowledgments 6

Introduction 7

CHAPTER ONE Early Newtonians 9

CHAPTER TWO Volunteers and Activists 17

CHAPTER THREE Public Servants 33

CHAPTER FOUR Businesspeople, Inventors, and Scientists 45

CHAPTER FIVE Religious Leaders and Groups 69

CHAPTER SIX Protectors 79

CHAPTER SEVEN Athletes 89

CHAPTER EIGHT Actors, Entertainers, and Musicians 99

CHAPTER NINE Artists, Writers, and Media 107

CHAPTER TEN Educators and Students 117

Bibliography 125

Index 126

ACKNOWLEDGMENTS

I would like to extend special thanks to Sara Goldberg and Cindy Stone, curator and former director, respectively, at Historic Newton. Without their help, I could not have told or portrayed the stories of Newton's earliest legends. Likewise, I want to thank Aaron Goldman in the mayor's office for assisting me with ideas, photographs, and everything else I needed, usually at a moment's notice. And, I would like to give a special shout-out to Mayor Setti Warren for his help in clearing impediments and for answering my imploring e-mails.

This book would not have been possible without the excellent resources at the Newton Free Library, including the Newton History collection at newtonfreelibrary.net. The library is among Newton's greatest gems, and I would like to acknowledge all the employees and volunteers who made my research such an easy and enjoyable endeavor.

I thank Greg Reibman for all of his great suggestions, feedback, and support. I am also grateful for the ideas that came from the passionate and engaged blogging community at *Village14.com*. You are all legends.

For help with photographs, I thank GateHouse Media and the Newton TAB, Leise Jones, the Boston Public Library, Chuck Proia, Roger Marrocco, Drew Hyman and Jen Nourse, Rick Mann, Jim Ready, the Library of Congress, Joyce Zakim, Peg Hannigan, David Sellers, Howard and Katy Haywood, Keith Jacobson, the Boston Red Sox, and everybody else who sent, scanned, or allowed me to take a photograph.

For ideas and information about legends, I cannot possibly include everyone but I especially want to acknowledge Tom Mountain and Katy Holmes for their tireless research on those who have served our country, and Police Lt. Bruce Apotheker for his suggestions on those who have served this city.

My editor, Erin Vosgien, deserves a special thanks for her patience and support, as does my husband, Dan Richards, for supporting me technically and emotionally. I also thank Mike Richards for his very valuable last-minute edits.

I cannot express enough gratitude for all I learned about the amazing people who live or have lived in this city. Men and women all over Newton welcomed me into their living rooms, trusted me with their photographs, and shared their stories. It was my honor to write about all of them.

INTRODUCTION

Identifying some 100 or so Newton residents who have made an impact on their immediate community or the community at-large was, without a doubt, the easiest part of writing *Legendary Locals of Newton*. Narrowing down the list was much more challenging. Charged with finding people who have made Newton their homes dating back to the first settlers in the mid-17th century, my task was at times daunting. Newton's houses have always been filled with determined and passionate people, illustrated perhaps by settlers' very first efforts at separating from Cambridge. It took many years and petitions for the Cambridge selectmen to grant the settlers, first, freedom from paying church taxes and then political separation in the way of incorporation as a town in 1688.

It was not until nearly two centuries later, in 1874, when managing a town of 15,000 with a board of selectmen and town meeting was getting too cumbersome, that Newton became a city. The decision to apply to the General Court for a city charter came about after debate over other propositions, namely, for annexation to Boston or for a division of the town. Town meeting voted 1,224 to 391 to change to a city form of government. According to the essay "From Village to City—A Political History" by Carole Fischberg, "Jubilant supporters of cityhood celebrated that night with a torchlight parade through all the villages, with music and fireworks accompanying them."

James F.C. Hyde, who led the drive for changing to a city government, was the first mayor of Newton when it became a city on January 5, 1874. *Legendary Locals of Newton* begins with Hyde, though chronologically he is not its earliest legend. Still, Hyde's biography shows a commitment and love for Newton that repeats itself time and again in this book. Public servants, activists, public safety officers, and educators all share or shared Hyde's dedication to this city.

In choosing the individuals and groups profiled here, I tried to pick people whose imprint on Newton was strong. In some cases, their stories extend well beyond Newton's 18 square miles. Some of the people are Newton natives, while others came here from other parts of the country or world. Still others lived in Newton for just a short time, but we are proud to call them one of ours.

These brief narratives barely illustrate the rich and colorful lives of the people described on these pages. Moreover, these pages hardly contain the number of legends I uncovered and would have liked to include. There is no shortage of stories to tell about our fine city; there was only a shortage of allotted words. In some instances, I mention people in chapter introductions that readers will not see profiled. It was my way of cheating—I was able to sneak in a few more legends without devoting more space to them.

Writing *Legendary Locals of Newton* was a humbling experience. Learning about the brilliant and creative minds that have argued about their visions of Newton, discussed the future of public education, protested wars, composed music, written novels, and helped runaway slaves was both inspiring and thrilling.

The town that began with 50 families is now a diverse, vibrant city housing 85,000 residents in its 13 villages. The railroads that once turned Newton into one of America's first suburbs are now part of a daily routine for many commuters. The city continues to draw new people who come for the location, the schools, and the quality of life. Fortunately for all of us, it also continues to be graced by volunteers like Audrey Cooper (page 24), stores like Newtonville Books (page 61), and teachers like David Gaita (page 121). Newton's legendary locals are as much a part of its history as its first meetinghouse. They make up the fabric of the city that we are so proud to call home.

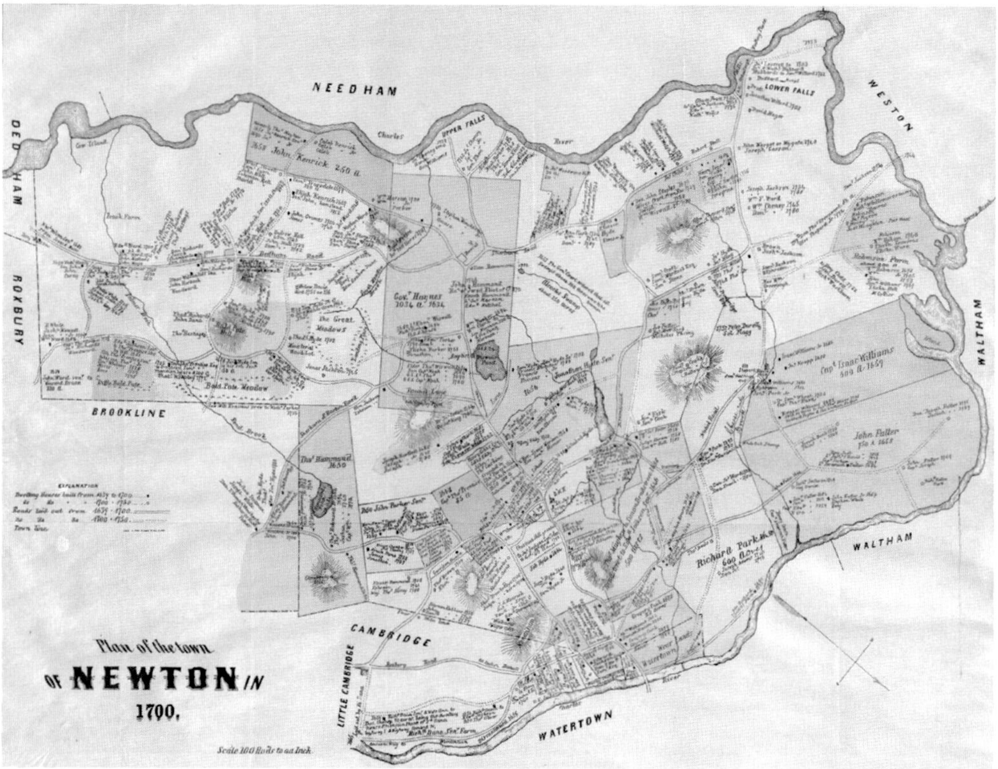

Newton Town Plan, 1700

This map from 1700 shows early development plans for the town of Newton. The map also delineates the roads and homesteads that existed at the time. (Courtesy of Newton Free Library.)

CHAPTER ONE

Early Newtonians

The first person to settle in what is now known as Newton was John Jackson in 1639. Over the next 10 years, a total of seven families settled: two Jackson families, two Hydes, one Fuller, one Park, and one Prentice. Many of them remained forces in Newton for generations.

This chapter touches on a few of Newton's early ancestors. Two—William Jackson and James Hyde—are direct descendants of the first settlers. Others, like John Farlow, attest to the philanthropy that helped build Newton.

Some of the historical figures that have spent time in the city—or more likely the town prior to its incorporation as a city—are not included in this chapter but they are worth mentioning. Paul Revere worked in a room in Newton Corner for some amount of time. George Washington is reputed to have stayed at a Newton Corner inn in 1789. The great Sioux chief, Sitting Bull, rode down Walnut Street to visit Governor Claflin. Charles Dickens walked from Back Bay to Newton Centre. Norse explorer Leif Erikson is said to have explored the Charles River.

Two legends who are relevant in Newton's history but whose stories are not contained in this chapter are Katharine Lee Bates and Rebecca Pomroy. Bates, a graduate of Newton High School, is the author of *America the Beautiful*. Rebecca Pomroy did not settle in Newton until age 55, after having been a nurse to Civil War soldiers and the family of Pres. Abraham Lincoln. In Newton, she founded the Home for Orphan Girls. Open only to Newton residents, girls without homes lived in a family-like environment, attended public schools, shared in household tasks, and remained there until they reached age 21.

James F.C. Hyde, Newton's First Mayor

Newton's first mayor, James Francis Clark Hyde, was no stranger to public service when he was elected to the city's top job in 1873. The seventh in line of descent from Newton's fifth permanent settler, the well-respected man held a number of elected positions. In the more than 50 times that his name was on the ballot, he was never defeated.

Hyde, a popular and accomplished mayor, successfully pushed for the Newton Circuit Railroad, which went into operation in 1886. He is credited with devising and setting in motion the pieces that would connect—through Newton Highlands—one railroad's existing tracks running from Chestnut Hill to Upper Falls with another's existing commuter line at Riverside. In doing so, travel became possible between Newton's villages, and a residential development boom was born.

Long before he was mayor, he was involved in many civic organizations. His love for gardening was impetus for Hyde to organize the Newton Horticultural Society and to serve a term as president. He also formed the Newton Centre Tree Club in 1852, which not only evolved into the Newton Centre Improvement Society but also proved to be the first improvement society in the country.

When James Hyde died in 1898, the *Newton Graphic* wrote in his obituary, "No man has occupied a more prominent place in the history of Newton or possessed a greater degree of respect of its inhabitants." (Courtesy of Historic Newton.)

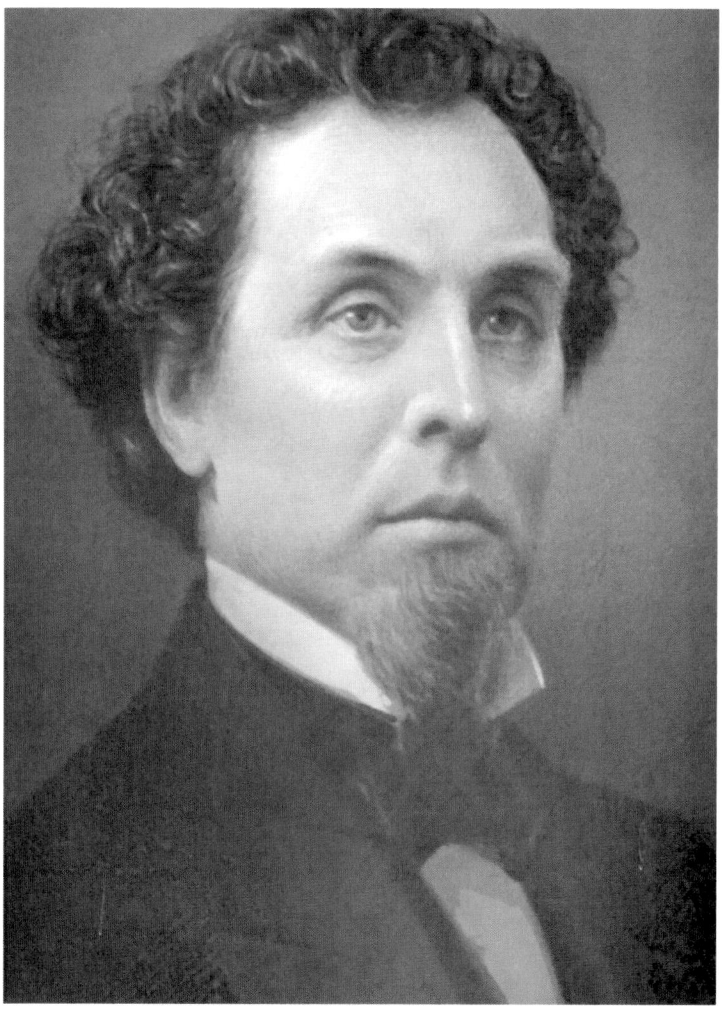

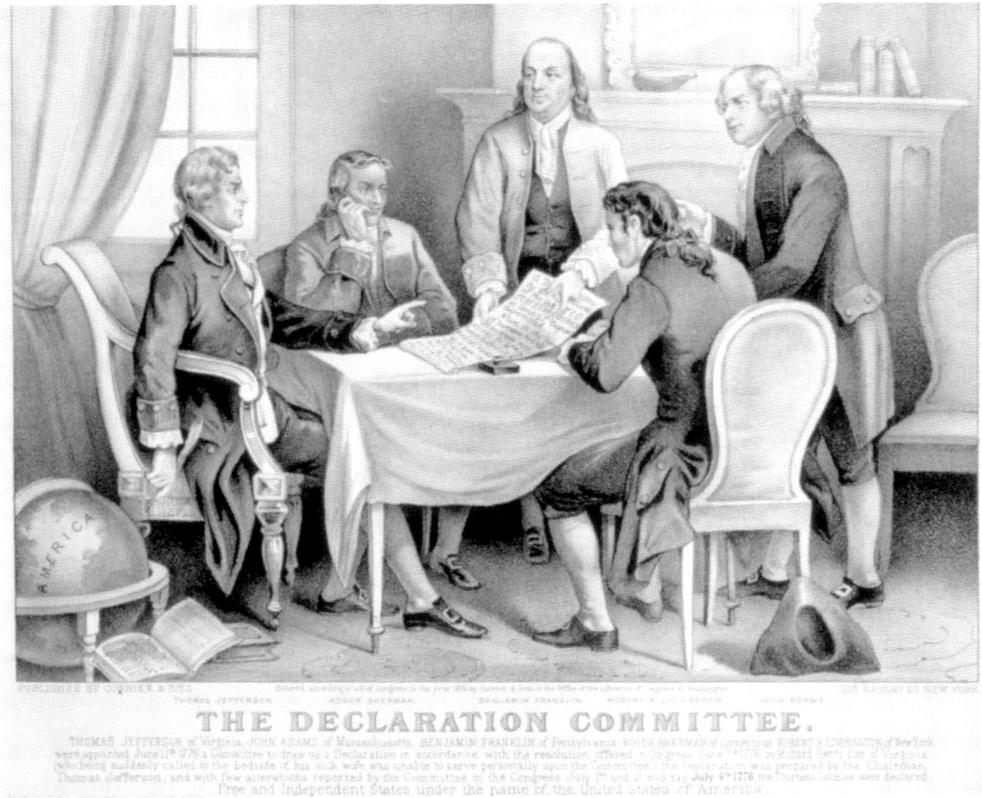

Roger Sherman, Founding Father

Roger Sherman (second from left), born in Newton on Waverly Avenue in 1721, not only signed the Declaration of Independence, but he also served on the Congressional committee that helped Thomas Jefferson draft the document. John Adams called Sherman "one of the most sensible men in the world." Sherman, who did not live in Newton long, was a US senator from Connecticut when he died in 1793. (Courtesy of Library of Congress.)

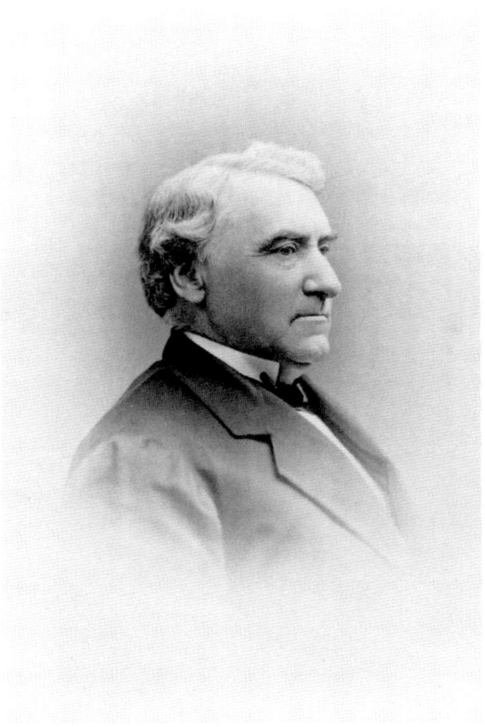

John Farlow, Businessman and Philanthropist

John Farlow was a railroad millionaire who donated a portion of his 40 acres in Newton Corner in the 1880s for the city's first public park. He also gave generously to the fund that formed what eventually became the Newton Free Library. (Courtesy of Historic Newton.)

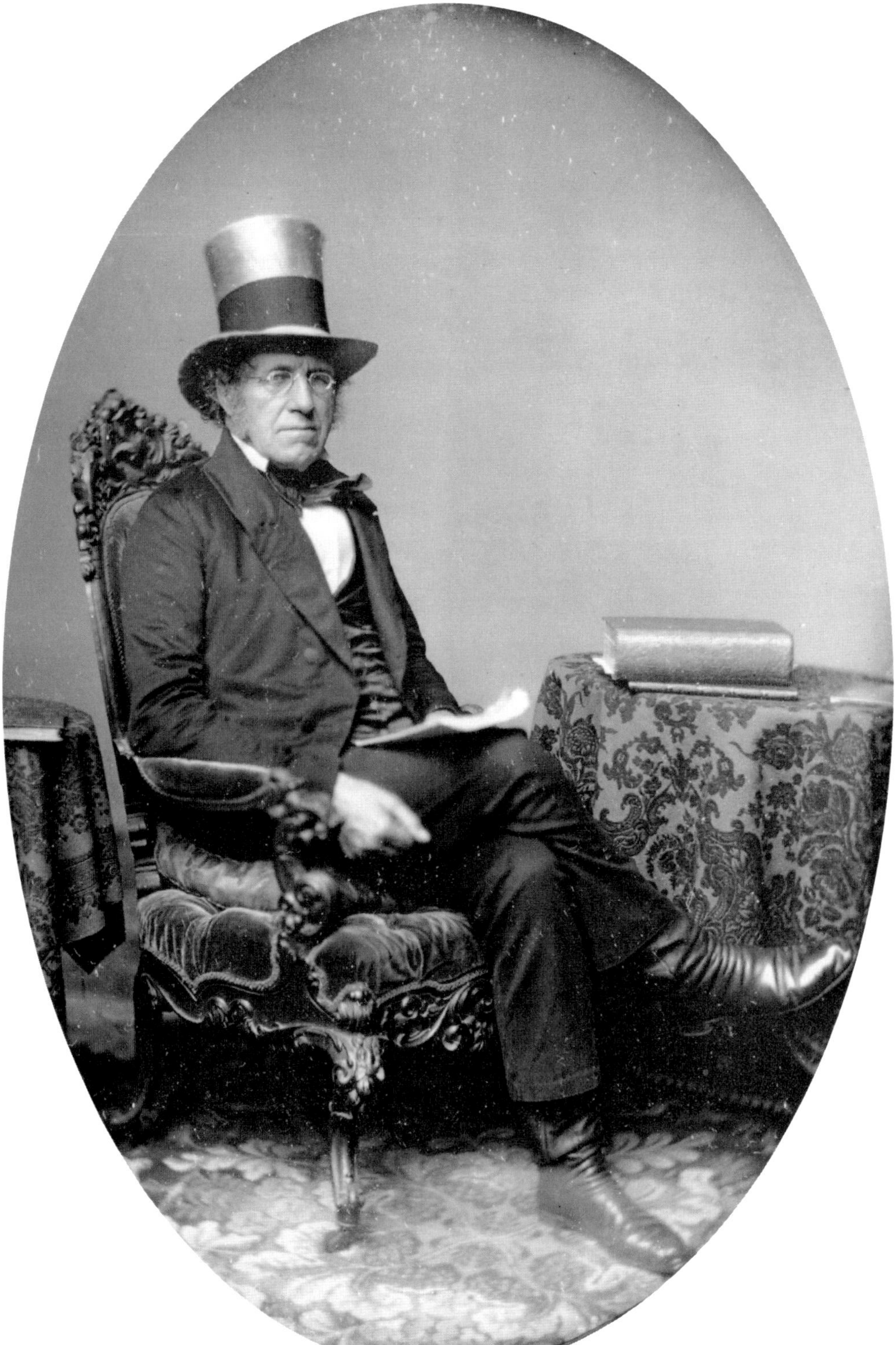

William Jackson, Local Politician and Abolitionist, 1783–1855

William Jackson's family can be traced back to the early 1600s when his ancestors were among the first settlers on the south side of the Charles River in Cambridge. In 1809, his father, Maj. Timothy Jackson, built the existing Jackson Homestead, pictured below, located at 527 Washington Street.

Among other vocations, William Jackson was a politician, serving as chairman of the Newton Board of Selectmen, a state legislator, and one of the city's foremost advocates for the creation of the Newton Temperance Society. He was also an abolitionist who turned the Jackson Homestead into a stop on the Underground Railroad.

Jackson's interest in railroads helped bring about the first passenger line between Newton and Boston. He served in the Massachusetts House of Representatives and was then elected as an Anti-Masonic candidate to Congress in 1832, where he served two terms. (Sketch by Stephen Winchester Dana Jackson; both courtesy of Historic Newton.)

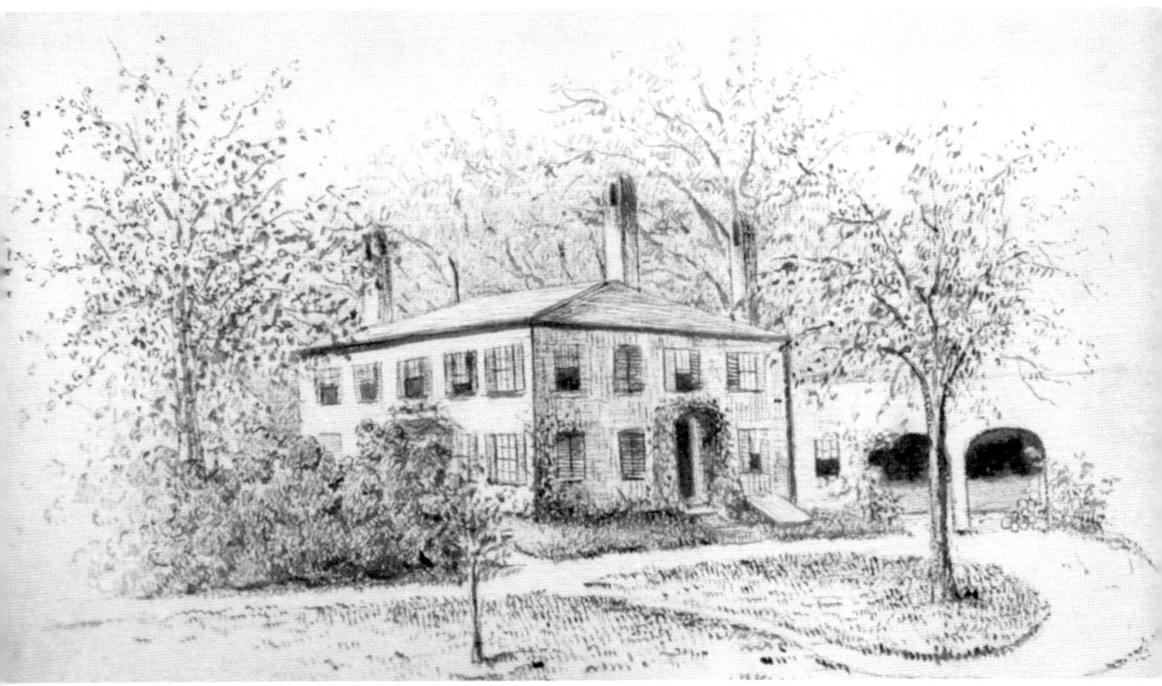

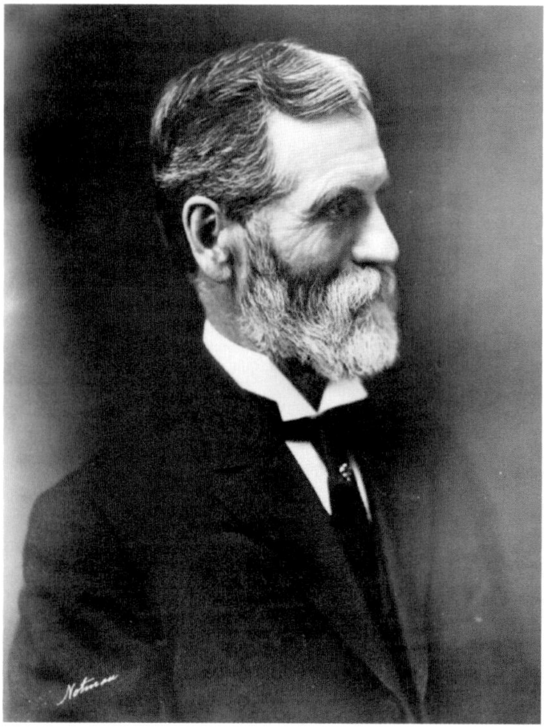

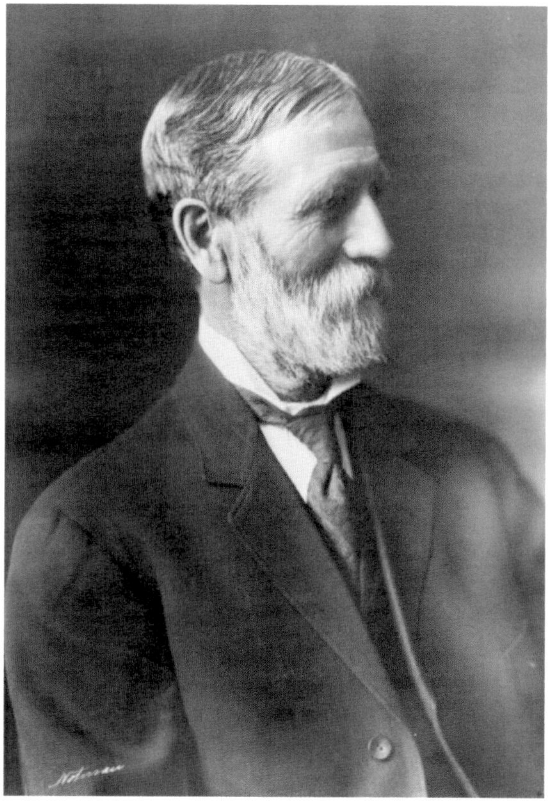

Francis Edgar and Freelan Oscar Stanley, Inventors

Identical twins Francis Edgar (opposite page, above) (1849–1918) and Freelan Oscar Stanley (opposite page, below) (1849–1940), respectively known as F.E. and F.O., were integral to both American and Newton business in the late 19th and early 20th centuries.

The brothers, who made Newton Corner their home for many years, invented the Stanley steam-powered automobile in 1897 for personal use. The auto attracted a lot of attention, giving the Stanleys unexpected business. They formed the Stanley Motor Carriage Company in 1902 and produced the cars in a factory off Galen Street, and the business took off.

The Stanley Motor Carriage Company of Newton built about 14,000 Stanley steam cars between 1898 and 1924.

F.E. Stanley is buried in the Newton Cemetery. His brother is buried in Maine. (Portraits courtesy of Historic Newton; photographs courtesy of Historic Newton and the Stanley Museum of Kingfield, Maine.)

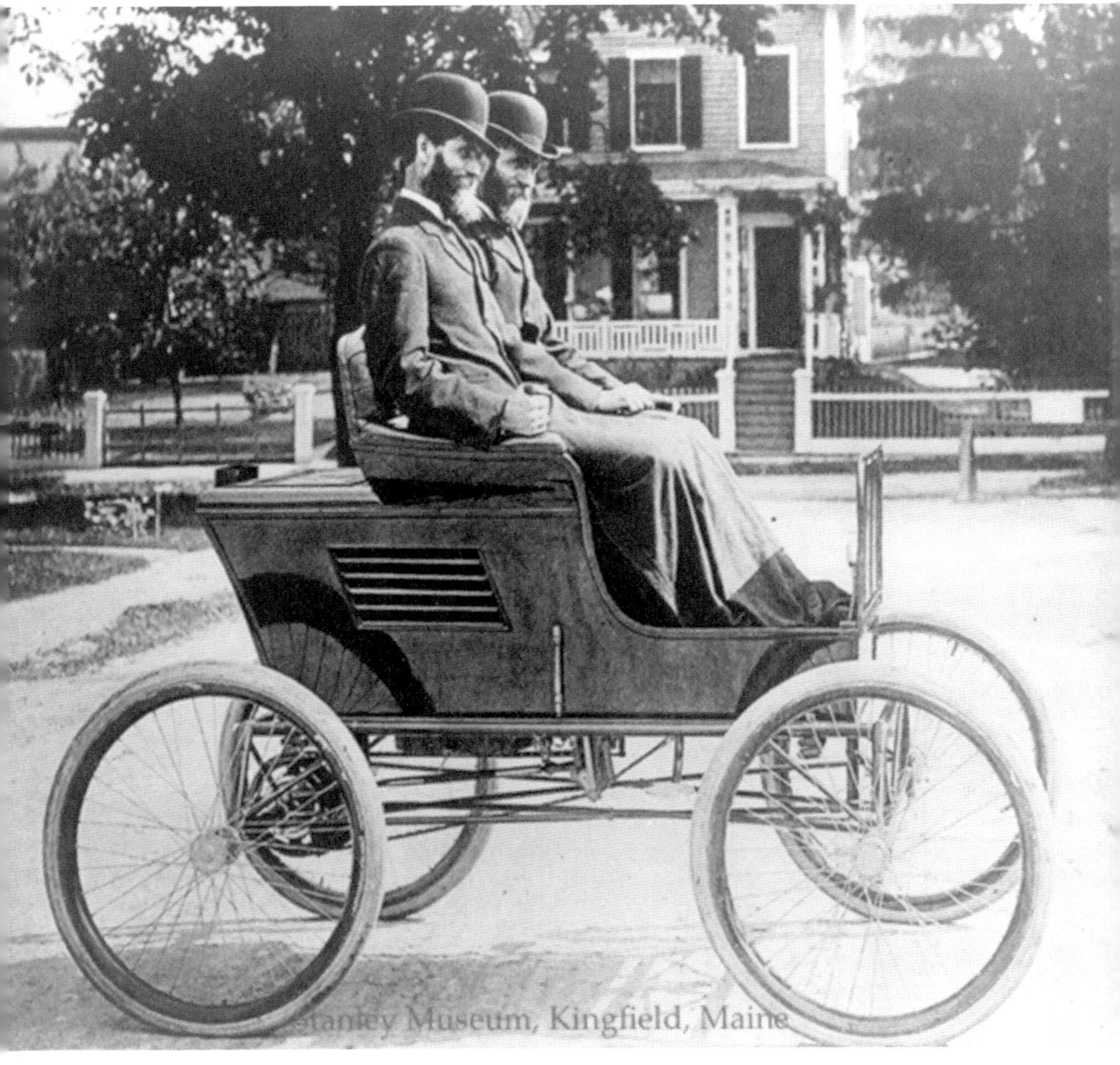

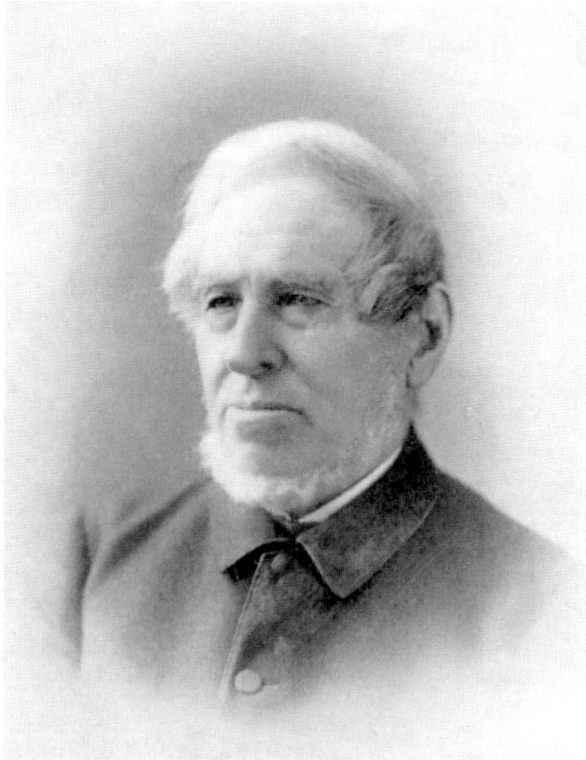

Samuel Francis Smith, Author of "America"
Samuel Francis Smith did not live in Newton in 1831 when he wrote the hymn "America," also known as "My Country 'Tis of Thee," but after he accepted a position as pastor of the First Baptist Church in 1842, he became well versed in Newton's history. Smith wrote *History of Newton, Massachusetts: Town and City from its Earliest Settlement to the Present Time, 1630–1880*. Smith died in 1895 at the age of 87. The tower on the First Baptist Church in Newton was given in memory of Smith. (Courtesy of Historic Newton.)

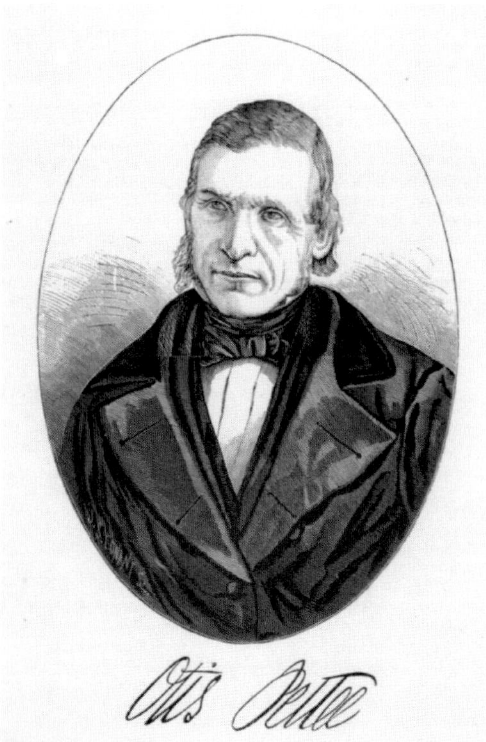

Otis Pettee, Helped Build Upper Falls
Employment at the Ellis Cotton Mills, and later the Elliott Manufacturing Company, is what drew Otis Pettee to Newton Upper Falls in 1817. After improving the machinery, he purchased part of the business and built his own cotton machinery plant. A few years later, he started an iron foundry that grew into a prosperous business.

Pettee established the Upper Falls Post Office in 1825 and served as its first postmaster. He was also instrumental in getting through the construction of the railroad from Brookline to Upper Falls.

Pettee lived in Newton Upper Falls until he died in 1853. (Courtesy of Historic Newton.)

CHAPTER TWO

Volunteers and Activists

Newton has never had a shortage of people willing to advocate for a cause about which they feel fervent. Just as passionate discussions fuel Newton's blog banter, government meetings, and dinner party discussions today, charged talk about suffrage, temperance, abolition, and education reform frequently filled the houses of Horace and Mary Peabody Mann, Nathaniel and Caroline Bassett Allen, and others in West Newton.

The activists and volunteers who live or have lived within the borders of our city rarely fail to impress, and capturing everything they have done on paper is all but impossible. Newton native Billy Starr founded the Pan-Mass Challenge, an athletic fundraiser that has raised $455 million for cancer research in 35 years. Louise Bruyn read the newspaper one morning in 1971, decided that Americans had become numb to the tragedy taking place in Vietnam and, 11 days later, began a 450-mile walk to Washington, DC, to tell the president to stop the war. Auburndale's Armando Rossi never waited to be assigned a task; if something needed to be done, he did it. Lenny Zakim, who poured his soul into fighting civil injustice and discrimination, left a legacy so enormous that one of the widest cable-stayed bridges in the world is named after him.

Worthy of mention and perhaps requiring a chapter by itself is the massive volunteer effort behind NewtonSERVES. Started as part of the millennial celebration during Mayor David Cohen's administration and led by director of cultural affairs Linda Plaut, NewtonSERVES is now an annual day of service where more than 1,000 volunteers complete dozens of community projects across the city. While not a person, NewtonSERVES is a legend that will define the Garden City for years to come.

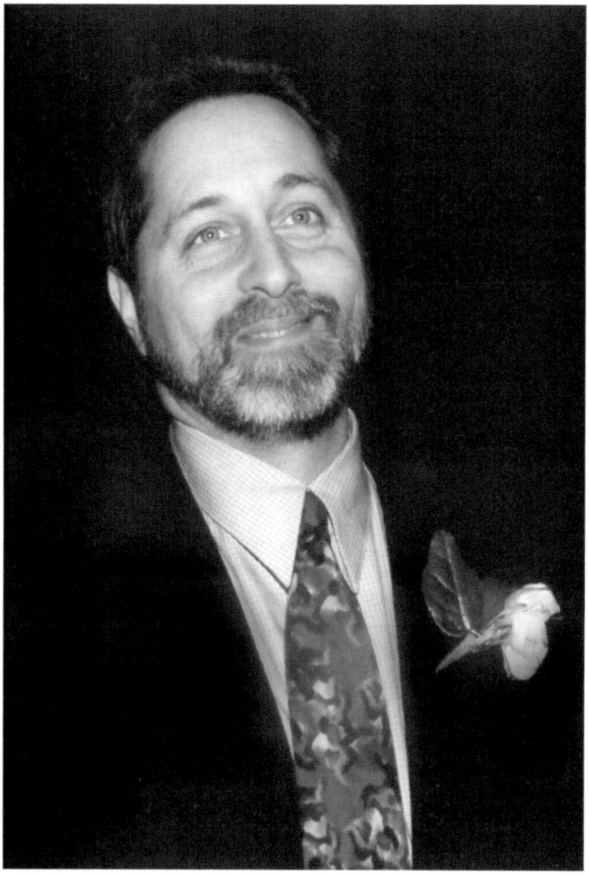

Leonard Zakim
Civil Rights Activist

There was one thing that Lenny Zakim could not tolerate: intolerance. The civil rights activist and executive director of the New England region of the Anti-Defamation League dedicated his life to uniting people—regardless of race, ethnicity, religion, or sexual orientation—in the battle against prejudice.

Zakim was said to have connections everywhere. He was known to call upon friends in politics, entertainment, sports, and religion to help promote his various causes and most often to teach tolerance and harmony.

Among other accomplishments, Zakim worked with leaders of several ethnic and religious groups to make significant advances in Catholic-Jewish relations and to develop Team Harmony, one of the country's largest anti-bigotry programs for teens.

Lenny Zakim also started a black-Jewish Passover seder in the early 1980s to help repair relations between the two groups. Six people attended the first seder, and 12 attended the following year. But the following year, with the help of the Rev. Charles Stith of Union United Methodist Church of Boston, 100 people attended the seder. By 1999, the year of Zakim's death at age 46, 650 people attended. Lisa Kessler photographed the black-Jewish Passover seder (opposite page, bottom image) in the late 1990s.

After Zakim was diagnosed with multiple myeloma, a rare cancer of the bone marrow, in 1995, he had a new purpose: He would set up a philanthropic organization to perpetuate his vision of social justice. The mission of the thriving Lenny Zakim Fund is to "identify, listen to, support and connect grassroots community organizations and programs operating below the radar screen of large charitable groups and government grants." By 2013, the Lenny Zakim Fund had given nearly $5.5 million to groups involved in coalition building across race, religious, and ethnic lines.

Zakim's dreams did not stop there. As a five-year patient at Dana Farber who was comforted by combining acupuncture, massage, Reiki, and other integrative therapies with chemotherapy and radiation, Zakim wanted to make integrative therapies available and affordable to all Dana Farber patients. Shortly before he died in 1999, Zakim announced the establishment of the Zakim P. Center for Integrative Therapies, which opened in 2000.

Zakim's friend and music hero Bruce Springsteen performed in 2002 at the dedication of the newly constructed Leonard P. Zakim Bunker Hill Memorial Bridge, one of the widest cable-stayed bridges in the world. (All courtesy of Joyce Zakim.)

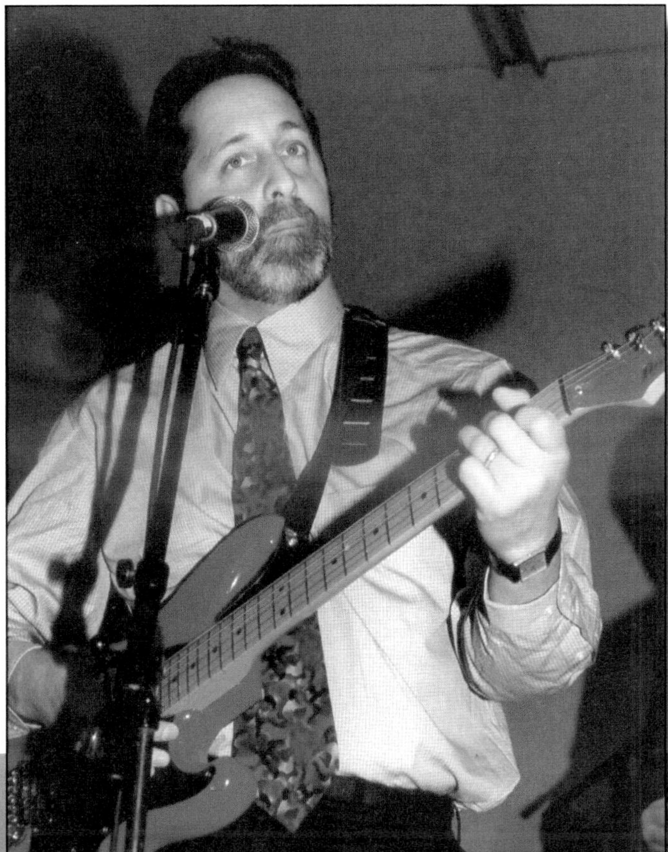

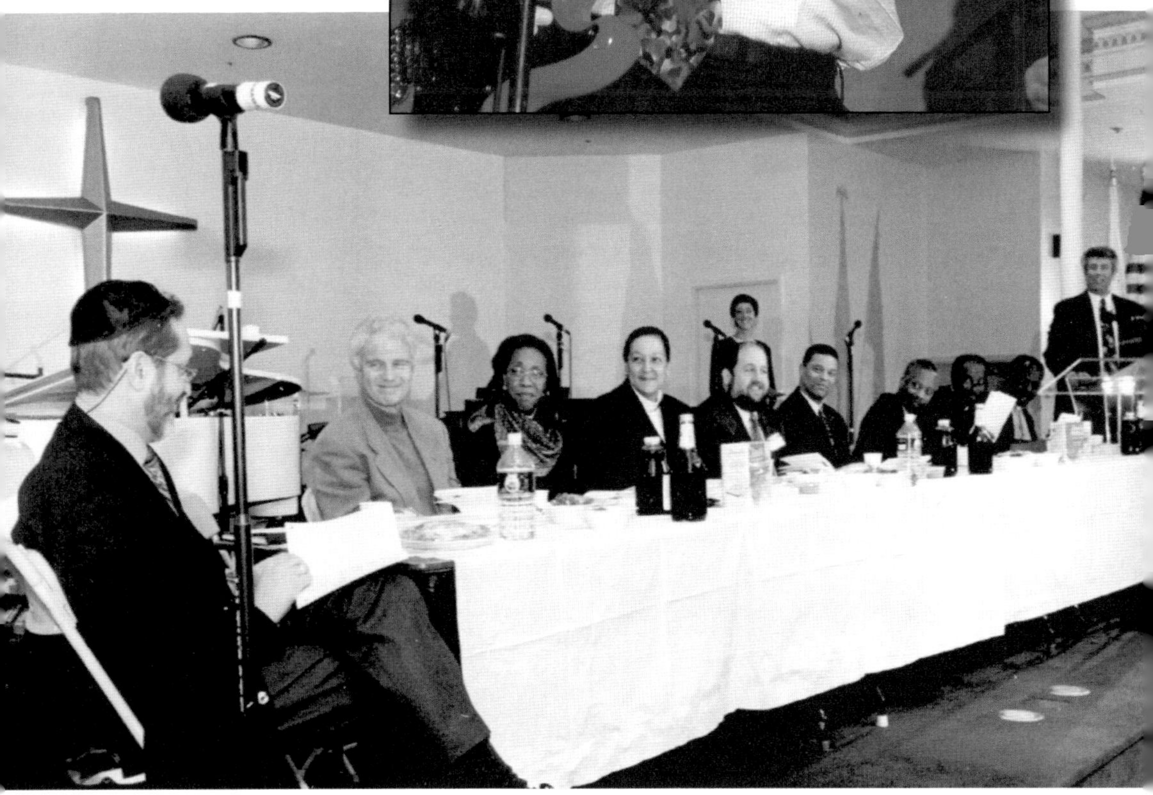

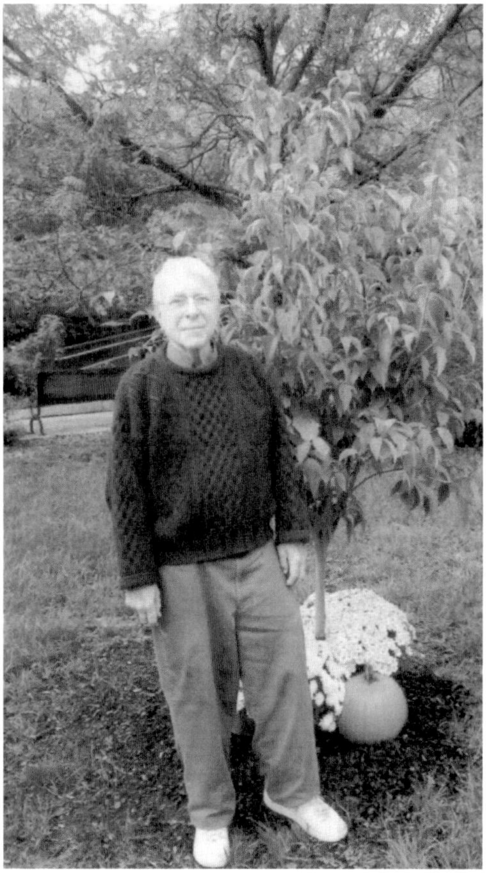

Armando Rossi, Auburndale's Unrelenting Volunteer

Renowned for his green thumb and seemingly endless thirst for volunteering, Armando Rossi was unofficially dubbed the "mayor of Auburndale" by the neighborhood. Rossi, who was born in Connecticut and moved to Auburndale in 1957, taught business and economics for 23 years at Newton North High School. He was a key player in opening the Auburndale Community Library after the city budget cut funding for the last four branch libraries in 2008. A tree is planted in his honor in front of the Auburndale Community Library. (Courtesy of the Rossi family.)

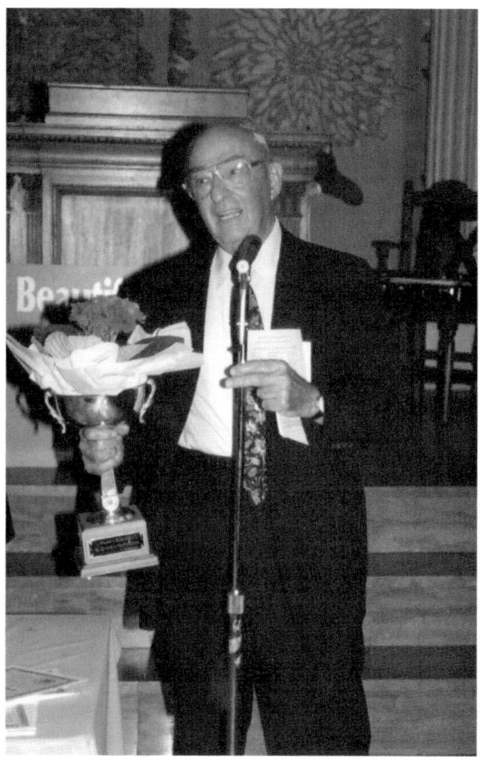

Leo Levi, Avid Gardener, 1915–2008

Credited by many with helping Newton reclaim its moniker "the Garden City," Leo Levi founded the Newton Pride Beautification Committee. He launched a citywide effort to plant flower bulbs, creating a catalog that was distributed to 30,000 households and sold four million bulbs. Levi started the Newton Tree Endowment Fund, headed an effort to plant 2,000 trees for the millennium, created a sunflower planting competition for school children, created the Newton Centre Garden, and organized the first inventory of Newton's street trees. (Courtesy of the City of Newton.)

Jeffrey Beatrice, Beloved Coach and Announcer

Kids loved Jeff Beatrice. Not just his 11 kids, but also the ones he coached over the years in various sports, including football, baseball, softball, and basketball. He was a big guy who made his presence known, and all of Nonantum appeared to enjoy his company. When he was not coaching or working as a certified public accountant, he announced for Pop Warner football games.

Everything came to an abrupt stop for his family, though, on October 23, 2009, when Beatrice, 49, who was under enormous financial stress, had a heart attack and died, falling into the arms of his wife, Elinor.

With seven of their children still living at home and a lien on the house in which Beatrice had been raised, Elinor was left with a huge financial mess. The bank intended to foreclose on the house, but the community refused to let that happen. Neighbors and friends held several fundraisers, collecting enough money to save the Beatrice home and demonstrating the power of community. (Courtesy of Elinor Beatrice.)

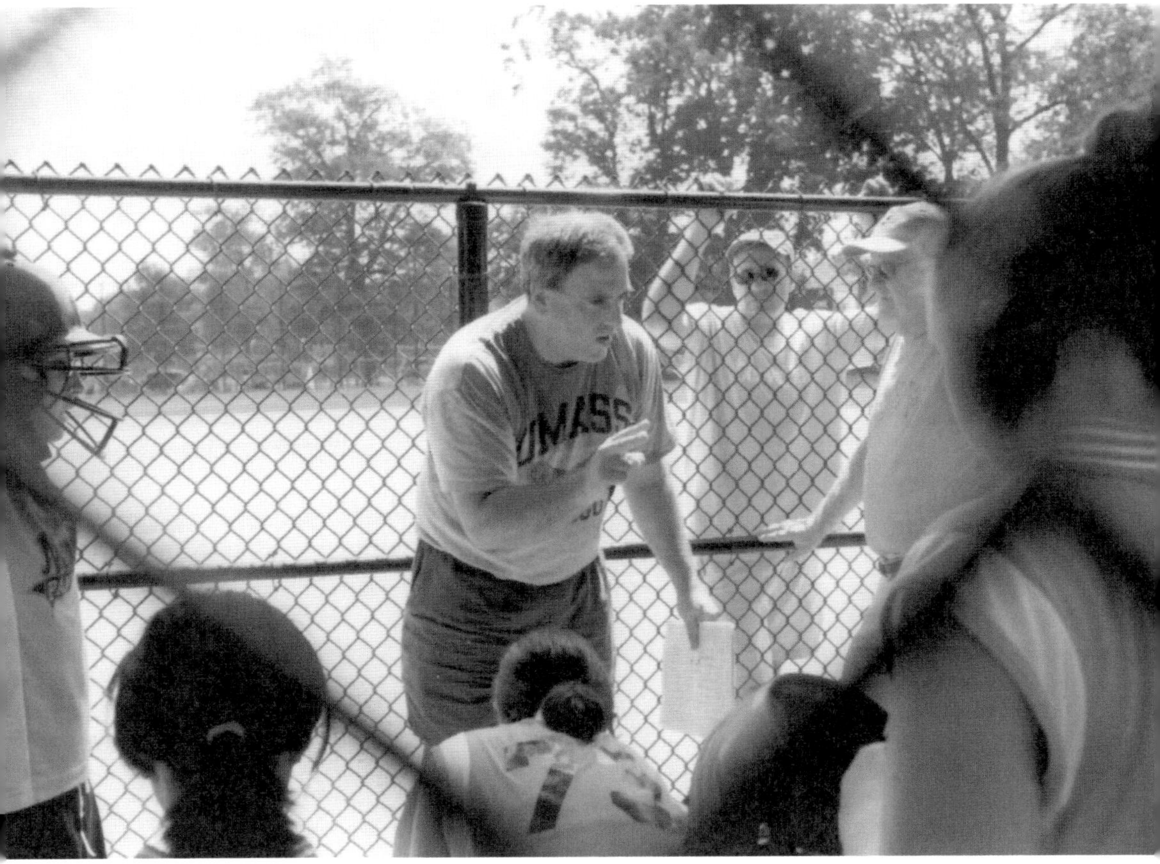

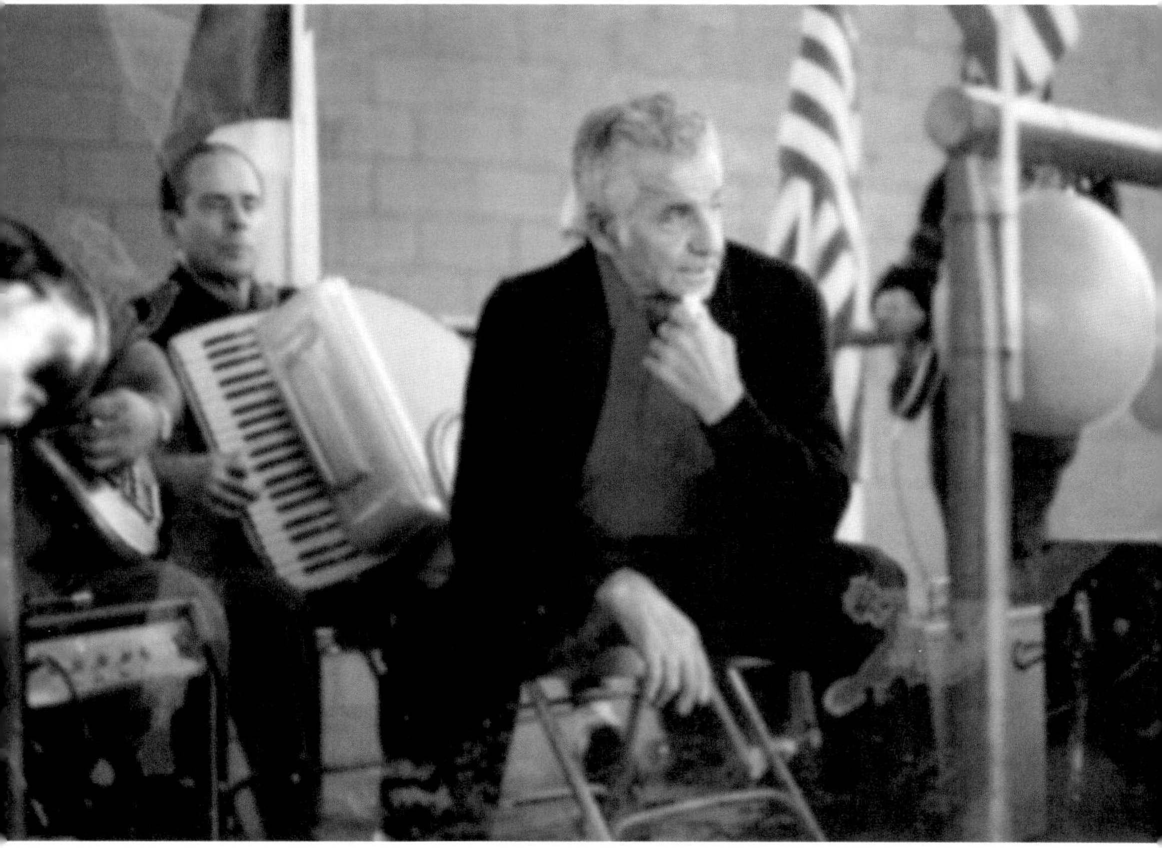

Anthony "Fat" Pellegrini (CENTER), "Mayor of Nonantum"

There have been few legends in Newton as entrenched as Anthony "Fat" Pellegrini (1925–2004). Born and raised on Clinton Street in Nonantum, Pellegrini's passion for his Nonantum neighborhood, The Lake, was apparent nearly every time he opened his mouth.

With a reputation as a Robin Hood–type character, but with a little more flavor to his language, Pellegrini was known for looking out for the little guy, particularly if the little guy lived in The Lake. He frequently carried with him a cigar box holding money he collected for those in need. His pet project, the Nonantum Children's Christmas Party Association, featured Christmas parties so festive that adults still gush over the ones they attended as children. Santa was flown in on a helicopter, and towering bags of presents were stuffed with toys for children who might otherwise have received very little, or nothing. Through his fundraising, he ensured that every senior citizen or family in need received a basket of food for the holiday. Every year, the holiday was celebrated with a parade and the erection of an 18-foot Santa Claus. Santa still towers over Nonantum every Christmas season.

Pellegrini, whose nickname "Fat" was earned as a chubby child even though he outgrew the baby fat as a young man, loved to flout authority and break rules. According to the *Boston Globe*, he and some friends once broke into the local pharmacy to steal a hospital bed and wheelchair for a dying neighbor, leaving a note promising to settle the debt later.

Pellegrini served in the Merchant Marines during World War II. He was a member of the American Legion, Sons of Italy, Newton Soccer Club, Newton Elks, and the St. Mary of Carmen Society. (Courtesy of the Pellegrini family.)

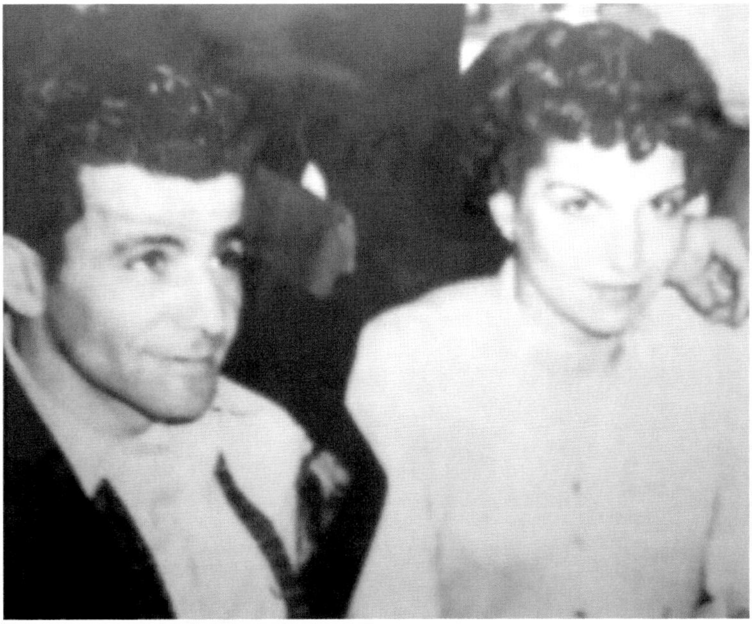

Newlyweds Anthony "Fat" and Joanne Pellegrini
Anthony Pellegrini and his first wife, Joanne Pellegrini, who died in 1997, are pictured here at the Monticello Dinner Theater & Night Club in Framingham. Pellegrini Playground in Nonantum is named in memory of Joanne. (Courtesy of the Pellegrini family.)

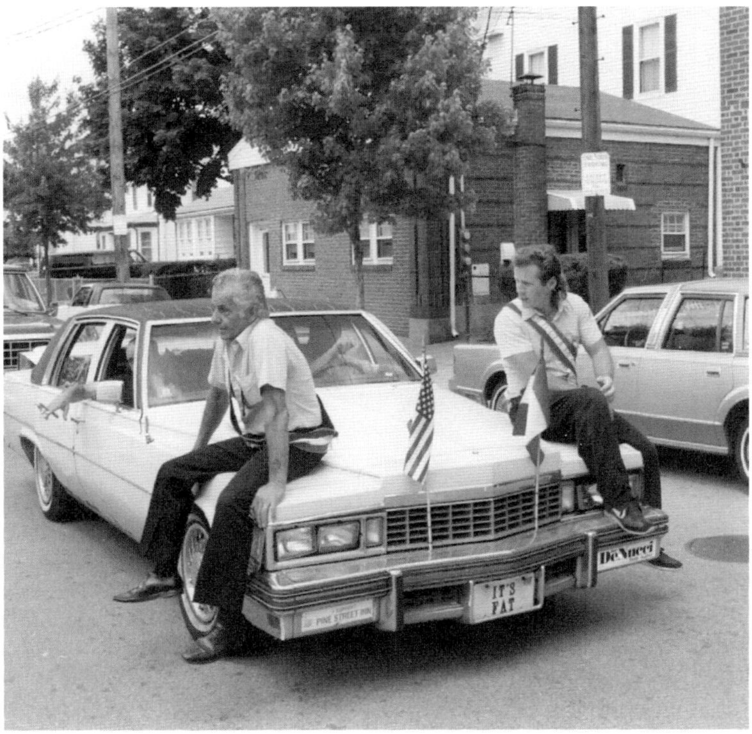

Anthony "Fat" Pellegrini (Left) and Roger Marrocco in Parade
Fat Pellegrini and Roger Marrocco sit atop Pellegrini's Cadillac in the processional in the 1990 St. Mary of Carmen Society Festival. As a member of the society and other organizations, Pellegrini helped scores of Nonantum families. (Courtesy of the St. Mary of Carmen Society.)

Audrey Cooper, Dedicated Volunteer

Few people have donated as much time to Newton as has Audrey Cooper, who turned 90 in March 2014. Born in Brookline, the West Newton resident and her late husband moved to the Garden City around 1950. Cooper worked as a secretary at Underwood Elementary School while her daughters were in school, planning to stay "just a couple of years," but she loved the job so much that she did not leave until her retirement 27 years and dozens, if not hundreds, of friends, later.

Upon her retirement, at the request of former mayor Ted Mann, she cochaired the effort to establish a senior center in Newton, spending two years raising money and bringing the center to life. She then served on the city's planning and development board and library board of trustees.

A member also of the Newton Community Service Center (NCSC) Board, Cooper cochaired the galas celebrating both the 75th and 100th birthdays of the center. She helped lead the Newton program for Head Start and served on the NCSC Youth Commission and Fair Housing Committee.

In 2009, Cooper received the Human Rights Award from the city, and in 2011, the Massachusetts Commission of Status of Women named her an unsung heroine for her 50 years of service on the NCSC's board of directors.

Cooper, who majored in political science at the former Pembroke College—the women's division of Brown University—continues to volunteer as a member of the Newton Council on Aging and continues to rave about the wonderful people living in Newton. (Photograph by Lisa Cassidy; courtesy of Wicked Local Newton.)

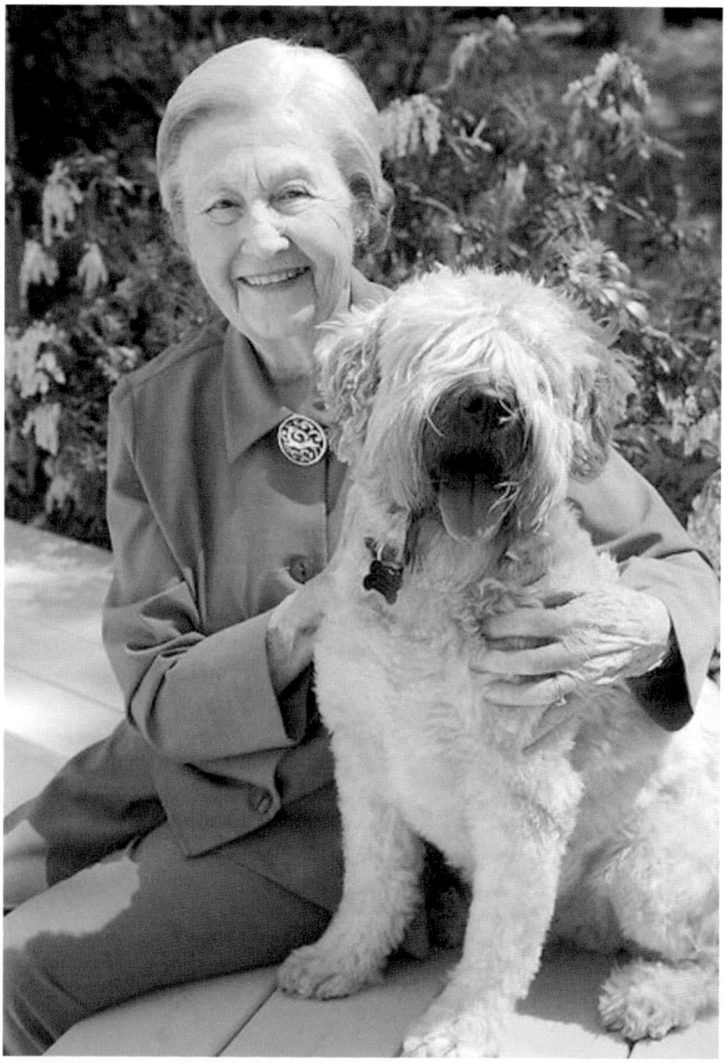

Louise Bruyn, Walked 450 Miles Opposing Vietnam War

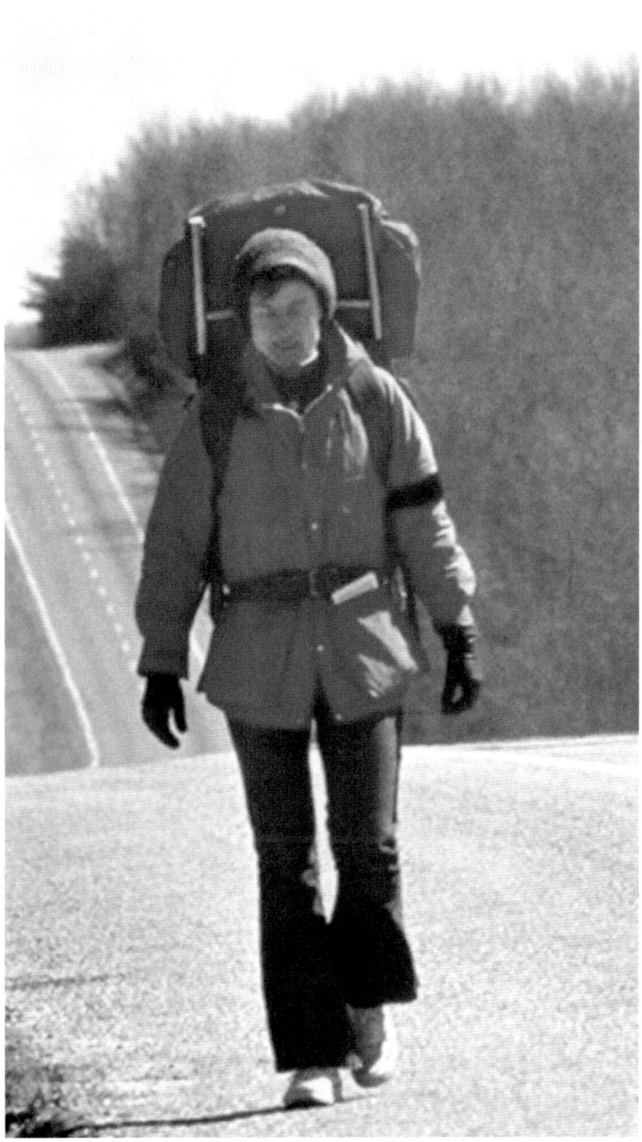

A February 6, 1971, *New York Times* opinion column made housewife, mother, and dance teacher Louise Bruyn realize that she, along with the rest of the country, had become anesthetized to the Vietnam War. Deciding that she needed to take action, she quickly devised a plan, and just 11 days later, she left her Newton Centre house on foot, carrying her necessities on her back, headed for the nation's capital. She brought with her a document for the president and members of Congress, the "Five Theses on American Foreign Policy"—a message written by Bruyn, her family, and friends—demanding that the foreign policy of the United States be redirected to world peace and law, rather than war.

During her 45-day trek, the mother of two 16-year-old daughters and an older son no longer living at home, walked 450 miles, sometimes alone, other times surrounded by friends, strangers, and flogged by media. She depended upon, and received, the kindness of strangers to take her into their homes, feed her, and provide her a warm bed. Along the way, she talked and listened to people about the atrocities happening in Southeast Asia.

When she arrived on the steps of the Capitol on April 2, 1971, with stacks of signatures supporting the "Five Theses" that she had collected along the way, Sen. Edward Kennedy and Congressman Robert Drinan were waiting to greet her. The media, including *Time* magazine, were on hand to interview her and a high school band heralded the end of her journey.

Kennedy commented that "no statement by any member of Congress can carry the sense of commitment that Mrs. Bruyn has conveyed." She talked of all the people who told her she was walking for them and of all the people everywhere who wanted an end to the war.

She waited five days without a response for her request for a meeting with President Nixon before flying home. In 2013, Bruyn published her story, *She Walked for All of Us*, hoping that it might convey the importance of being active.

Bruyn remains active in city affairs, including Green Decade/Newton, which she founded in 1990. (Courtesy of Louise Bruyn.)

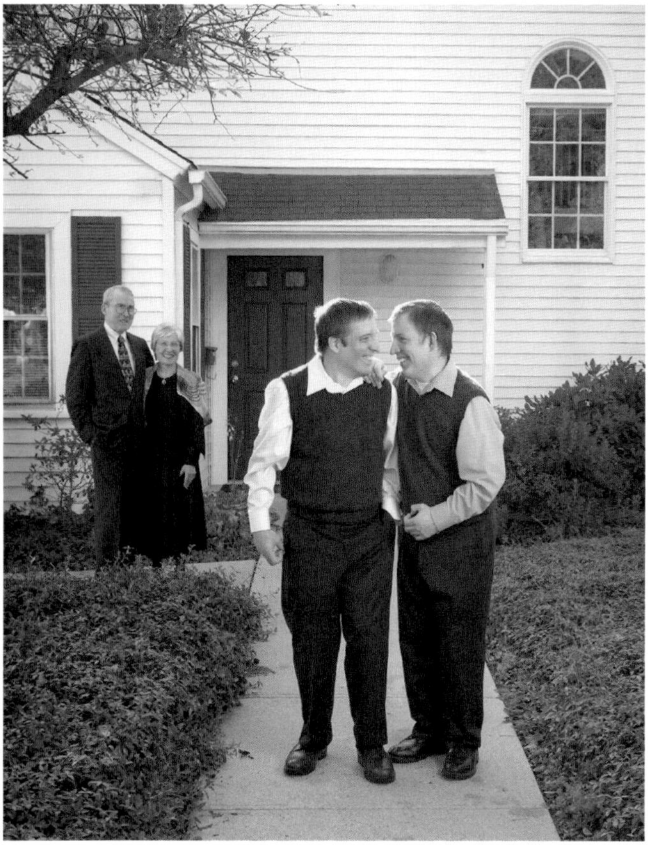

Carol Beard (BACKGROUND), Understanding Our Differences Founder

Newton resident Carol Beard, the mother of twin sons with intellectual disabilities, was not alone in her belief that successful inclusion of children with disabilities in the Newton public schools required an understanding community. In 1978—a dozen years before Congress passed the Americans with Disabilities Act—Beard, along with four other Newton parents of children with disabilities (Gwendolyn Fineberg, Linda Marsh, Trina Schickel, and Rita Sheehy), founded the Understanding Handicaps Program, now Understanding Our Differences.

Newton public schools social worker Catherine Kosa, Burr School principal Ella Mae Gay, and Williams Elementary teacher Toni Miller joined the effort to develop a program that would increase the understanding of both students and parents. Working off curriculum written by Newton resident Susan Bookbinder, these founding members, with a small nucleus of other parents, wrote the original Understanding Handicaps' curriculum, which included five units: blindness, deafness, physical disabilities, mental retardation, and epilepsy. Mary Margaret Pappas served as the first executive director.

Today, Understanding Our Differences is an independent nonprofit organization providing award-winning disability awareness education at the elementary school level. Between 2011 and 2014 in Newton, the program educated more than 9,000 elementary school students, trained about 1,000 parent volunteers, and provided disability education and awareness in seven areas: autism spectrum disorder; blindness and low vision; chronic medical conditions including allergic conditions, asthma, diabetes, and epilepsy; deafness and hard of hearing; intellectual disabilities; learning disabilities; and physical disabilities. The curriculum has been distributed to more than 200 schools nationwide.

In 1996, Beard and her husband donated their house to Newton Wellesley Weston Committee for Community Living, Inc., to be used as a group home. (Photography by Drew of Newton, Jenny Nourse Photography of Canton.)

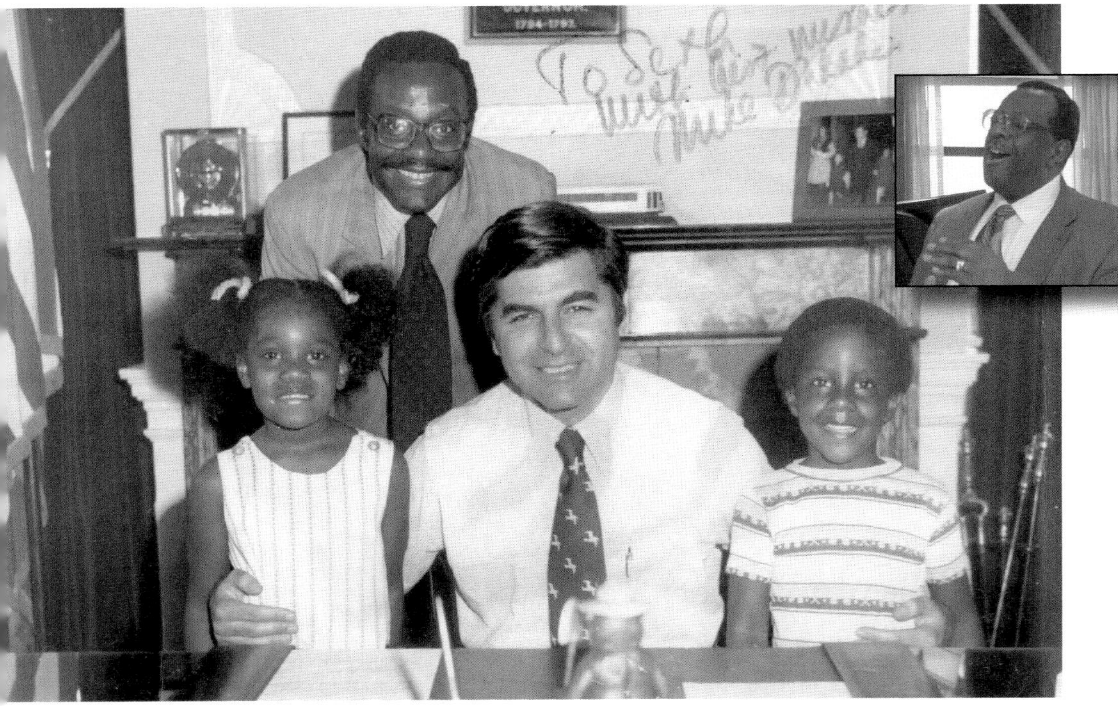

Joseph Warren with His Twins and Gov. Michael Dukakis

Born in Harlem, Joseph Warren's decision to move his young black family to Newton was a big step. Shortly after their arrival in 1972, his wife and children were the target of both rocks and racial slurs. Not a shy man, Warren called city hall and shared his feelings. Upon returning the call, Mayor Ted Mann recruited him to help ease racial tensions in the city, forging a bond between the two and launching Warren's continued commitment to Newton.

The first time Warren left Harlem, it was to join the Air Force, serving in Korea. When he returned home to see gangs ruling the streets, he became a youth outreach worker in his own neighborhood, a choice that would resonate throughout his career.

Soon after, he attended college at North Carolina Agricultural and Technical University, where he jumped into the civil rights movement. He marched, received death threats, and served jail time but kept fighting for justice.

After graduating college, he moved to Massachusetts to attend Brandeis and pursue his true passion: providing a path for success for the disadvantaged. He ran the university's Upward Bound program. His motto, "Failure is not an option," was reflected in the success and accomplishments of the students who served others. Warren earned his master's degree in social research in 1972 and his doctorate in economics and social welfare in 1983, both at Brandeis.

An active member of the Democratic Party, he established a political advocacy group in 1979 to improve the social and economic circumstances of minority communities across the country. He served in both Dukakis administrations, creating a relationship between his family and the Dukakises that spanned generations. He was also a senior adviser to Michael Dukakis during the 1988 presidential campaign.

As director of community affairs for Northeastern University in the early 1980s, Warren created the Balfour Academy for providing inner city youth with after-school tutoring and college preparation. He established a job training consultant firm to help disadvantaged people, and he launched an intensive tutoring program for at-risk youth and their families from Northeastern neighborhoods. Warren also taught African American studies.

Warren died in April 2010 just three months after his son, Setti Warren, was inaugurated as Newton's first African American mayor. (Both courtesy of Mayor Setti Warren.)

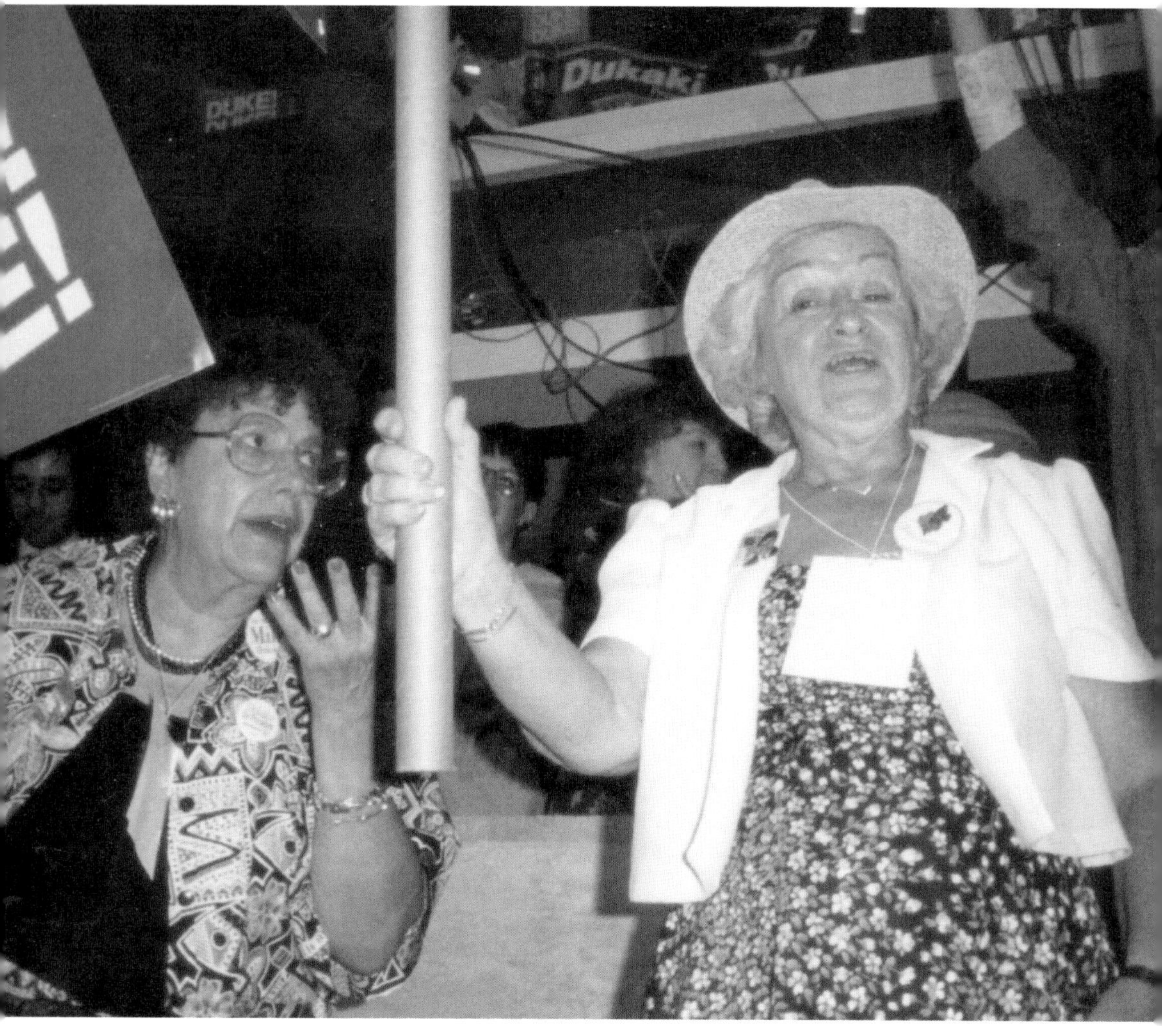

Margaret Hannigan, Godmother of Newton Politics

Well into her 90s, Peg Hannigan retains the title she earned decades ago—the "Godmother of Newton politics." Democratic candidates place a great deal of value on support and advice from Hannigan. A positive public comment from the Godmother carries a lot of weight.

Her kingdom stretches even farther than Newton. Not only does she know practically every Democrat who has held statewide office in Massachusetts in the last 50 years, but also many of them have come to her for her wisdom and blessing. She has boxes full of photographs and personal correspondence to prove it. Candidates such as John Kerry, Barney Frank, Joe Kennedy III, Mike Dukakis, Setti Warren, and Steve Grossman have all spent hours talking with the Godmother.

Hannigan was introduced to Newton politics in the 1970s during the construction of the Massachusetts Turnpike, which was literally dividing the city. Father Loscocco of Our Lady Help of Christians Parish asked for her leadership help in redrawing wards and precincts. Hannigan responded with, "Excuse me, Father. I have no idea what you're talking about."

Today, Hannigan, who chaired the Democratic City Committee for 10 years, recalls many fellow Democrats by the ward in which they live before she remembers their names. She never ran for office because she knows her limitations, and she's proud that Nonantum patriarch Fat Pellegrini liked to call her "one tough Irish broad." (Courtesy of Peg Hannigan.)

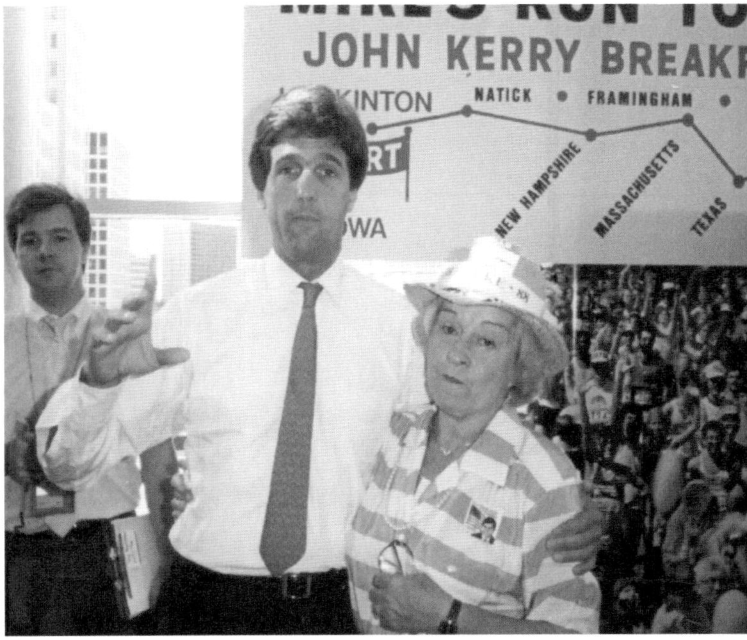

Peg Hannigan with Sen. John Kerry
Peg Hannigan owns boxes filled with photographs of herself with Massachusetts Democrats. Among her many political friendships is Secretary of State John Kerry, who was the US senator from Massachusetts when this photograph was taken. (Courtesy of Peg Hannigan.)

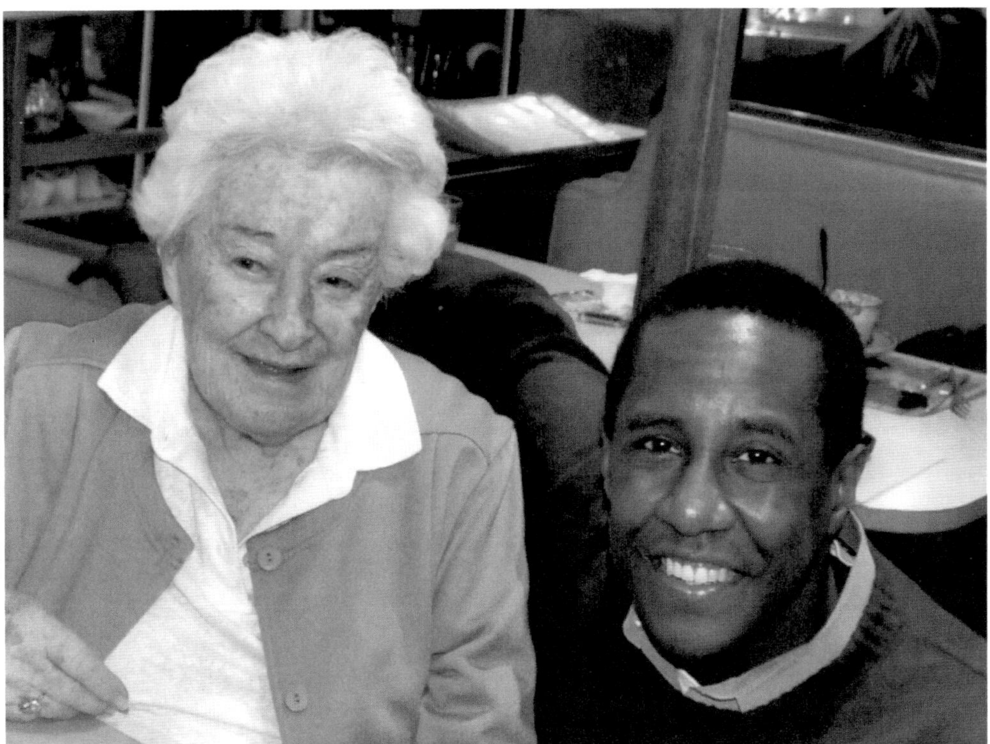

Peg Hannigan with Mayor Setti Warren
Peg Hannigan has known Mayor Setti Warren since he was six years old. She worked with his father, Joe Warren, on Gov. Michael Dukakis's run for president in 1988, and she endorsed Setti Warren when he ran for mayor of Newton. (Courtesy of Peg Hannigan.)

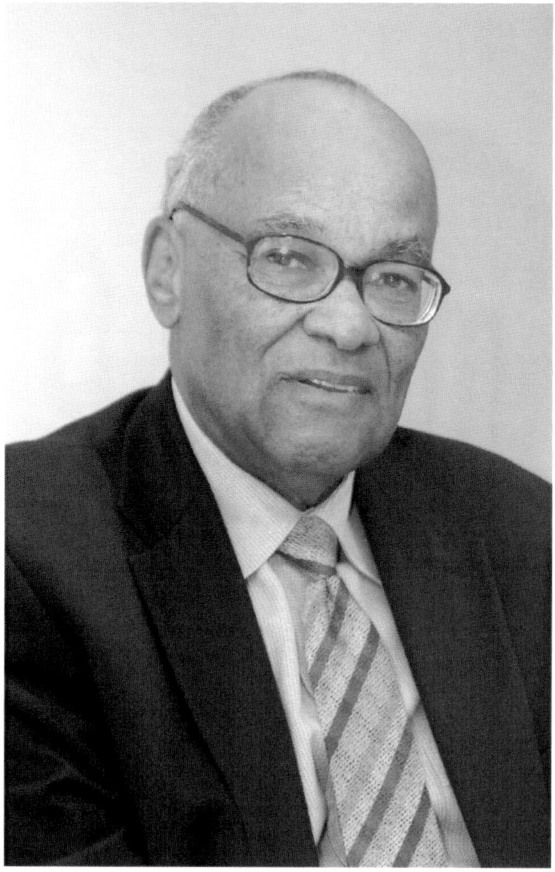

Hubert Eugene Jones, Social Justice Leader
As director of the Roxbury Multiservice Center in the late 1960s, Hubie Jones, noticed a disturbing pattern among school-aged children and took action. He investigated and published a report showing that the Boston Public Schools were systematically excluding 10,000 or more children because they were physically or mentally disabled, had behavioral problems, did not speak English, or were pregnant. The resulting report, "The Way We Go To School: The Exclusion of Children in Boston," led to the enactment of two landmark laws in Massachusetts, the Special Education Law and the Bilingual Education Law. The task force that Jones chaired is now Massachusetts Advocates for Children.

More recently, Jones founded the Boston Children's Chorus, a passion that he pursued after he was mesmerized by a performance by the nationally renowned Chicago Children's Choir. He returned to Boston determined to replicate the program with the mission of uniting young people across differences in race, religion, and economic status. The Boston Children's Chorus (BCC) launched in 2003 with 20 children; the 2013–2014 chorus comprised nearly 500 singers participating in 12 different choirs. Jones's work with the BCC won him the 2010 Purpose Prize, a monetary award presented to individuals over age 60 who find new ways to solve difficult social problems.

The BCC was the winner of the 2013 National Arts and Humanities Youth Program Award by the President's Committee on the Arts and Humanities and the recipient of the 2011 Margaret Hillis Award for Choral Excellence by Chorus America, an award that also represents a commitment to outreach, education, and/or culturally diverse activities.

Jones, who also served as the first African American dean of Boston University's School of Social Work, was a cofounding board member of City Year, a national nonprofit organization that helps young people spend a year serving their communities. (Courtesy of Hubie Jones.)

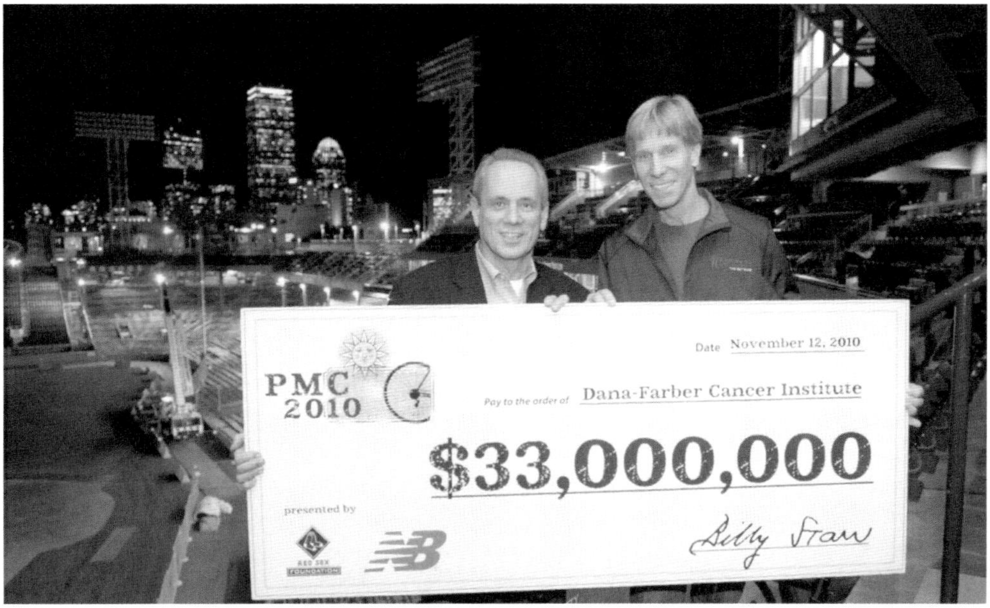

Billy Starr, Founder of Pan-Mass Challenge

Newton native Billy Starr started the Pan-Mass Challenge in 1980 as a weekend ride across Massachusetts with a group of cycling friends. Because his mother had died from cancer, Starr decided to use the ride to raise money for cancer research. With that, the largest athletic fundraiser in the country emerged. The annual weekend ride now draws about 5,500 cyclists and has raised $414 million in total through 2013. Starr, Newton South graduate and executive director of the PMC, rides every year. He is pictured on the right with Red Sox owner Larry Lucchino in 2010. (Courtesy of the PMC.)

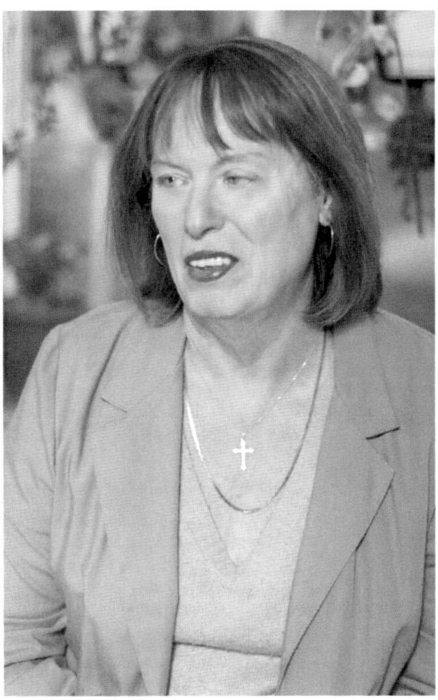

Holly Ryan, First Openly Transgender Public Appointee

Holly Ryan's appointment as Newton's first openly transgender member of the Human Rights Commission in 2012 was not about her. Rather, it was about accomplishing something for her community. Ryan, who was born male but knew she identified female by age 7, transitioned in her early 40s. As chairperson of the Massachusetts Transgender Political Coalition, Ryan helped the state create legislation that would protect transgender people from discrimination. The vice chairwoman of the Newton Democratic City Committee was also instrumental in working with the state Democratic Committee to attain lesbian, gay, bisexual, and transgender (LGBT) representation. (Photograph by Kristin L. Caffray.)

Howard Zinn, Historian and Activist

Howard Zinn (1922–2010) was a historian, political activist, author, and an early opponent of US involvement in Vietnam. A professor in the political science department at Boston University from 1964 to 1988, he was revered by the political left for his views on civil rights and his perspective on American history. Of the more than 20 books he wrote, his most popular, *A People's History of the United States*, presented a previously untold, or at most whispered, picture of American history that centered on the oppressed. *People's History* gained fame when actor Matt Damon, who was a Newton neighbor of Zinn's as a child, mentioned the book in his award-winning movie *Good Will Hunting*. Many people credit the book for changing the way people look at American history. (Photograph by Frank Curran for Boston University.)

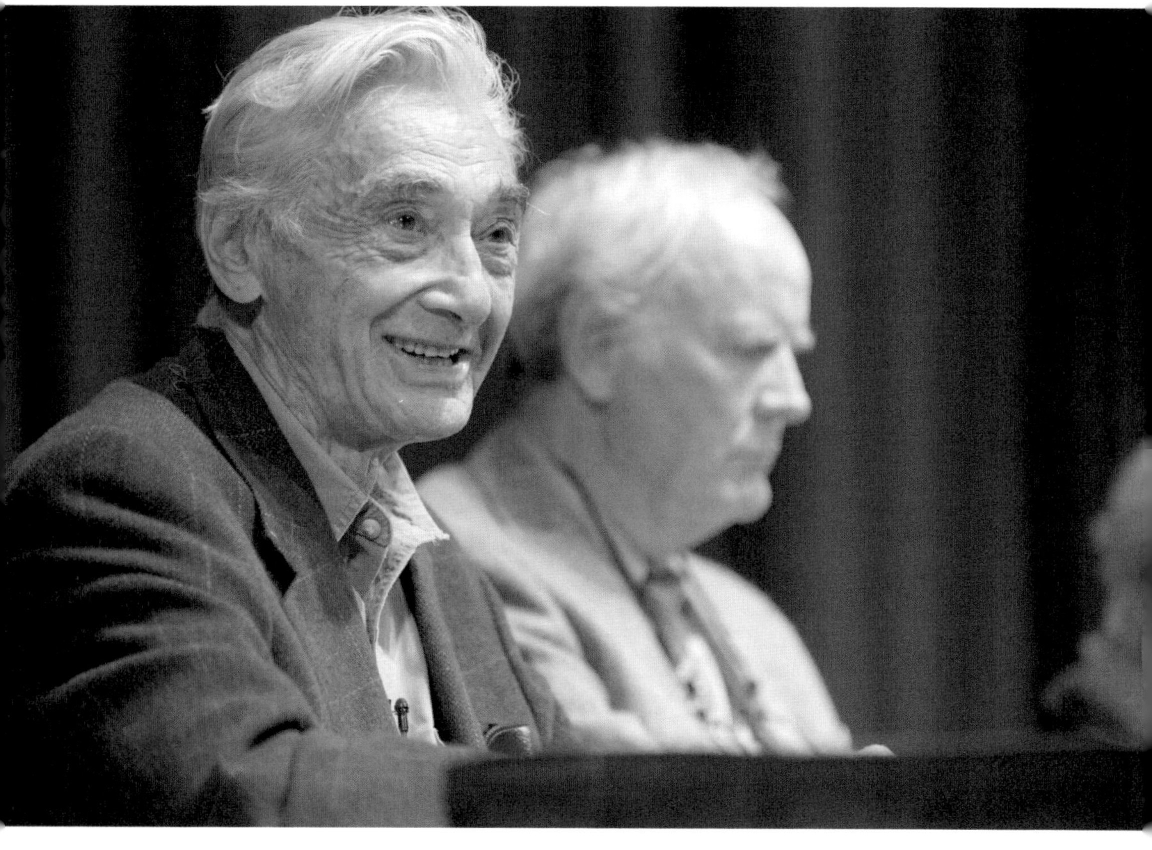

CHAPTER THREE

Public Servants

Countless people have devoted their careers and their lives to making the city of Newton, the state of Massachusetts, and even the country run properly. Many politicians who began their careers on the Newton Board of Aldermen moved on to wider stages. Leverett Saltonstall, once an alderman, was the 55th governor of Massachusetts and a 22-year member of the US Senate. Mayor David Cohen was first elected to the Newton Board of Aldermen when he was 24 years old. Before John Weeks was elected Newton's 14th mayor, he sat on the board of aldermen. He went on to serve in the US House of Representatives and Senate and was later appointed secretary of war by Pres. Warren Harding.

In this chapter, readers will learn about a lot of firsts, like Newton's first African American mayor, first woman alderman, and first female legislator. Located elsewhere in this book is Kathy Jones (see page 121), the city's first black school committee member.

Of course, a book about Newton legends would not be complete without pages dedicated to Mayor Ted Mann, the man Sen. Edward Kennedy once called "a Republican that all Democrats could love."

Too plentiful to include are all the city workers whose work is legendary but whose names rarely make the spotlight. Lillian Shapiro Radlo, who died in 1984, was not only secretary to the Newton School Committee, administrative assistant to the superintendent of schools, and director of community relations for the school department but she also was a civic leader who helped found Temple Shalom. Judy Anderson, whose enthusiasm for her work at the department of cultural affairs and the Newton Cultural Council was legendary, had a sign near her desk that read, "Love what you do and you will never work a day in your life." Ernie Peltier, a beloved custodian who has worked at Newton South High School since it opened in the fall of 1960, has hardly missed a day of school. This chapter is for all of them, too.

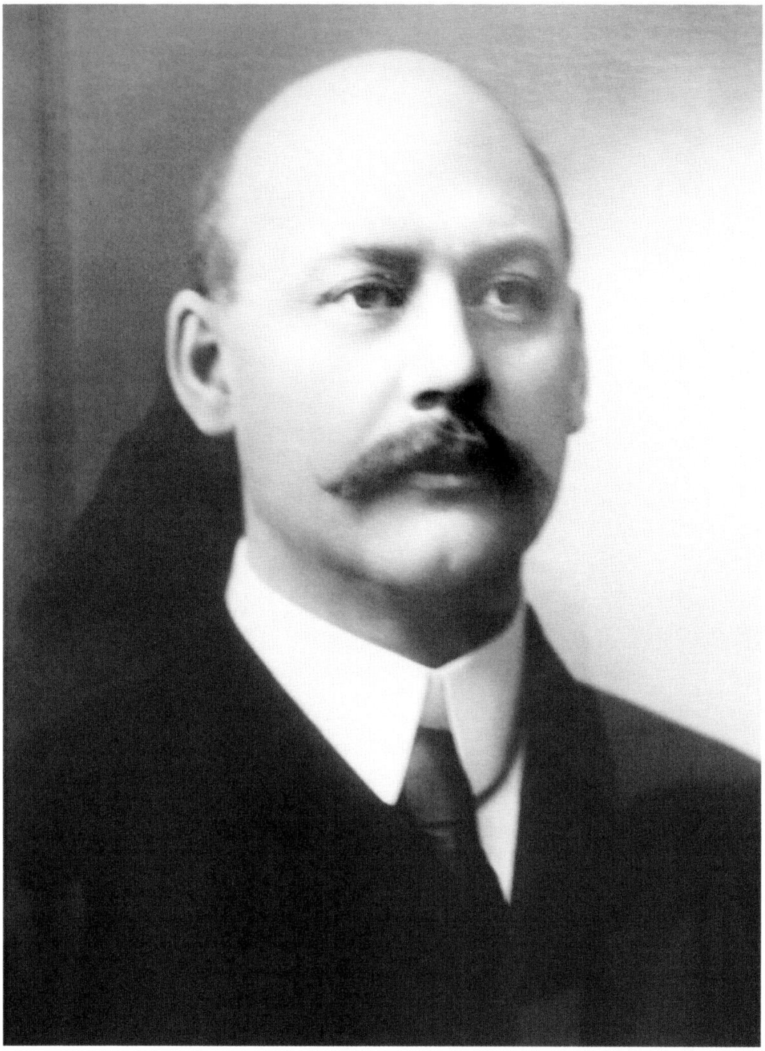

John Weeks, Mayor, Legislator, Secretary of War

A graduate of the US Naval Academy, John Weeks (1860–1926) was born in New Hampshire. He served in the Navy for two years before moving to and settling in Newton.

He worked in banking and brokerage in Boston, and he later became involved in Newton politics, first serving on the Newton Board of Aldermen and then serving as mayor from 1902 to 1903. Elected to Congress in 1904, Weeks represented the 12th Congressional District from Massachusetts from 1905 to 1913, when he entered the Senate. Among his accomplishments in Congress was the Weeks Act in 1911 that created the foundation for the US National Forest System.

Weeks remained in the Senate for six years and was defeated when he ran for reelection in 1918.

Pres. Warren G. Harding appointed Weeks secretary of war in 1921, and Pres. Calvin Coolidge kept him in that position when Harding died in office. Weeks retired due to poor health in 1925 and died on July 12, 1926. He was buried in Arlington National Cemetery.

Weeks's namesakes in Newton include the former Weeks Junior High School (now Weeks House) and Weeks Field.

John Weeks's son, Sinclair Weeks, served as mayor of Newton from 1930 to 1935. (Courtesy of Historic Newton.)

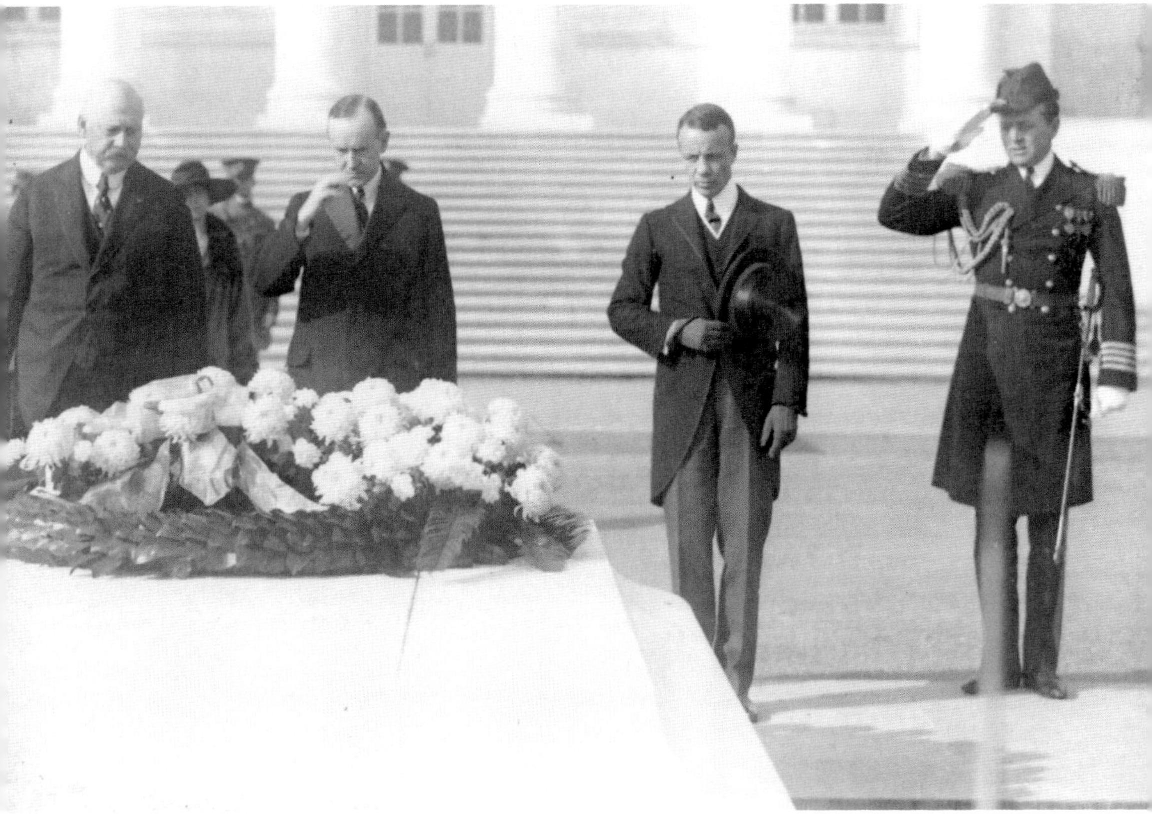

John Weeks (Far Left) with President Coolidge (Second to Left)
Secretary of War John Weeks, Pres. Calvin Coolidge, and Asst. Secretary of the Navy Theodore Roosevelt Jr. visit the Tomb of the Unknown Soldier on Armistice Day in 1923. (Courtesy of Library of Congress.)

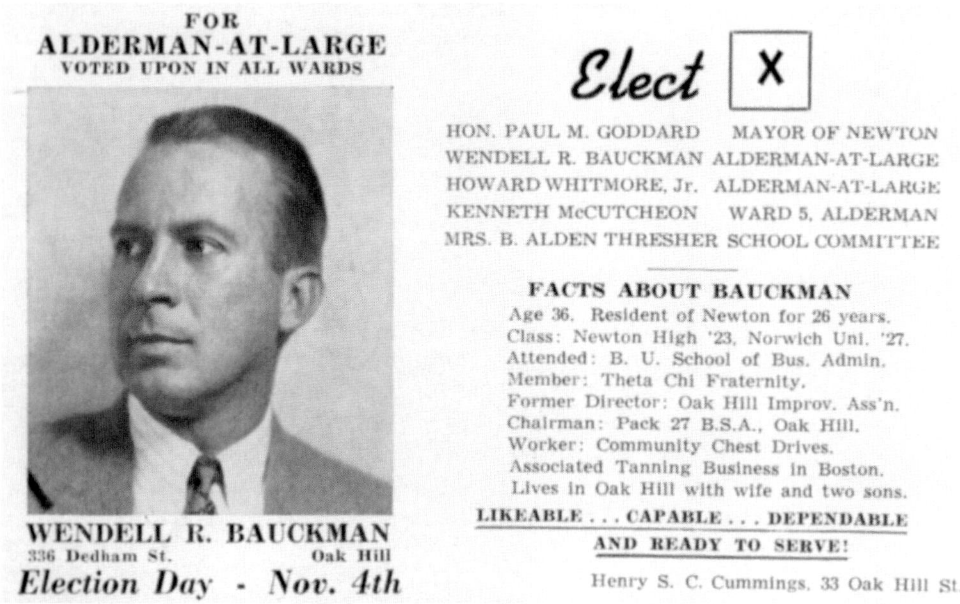

Wendell Bauckman, Longest-Serving Alderman
Wendell Bauckman's record on the Newton Board of Aldermen is likely to stand for a longtime. When the Oak Hill Republican died in office, he had served on the board for 55 years, making him the longest-serving alderman in the city's history. He served as president of the board for 24 of those years. In 1995, when Bauckman had served 53 years, the *Boston Globe* estimated that he had spent close to 20,000 hours attending meetings at city hall. Bauckman died in 1997 at the age of 91. (Courtesy of Historic Newton.)

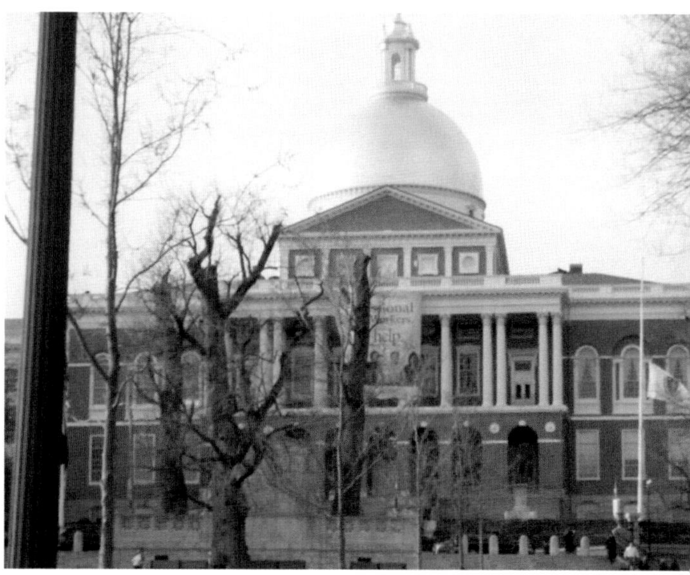

Margaret Spear, Newton's First Female Legislator
Margaret Spear (1882–1957) was Newton's first female state legislator. A Wellesley College graduate who lived in Newtonville, she was elected to the House of Representatives in 1940, representing the 5th Middlesex District and focusing on welfare and education. Spear also served as secretary in the Newton Republican City Committee for 12 years. She retired in 1950 due to ill health. (Photograph by Gail Spector.)

Adelaide Ball, First Alderwoman

In 1953, Adelaide Ball (1898–1983), who was born and lived her entire life in Newton Corner, was the first woman to be elected to the board of aldermen. She was also the first female president of a boys' club in America and the first woman elected president of the Newton Community Council.

Her Newton roots ran deep. She was a descendant of Deacon John Jackson, reputed to be the first permanent settler of Newton. Her maternal grandparents, the Buckinghams, were one of Newton's oldest families, and her grandfather, the Reverend Buckingham, officiated at the wedding of Theodore Roosevelt in 1880.

Ball lost the Ward 1 alderman seat in 1957 but was elected as alderman at-large in 1959 and retained that seat until she retired in 1971. (Courtesy of Historic Newton.)

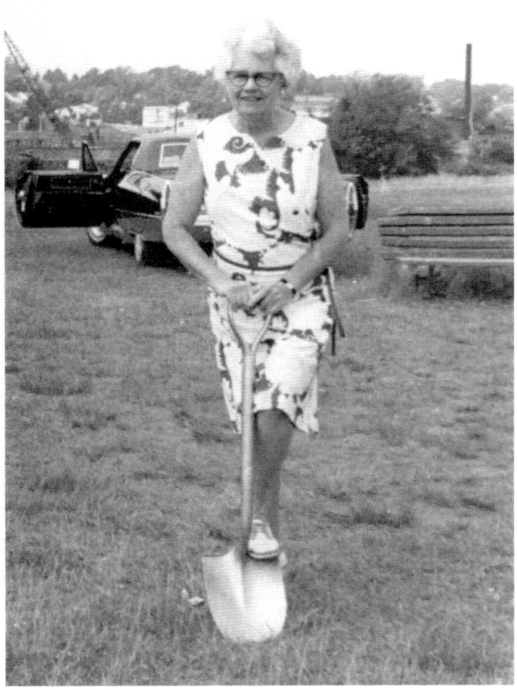

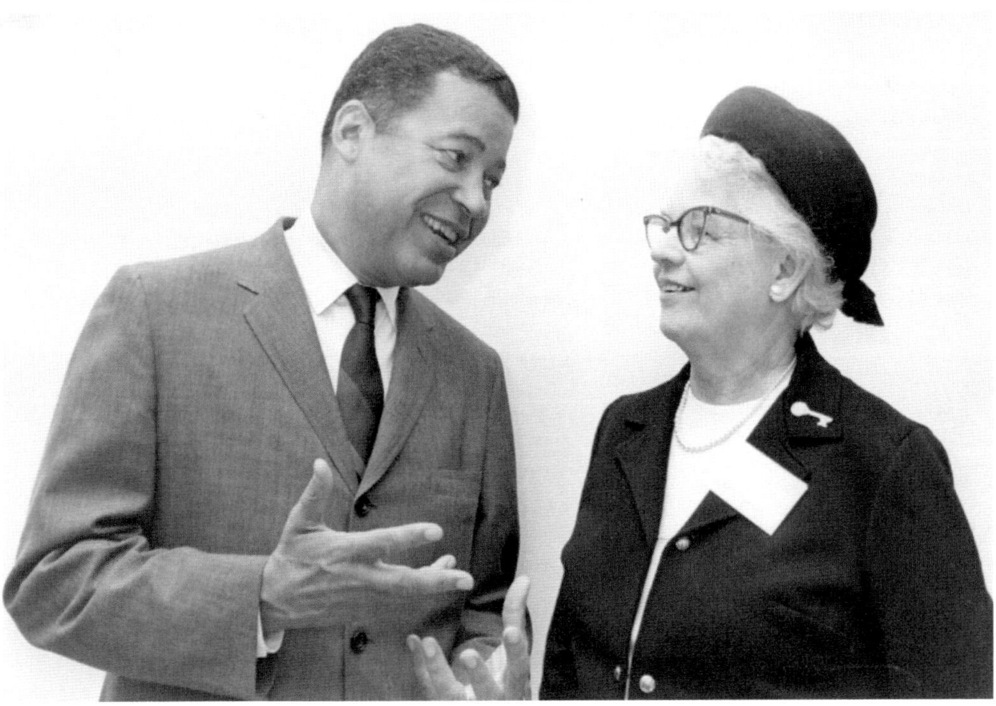

Adelaide Ball with US Senator Edward Brooke

Adelaine Ball sat on or led dozens of committees for the city, including the Charter Commission, Newton Women's Republican Club, and the Newton Housing Authority. She was an integral part of the establishment of the Newton Council for the Aging. (Courtesy of Historic Newton.)

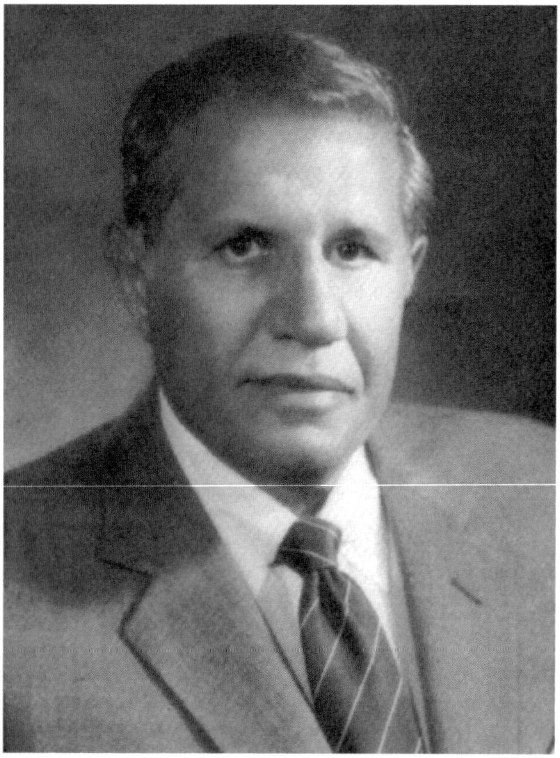

Ted Mann, Newton's Longest-Serving Mayor
Ted Mann was everybody's mayor. A liberal Republican in a city teeming with Democrats, he was Newton's first Jewish mayor. Before he became Newton's longest-serving mayor, he spent eight years on the board of aldermen and another eight in the State House as a representative. Where other 38-year politicians might have garnered more animosity along the way, Mann left an imprint on the city filled with affection and devotion. David Nyhan from the *Boston Globe* called him the "pied piper of optimism" and a "municipal treasure." Newtonians who knew him have at least one favorite story about "Teddy Mann."

Mann, who served as the city's chief executive from 1972 until he died in office from leukemia in 1994, was known for returning phone calls from constituents. He jumped on opportunities to engage people to volunteer, and he had a knack for bringing people together to work toward a common goal. He was said to drive the streets as if he owned them, looking for potholes and other flaws in the operation of the city of which he was so proud. He took calls at home from constituents, enjoying the banter.

In a video made for the 38th annual Mayor's Prayer Breakfast, an event launched by Mann, Mayor Setti Warren tells of Mann calling him into his office when Warren was just a high school student. Instead of leaving problem solving to adults, Mann enlisted the help of the African American teen—and class officer—to ease racial tensions at Newton North. Warren's predecessor, David Cohen, describes Mann as someone who could always find the best in people. "He did not have to work at it. It was something he did naturally. He was a wonderful human being."

Mann, a World War II veteran, made many contributions to the city, including establishing a reputation as a safe, well-run city with excellent schools. He oversaw the construction of the Newton Senior Center during his tenure, and he persevered to see the construction of a new main library, which was dedicated in his honor shortly after his death. He chaired the Massachusetts Bay Transportation Authority (MBTA) Advisory Committee and served three terms as president of the Massachusetts Mayor's Association. He was a longtime member of the US Council of Mayors and a nine-time recipient of the council's commendation for "outstanding leadership in the development and support of citizen volunteerism." (Courtesy of the Mann family.)

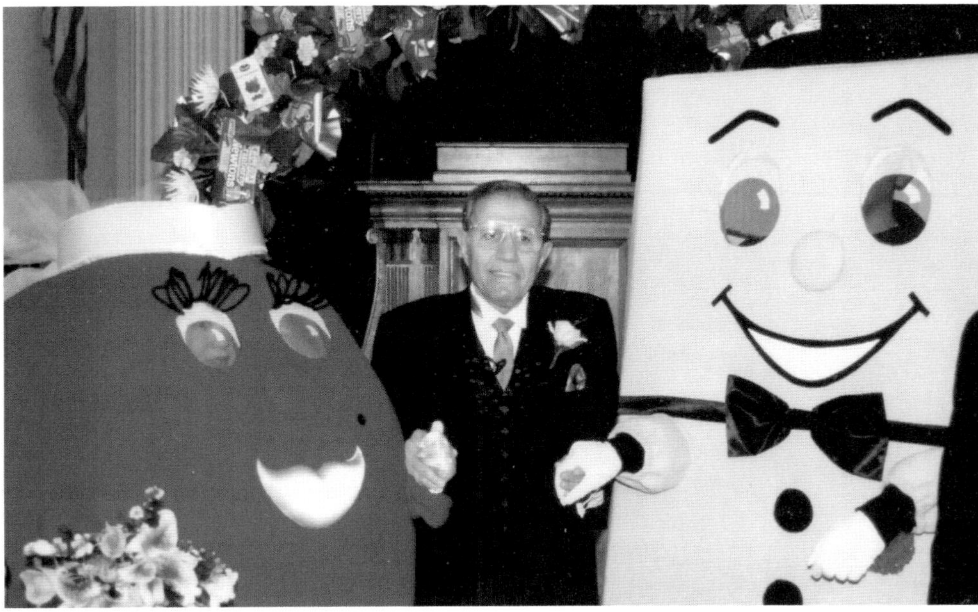

Ted Mann Marries the Cranberry and Fig in Mock Ceremony
Mann loved to raise money for his city. In May 1991, when Nabisco was celebrating the Fig Newtons' centennial in Newton, Mann arranged for a $30,000 scholarship endowment for Newton High School students from Nabisco. Two years later, Mann presided over a mock marriage ceremony joining the cranberry and the Newton cookie. Nabisco's wedding present to the city was an $8,000 donation to the Newton Pride Committee. (Courtesy of the Mann family.)

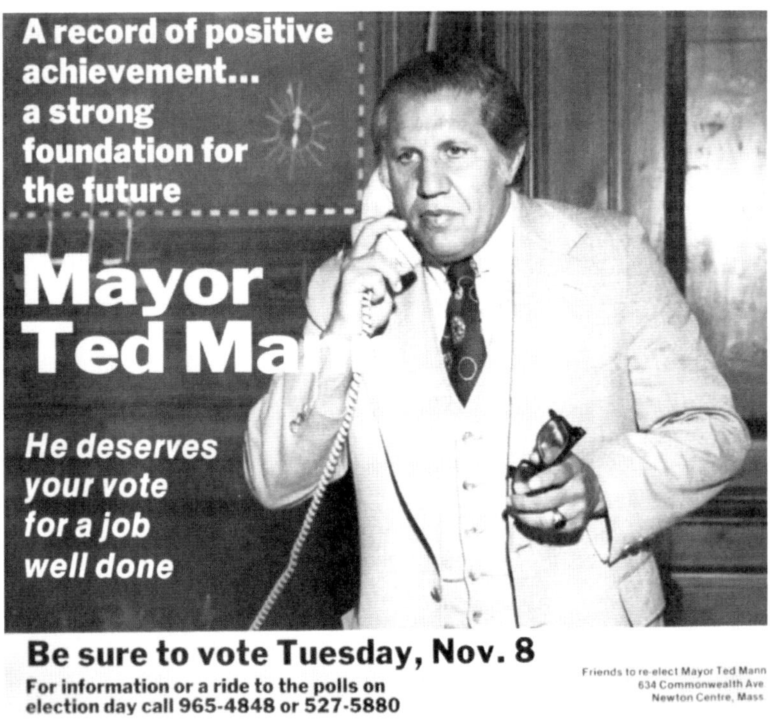

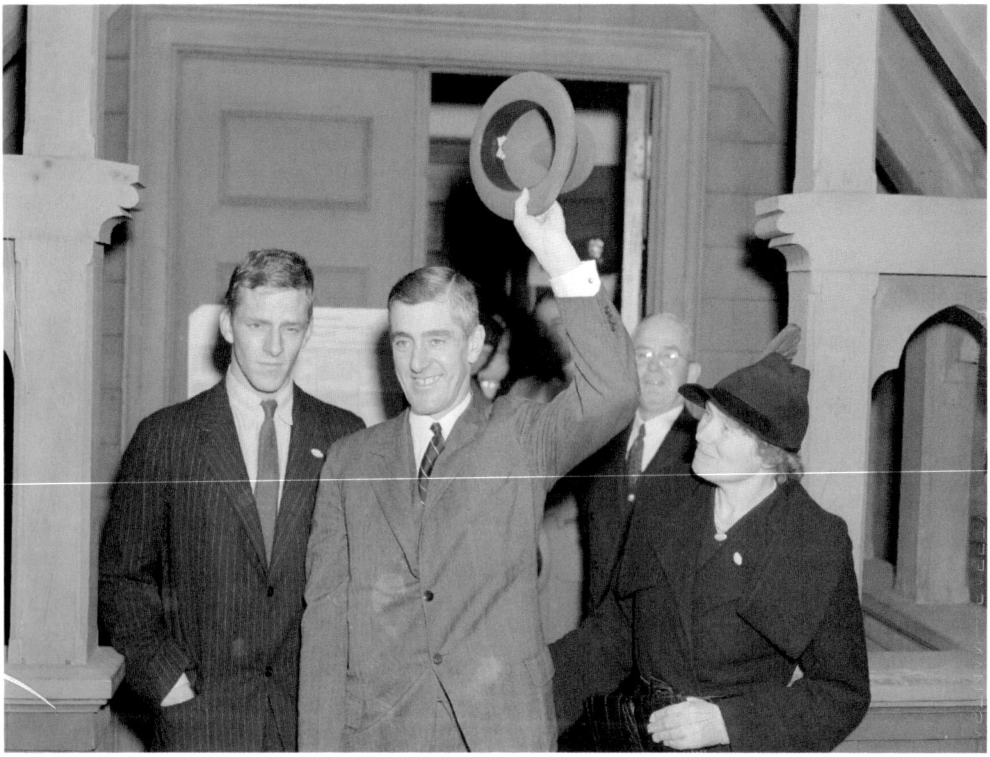

Leverett Saltonstall, Governor and Senator
Born in Chestnut Hill in 1892, Leverett Saltonstall's ancestry can be traced to the *Mayflower.* His political career started on the Newton Board of Aldermen, where he served for two years. The Republican was elected to the Massachusetts House of Representatives in 1923 and stayed there until 1936, serving the last seven years as speaker. In 1938, he was elected governor, and in 1944, he was elected to the US Senate to fill the vacancy caused by the resignation of Henry Cabot Lodge. He remained there through 1966, when he did not seek reelection. (Courtesy of the Boston Public Library/Leslie Jones Collection.)

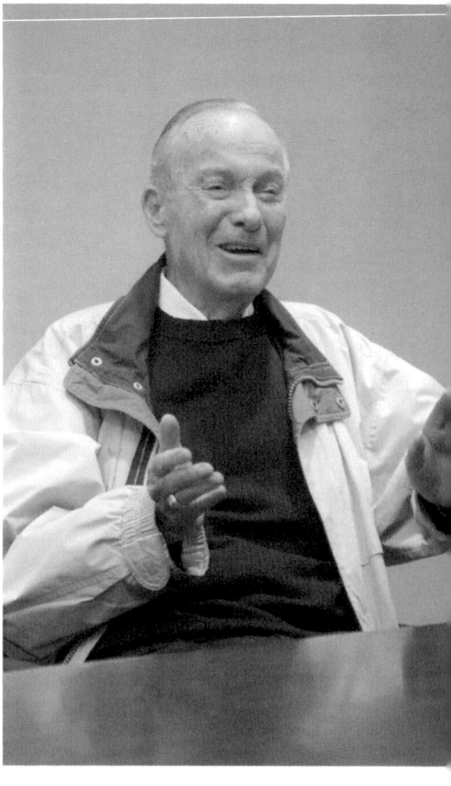

Carleton Merrill, Alderman and Veteran
First elected to the Newton Board of Aldermen in 1950 following his service in the Pacific during World War II, Carleton Merrill dedicated his life to serving veterans, his country, and Newton. His quarter-century on the board of aldermen was divided into three stints, with a 33-year position, from 1962 to 1995, as the city's director of veteran services separating them. The popular alderman often walked around with a stash of Vote Merrill wooden nickels in his pocket. Merrill died in January 2013. He was 88. (Photograph by Erin Prawoko; courtesy of Wicked Local Newton.)

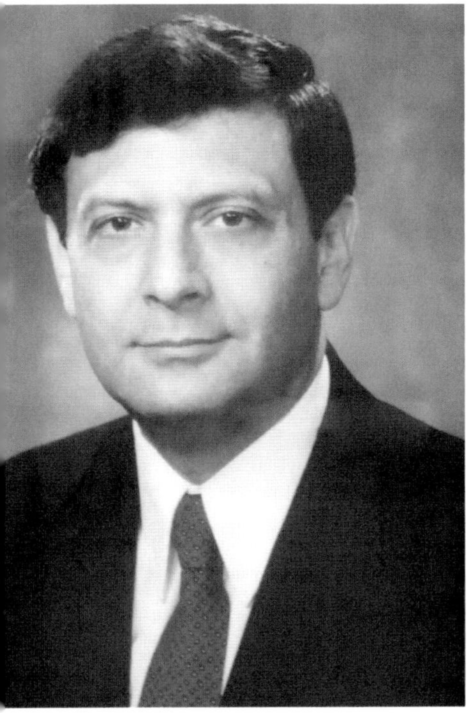

Mayor David Cohen

David Cohen spent his entire career serving the city he loved. He was an alderman for seven years, state representative for two decades, and mayor for 12 years.

As legislator, the Newton native embraced causes that won him popularity with his progressive Newton constituency. A liberal mayor, he hosted and celebrated the city's first gay marriage. In 2002, he made history by convincing voters to pass Newton's first Proposition 2½ override to increase property taxes. He also began a long-overdue process of renovating the city's schools, including a controversial rebuild of Newton North High School. He opted not to run for a fourth term. (Courtesy City of Newton.)

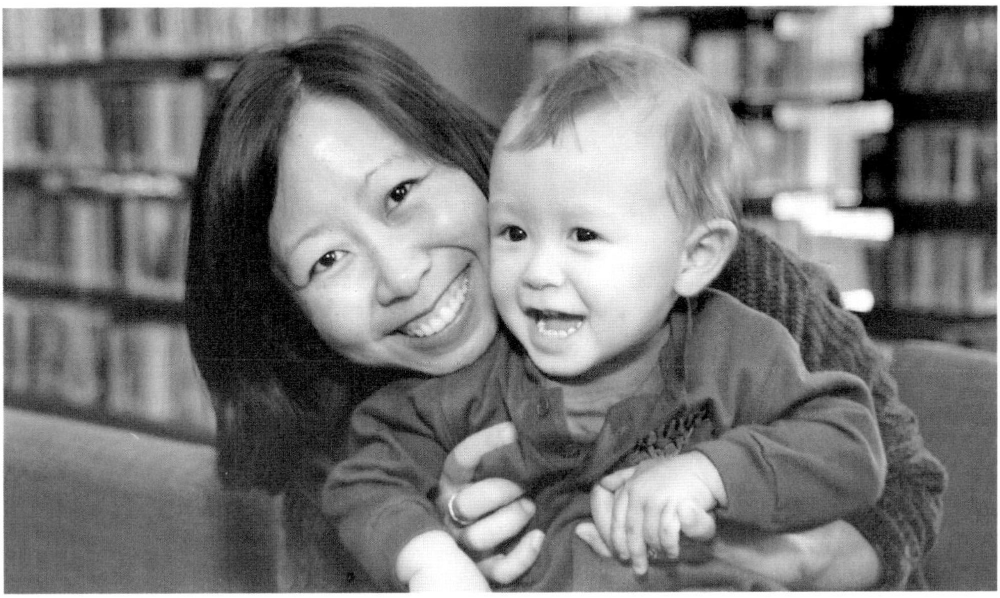

Alderman Amy Sangiolo

When Alderwoman Amy Sangiolo ran for office in 1997, a former alderman suggested she not use her photograph on her campaign literature because voters might be dissuaded by her Asian American appearance. Instead of taking that advice, she made her photograph prominent and added origami images to emphasize her ethnicity. She won by 12 votes, in a recount, and eight terms later, she is believed to be the longest currently serving Asian American elected official in Massachusetts. (Courtesy of Amy Sangiolo.)

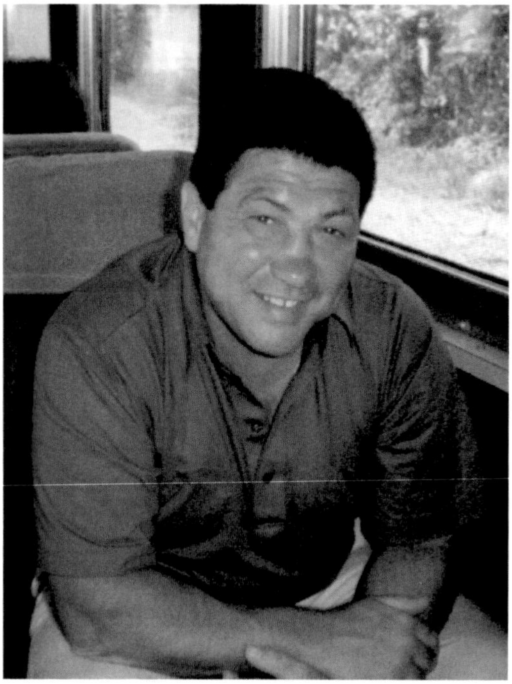

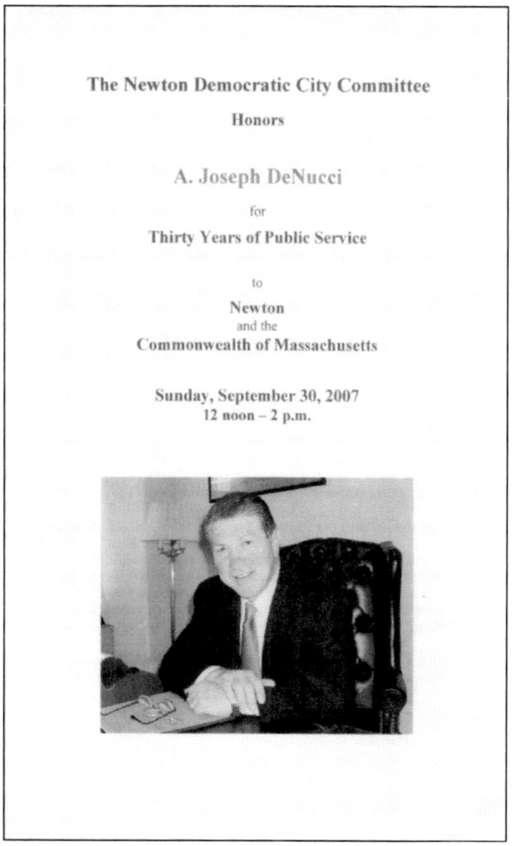

The Newton Democratic City Committee

Honors

A. Joseph DeNucci

for

Thirty Years of Public Service

to

Newton

and the

Commonwealth of Massachusetts

Sunday, September 30, 2007

12 noon – 2 p.m.

Joe DeNucci, State Auditor and Champion Boxer

Joe DeNucci was always quick on his feet. Long before he was elected to the powerful position of state auditor in 1986 and even before he won a seat representing parts of Newton and Waltham in the State House of Representatives, he was a champion middleweight boxer and two-time Golden Glove winner. The Newton native fought until he was 34 years old, consistently ranking as one of the top middleweights in the world. He holds the record for the most fights in the old Boston Garden and had a career record of 54-15-4. He twice fought Emile Griffith, a six-time world champion who had killed welterweight champ Benny Paret in the ring a decade earlier.

When he retired after 24 years as state auditor in 2010, DeNucci had been a much-beloved fixture at the Massachusetts State House for more than five decades. The son of an Italian working-class family, he started low on the totem pole as a legislative page at age 16 and worked his way up to legislative aide. He left that job when he was elected state representative in 1976, serving six years as chairman of the human service committee.

DeNucci was inducted into the National Italian American Sports Hall of Fame in Chicago in 2004. (Photographs courtesy of Peg Hannigan.)

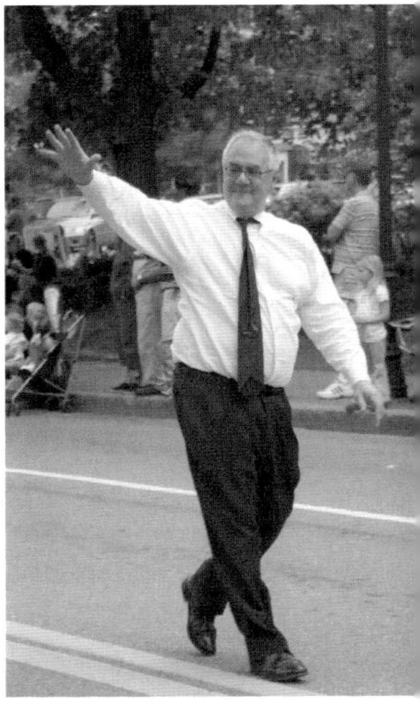

Congressman Barney Frank

Newton liberals were very supportive when Barney Frank made history in the May 30, 1987, edition of the *Boston Globe*, becoming the first member of Congress to voluntarily declare that he was gay.

Frank, at times a controversial figure for his liberal opinions and quick, sometimes unrestrained, wit, became a high-ranking, high-profile member of the House of Representatives during his 32-year stay. By the time he announced his retirement at Newton City Hall in November 2011, he had served as chair of the House Financial Services Committee and had become a liberal icon in the nation's capital. A cosponsor of the 2010 Dodd-Frank financial reform act, Frank's humor, intelligence, and work ethic helped him advocate for some of the issues about which he was most passionate, including gay and civil rights, low-income housing, banking reforms, and late in his tenure, reduced military spending.

Prior to running for Congress, Frank was a Massachusetts state representative from 1973 to 1980 and chief of staff to Boston mayor Kevin White. (Photograph by Jim Ready.)

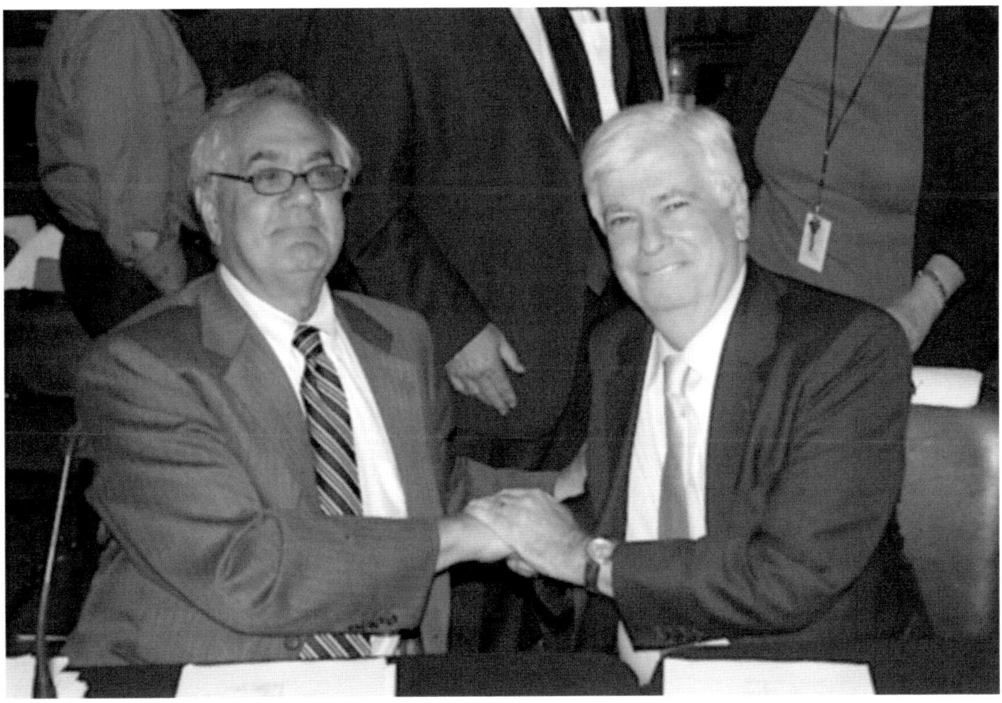

Barney Frank and Christopher Dodd at a Press Conference

Congressman Barney Frank and Sen. Christopher Dodd signed the Dodd–Frank Wall Street Reform and Consumer Protection Act "to promote the financial stability of the United States by improving accountability and transparency in the financial system, to end 'too big to fail,' to protect the American taxpayer by ending bailouts, to protect consumers from abusive financial services practices, and for other purposes" on July 21, 2010. (Photograph by Jim Ready.)

Mayor Setti Warren

Setti Warren's high school classmates from Newton North High School probably were not surprised to see their class president elected mayor of Newton in 2009. After all, the late Mayor Ted Mann had solicited Warren's help in easing racial tensions at the school and Warren had won the class president election all four years of high school.

But Warren was not a known quantity to the residents of Newton when he decided to challenge incumbent mayor David Cohen (who eventually decided not to run for reelection). He faced a five-term state representative who had been an alderman for eight years and—if elected—would have been the first female mayor, two well-known aldermen, and a lesser-known businessman. By knocking on the doors of many thousands of households, Warren, an Iraqi war veteran, won the hearts and votes of enough Newton residents to earn himself a desk in the executive office.

In doing so, Warren made history not just because he was Newton's first African American mayor, but he also became the first African American mayor voted into office in a city that had also elected both an African American governor (Deval Patrick) and president (Barack Obama).

In his first term, Warren was credited with changing the city's financial trajectory by fixing a structural budget deficit that was decades in the making.

Warren easily won reelection to his second term in 2013. (Courtesy of City of Newton.)

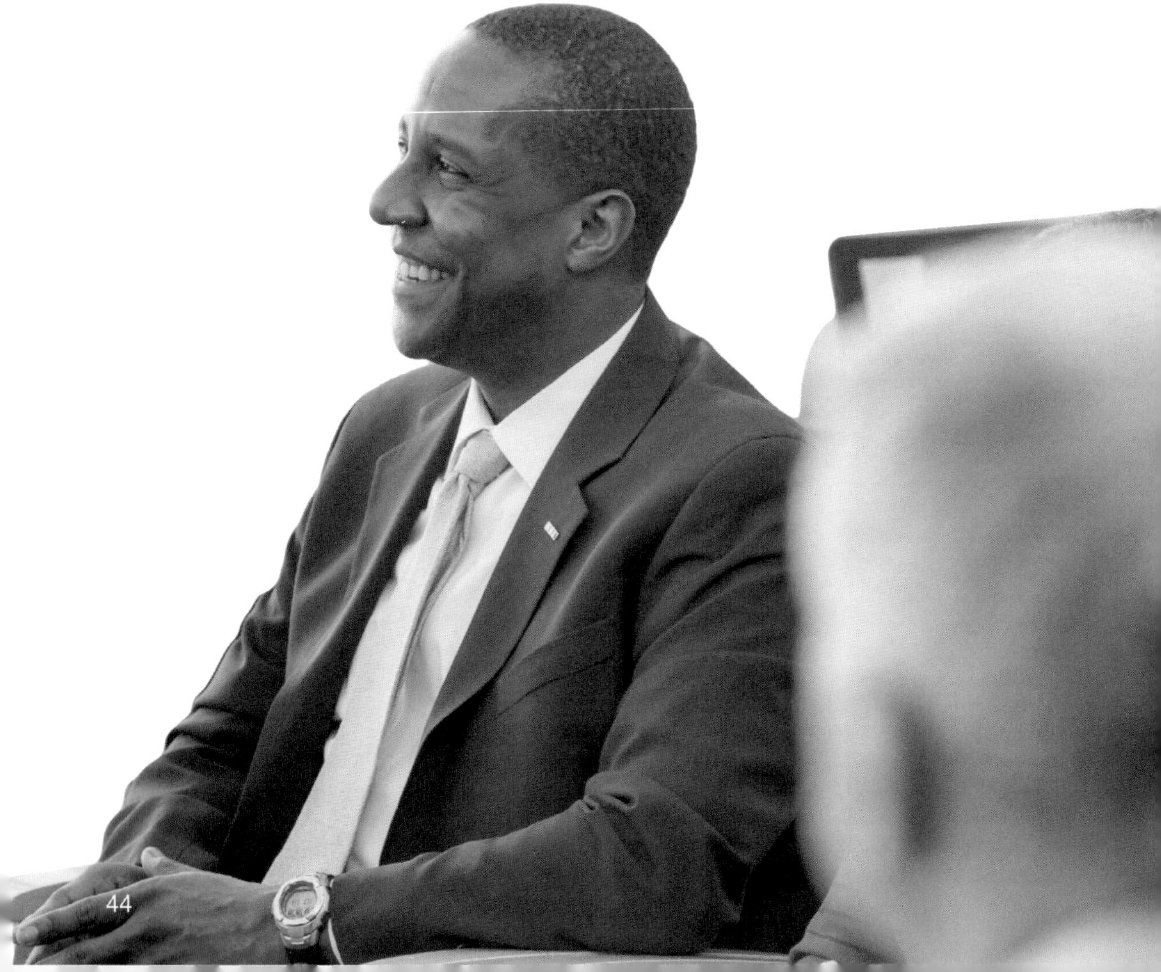

CHAPTER FOUR

Businesspeople, Inventors, and Scientists

A community is a sum of all of its parts, and Newton's businesses are as much a part of the city's fabric as are its people. Small shops often described as hidden gems are the heart of the city's villages. Better-known businesses like Cabot's Ice Cream, the Barn, and the West Newton Cinema regularly draw visitors from both inside and outside Newton. Not only is Newton in the unusual, and fortunate, position of being home to two independent bookstores, but as Newtonville Books owner Mary Cotton likes to say, both stores are uniquely named—Newtonville Books is no longer in Newtonville, and the New England Mobile Book Fair is not traveling anywhere. The investment that Newton's business community makes in supporting the city can be seen on the backs of Little League T-shirts, during school fundraisers, and on the sponsorship lists at public events.

The houses hold brilliant people who are discovering, inventing, developing, and creating all the time. Jim Koch, chief executive officer (CEO) and founder of the Boston Beer Company, brewed the first batch of Sam Adams in his Newton kitchen. At least four people have won a Nobel Prize while living in Newton. Newton entrepreneur Stephen Kaufer launched TripAdvisor, likely the largest travel site in the world. Ray Kurzweil, inventor of the first machine to translate print into computer-spoken words and an inductee of the National Inventors Hall of Fame, is a Newton resident. Century Bank founder Marshall Sloane, who with his wife, Barbara, is a philanthropist dedicated to giving back to his community, lives in Chestnut Hill.

Newton is also fortunate to have an independent, family-owned pharmacy. Located in Auburndale, Keyes Drugs is owned by pharmacists and brothers Raied and Saad Dinno, whose father bought the store in 1985.

This chapter will introduce the reader to just a few of Newton's business legends.

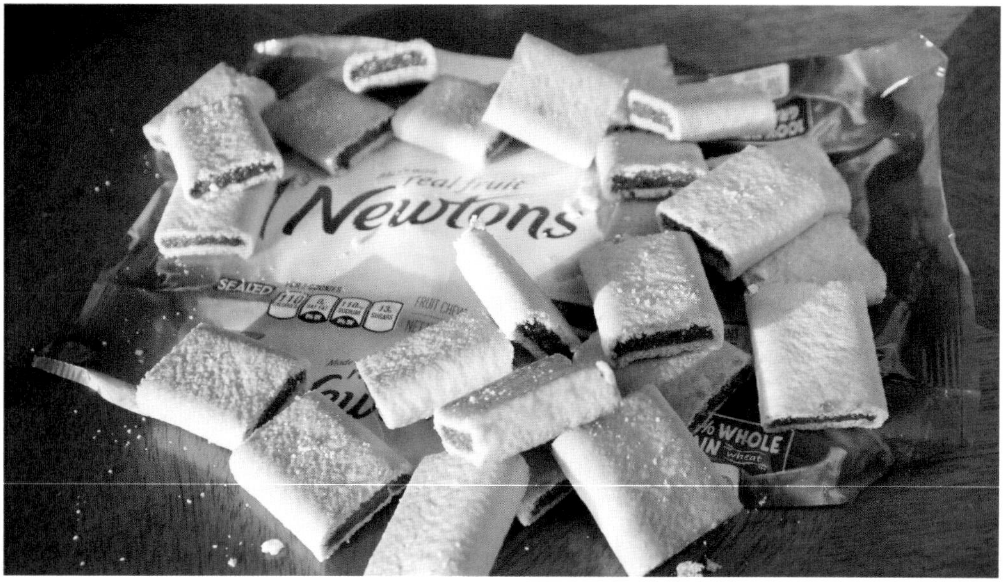

Fig Newton, Our Own Cookie

One of Newton's favorite claims to fame is the Fig Newton, a soft cookie filled with fig jam that is named after the city of Newton. Charles Roser, a cookie maker born in Ohio, created the Fig Newton recipe. Kennedy Biscuit Works used a machine invented by James Henry Mitchell in 1891 to mass-produce the cookies. In keeping with its tradition of naming cookies after the surrounding cities and towns of Boston, Kennedy Biscuits originally named the cookies "Newtons" and, later, changed the name to "Fig Newtons." (Photograph by Amit Lahav.)

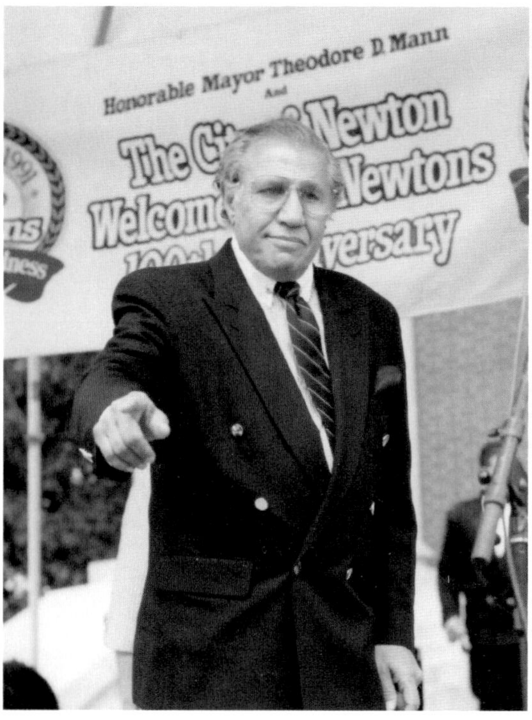

Mayor Ted Mann at Fig Newton's 100th Anniversary

Nabisco hosted a big celebration in honor of the Fig Newton's centennial in Newton in May 1991. Entertainment included country singer Juice Newton and dancing by commercial character Mr. Big Fig. More than 300 people attended the gala, which featured many Fig Newtons for people to devour and one 100-inch Fig Newton. (Courtesy of the Mann family.)

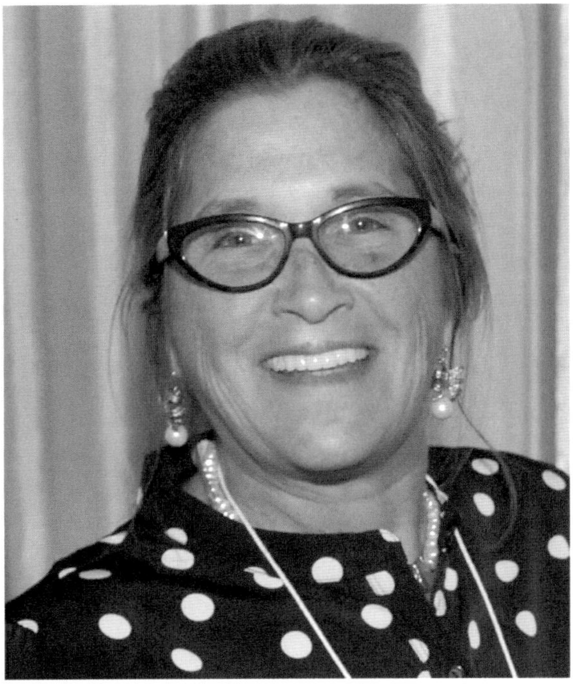

Seana Gaherin, Dunn-Gaherin Food & Spirits
Seana Gaherin and Robert Dunn opened Dunn-Gaherin Food & Spirits, an Irish pub located in a 260-year-old building, in 1991. Considered by many to be one of Newton's hidden gems, Dunn-Gaherin's cozy atmosphere, comfort food, and friendly staff draw customers from beyond its Upper Falls location. While Gaherin does not live in Newton, it seems like she never leaves. Gaherin, who is chair of the Newton-Needham Chamber of Commerce, is active in Friends of Hemlock Gorge, Project Hope, Feast of the Falls, and the annual For Pete's Sake Road Race. (Courtesy of Seana Gaherin.)

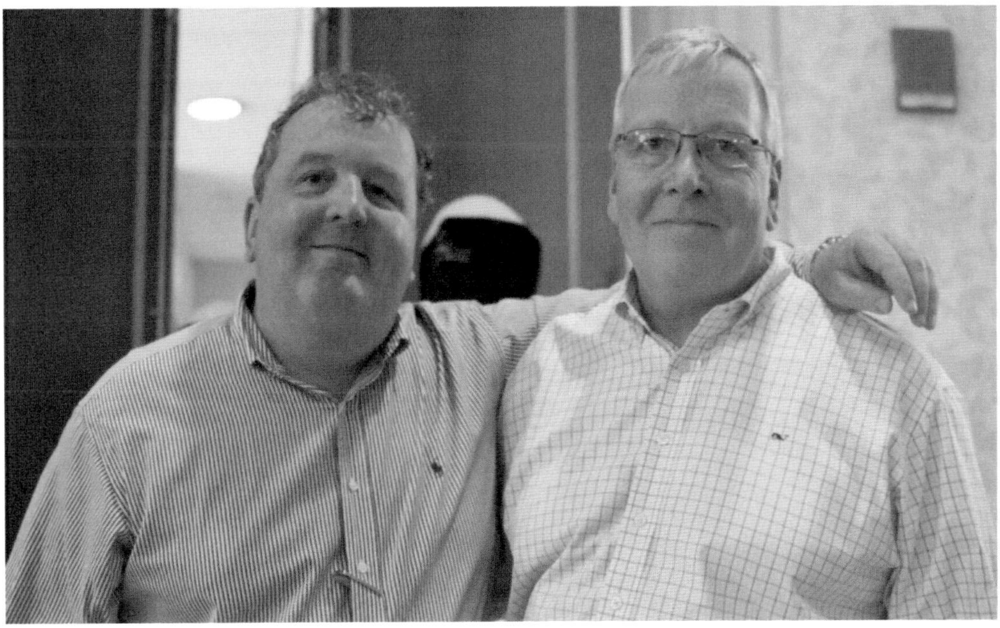

Karl and John O'Hara, O'Hara's Food & Spirits
Karl (left) and John O'Hara opened their first restaurant, O'Hara's Food & Spirits, with their father in 1985. The Newton Highlands pub, popular with the neighborhood and professionals for its good food, draught beer, and welcoming atmosphere, caught on fast. In 2002, the brothers opened the equally popular Paddy's Pub across the city in West Newton. Paddy's, named for the family patriarch, is well known for hosting the annual Paddy's Pub Shillelagh Shuffle Road Race, part of the New England Runner Pub Series. The three-mile run benefits Athletes Unlimited. (Photograph by Rachel Lebeaux.)

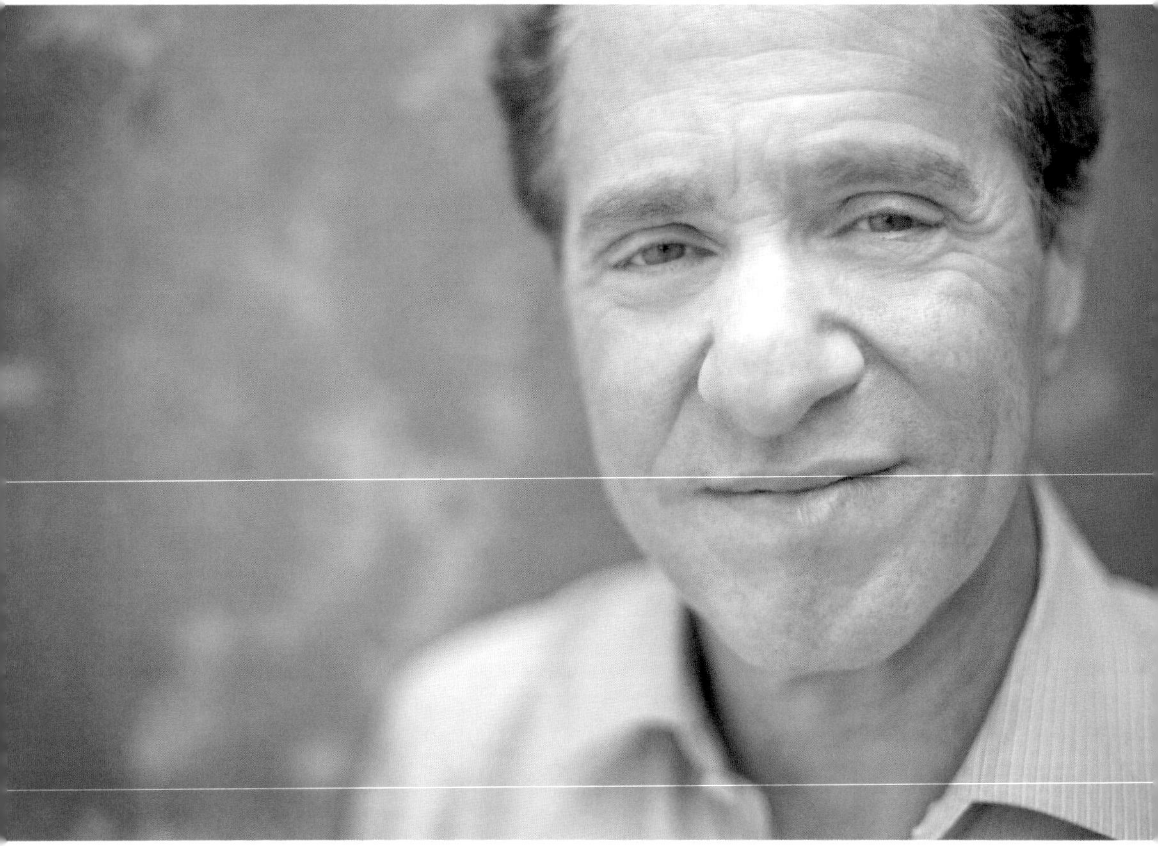

Raymond Kurzweil, Inventor and Futurist

Considered by many to be one of the world's leading inventors, thinkers, and futurists, Newton Highlands resident Ray Kurzweil's biography credits him with an impressive number of inventions. He was the principal inventor of the first optical character recognition (OCR) for transforming the written word into data, the first print-to-speech software for the blind, the first charge-coupled device (CCD) flatbed scanner, the first text-to-speech synthesizer, the first music synthesizer capable of recreating the grand piano and other orchestral instruments, and the first commercially marketed large-vocabulary speech recognition system.

Kurzweil, who was inducted into the National Inventors Hall of Fame in 2002, is the recipient of the $500,000 Lemelson–Massachusetts Institute of Technology Prize, the world's largest award for invention and innovation. He has received honors from three US presidents, including the 1999 National Medal of Technology, the nation's highest honor in technology. He has also received many other national and international awards, and honorary doctorates.

Kurzweil has written seven books, making the New York Times best-seller list with *The Age of Spiritual Machines* and *The Singularity is Near: When Humans Transcend Biology*. He espouses the theory that technology is accelerating so fast that the Singularity, the point at which there will be no distinction between humans and machines, is just three decades away.

Microsoft's Bill Gates called Kurzweil "the best person I know at predicting the future of artificial intelligence."

He joined Google as director of engineering in 2012. (Courtesy of Ray Kurzweil.)

Paul Levy, Patient Care Advocate, Soccer Lover, Blogger

Paul Levy has had a busy career. As CEO of Beth Israel Deaconness Medical Center (BIDMC) in the early 2000s, Levy avoided the massive layoffs that were taking place in hospitals across the country by collaborating with his employees to make sacrifices at all levels, saving the jobs of the lowest-paid workers. At the Massachusetts Water Resources Authority, many credit him for leading the Boston Harbor Cleanup. He also spent several years as executive dean of administration at Harvard Medical School. He chaired the Massachusetts Department of Public Utilities, directed Arkansas's Department of Energy, and taught environmental policy at Massachusetts Institute of Technology (MIT) for seven years.

Levy, who calls himself an "infrastructure nut," mixed things up at BIDMC when he embraced social media as a vehicle for reaching out to his employees. He began writing a blog, *Running a Hospital*, that included his thoughts on health-care issues, hospitals, medicine, and pretty much whatever else was on his mind. He was one of the first executives in the country to blog and was, perhaps, the very first to use his blog to rally employees to understand the organization's financial problems and brainstorm solutions in order to make shared sacrifices with management.

Locally, residents have been more likely to find Levy dressed in cleats and soccer attire than in a business suit. Levy has coached girls' soccer teams to championships, refereed almost too many Newton soccer games to count, and continues to play pick-up soccer himself. He chaired Mayor David Cohen's Blue Ribbon Commission that studied city finances in 2006–2007.

Levy is the author of *Goal Play: Leadership Lessons from the Soccer Field* and *How a Blog Held Off the Most Powerful Union in America*; he was the coauthor of *How to Negotiate Your First Job: 8 Steps That Will Create Value for You and Your New Employer.* After 10 years running BIDMC, Levy left in 2012. He continues to blog as *Not Running a Hospital.* (Courtesy of Paul Levy.)

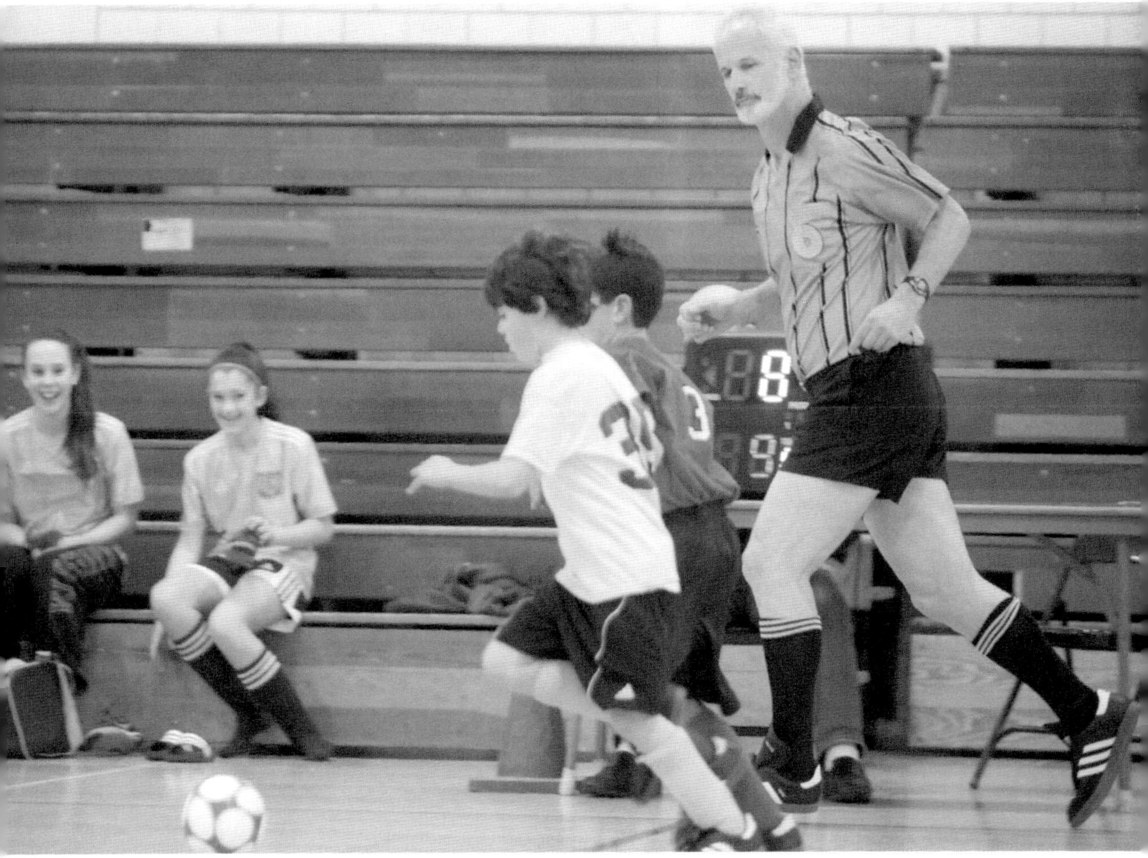

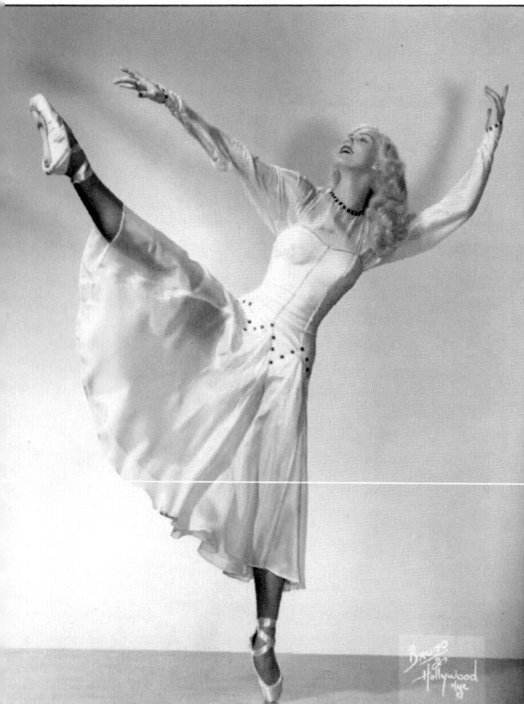

Paulette Harwood, Paulette's Ballet Studio

It is not easy to find a dancer in Newton who has not taken at least one class at Paulette's Ballet Studio on Oak Street in Upper Falls. Paulette Harwood, who opened her dance studio in 1960, has seen thousands of girls, boys, and adults cross the threshold onto her hardwood floors since she first hung her sign on the brick building.

Harwood started dancing as a young girl with her first professional job at 14 years old. She danced in the popular New York establishments Lou Walter's Diamond Horseshoe and the Copacabana, and was a soloist in the Radio City Music Hall Ballet Company.

Harwood has also choreographed dances for performances all over Massachusetts, including for the Boston Celtics cheerleaders. She has designed and sewed costumes for Miss America and Miss Massachusetts contestants, and she is known for the creative and dazzling costumes she designs for her students. (Both courtesy of Paulette Harwood.)

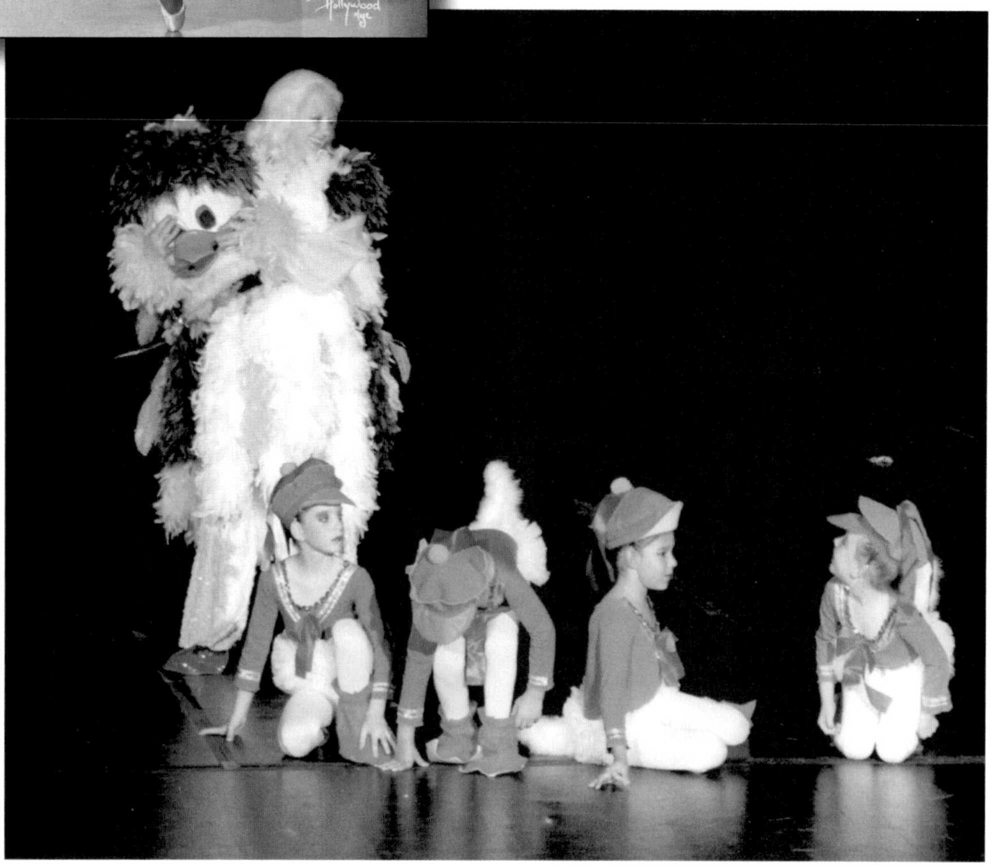

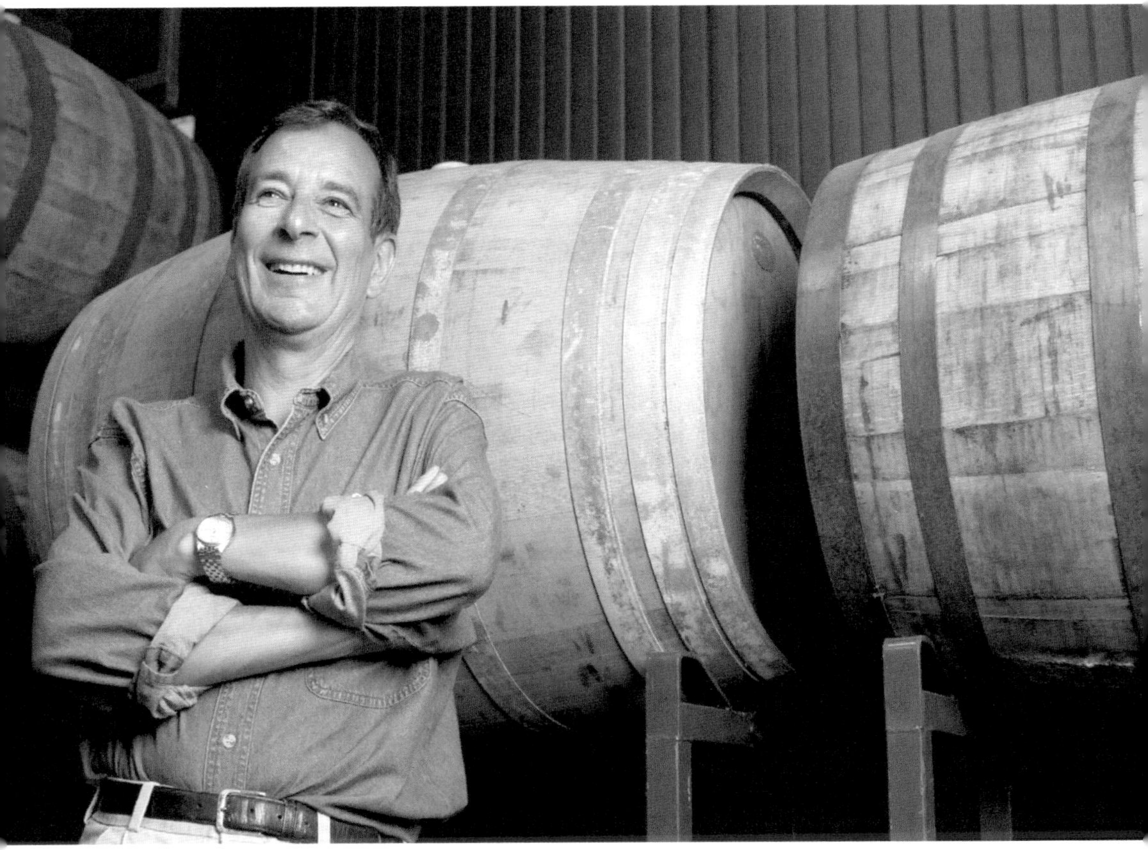

Jim Koch, Sam Adams Brewer

Although Jim Koch started his career in management consulting, the beer business was always on his radar. Five generations of Kochs had run breweries, but the family brewing recipes had not been used since the Louis Koch brewery closed during Prohibition. In 1984, when domestic beers were mostly pale lagers from mass-market brewers and the selection of imports was limited, Koch's instincts told him that the time was right to offer beer drinkers something different.

Koch went to work in his Newton kitchen with his great-great-grandfather's recipe from a St. Louis family brewer in the 1870s. The following spring, he filled his briefcase with bottles from his sample brew and pounded the pavement, visiting Boston bars and restaurants and asking managers to serve his beer, Samuel Adams Boston Lager.

Koch named the beer after Sam Adams, the patriot, because Adams was a revolutionary thinker and a brewer who had inherited his business from his father.

In April 1985, Samuel Adams Boston Lager made its debut in 25 Boston bars. By the end of the year, sales had reached 500 barrels, and by 1988, when the company built a small brewery in Boston, sales hit 36,000 barrels.

From those humble beginnings, Boston Beer became a leader in the growth of microbreweries across the country.

By 2013, Boston Beer Company was making more than 30 styles of craft beer. That same year, the Bloomberg Billionaires Index estimated Koch's net worth at more than a billion dollars, making him the first person to become a billionaire off the craft-beer business. (Courtesy of Boston Beer Company.)

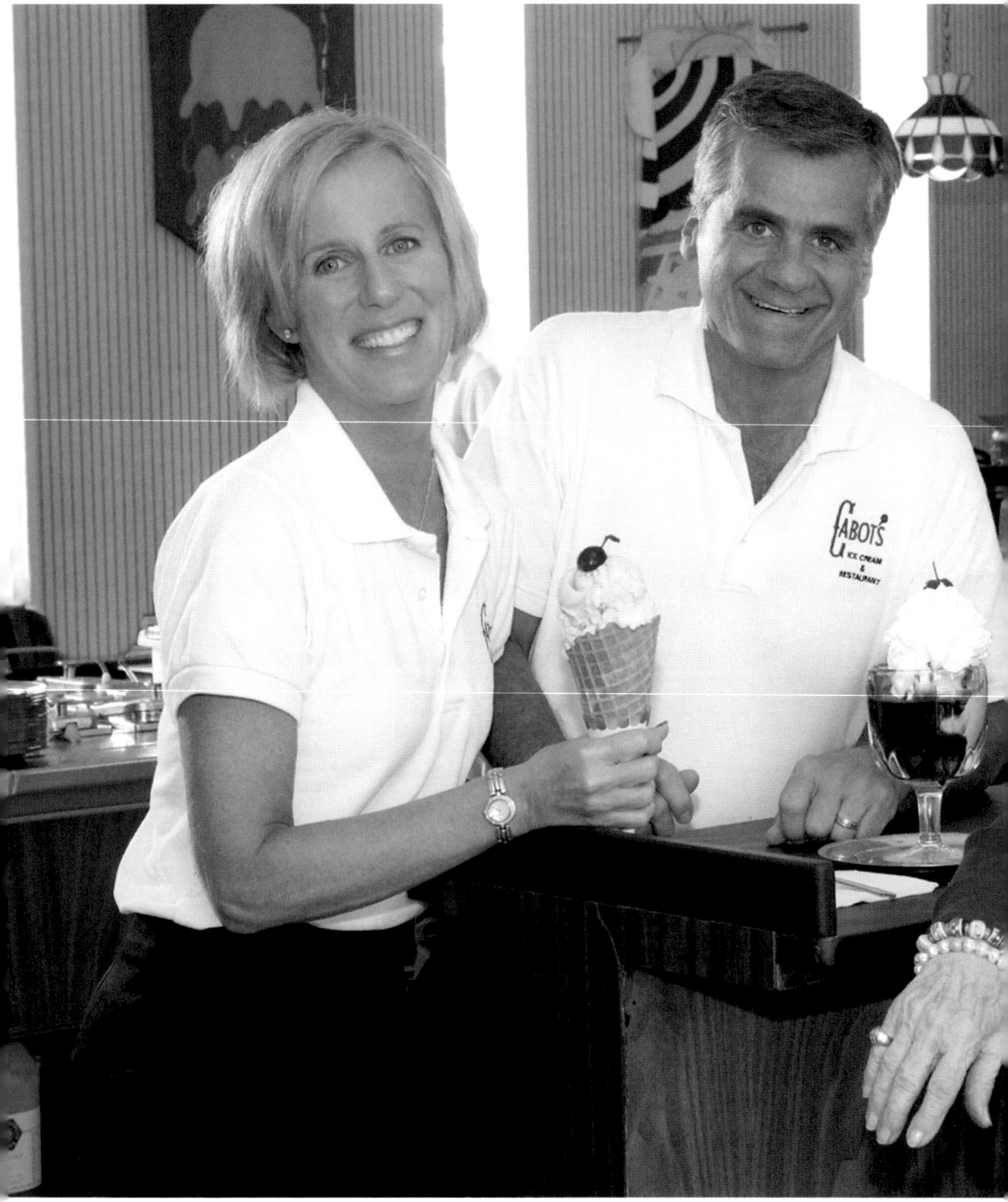

The Prestejohn Family, Cabot's Ice Cream and Restaurant
Ask Newton natives about happy childhood memories, and they'll almost always share one answer: going for ice cream at Cabot's. Catherine (seated) and Joseph Prestejohn (1923–1987) bought Cabot's Ice Cream from its prior owner in 1969 when they moved to Newton. Diners have filled the booths, counter seats and tables at the popular, old-fashioned style ice cream parlor and restaurant ever since.

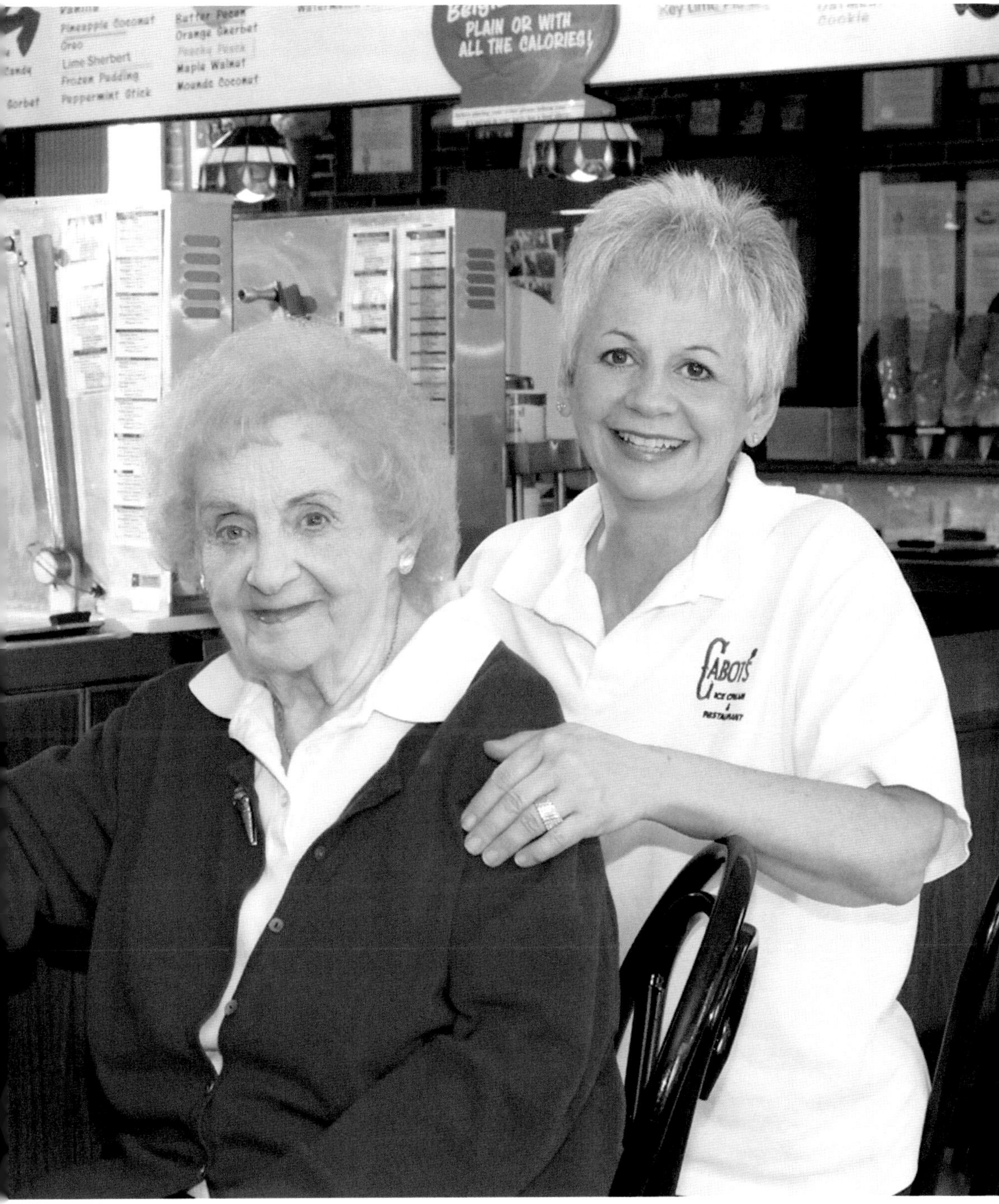

The Prestejohn family (shown here) is known for its generosity with both ice cream and time, and Cabot's is famous for its large portions, creative and unusual specialties, and delicious ice cream. Catherine Prestejohn—who seemed to always sit perched upon the same stool behind the counter and knew many customers by name—died in 2013. (Photography by Drew of Newton, Jenny Nourse Photography of Canton.)

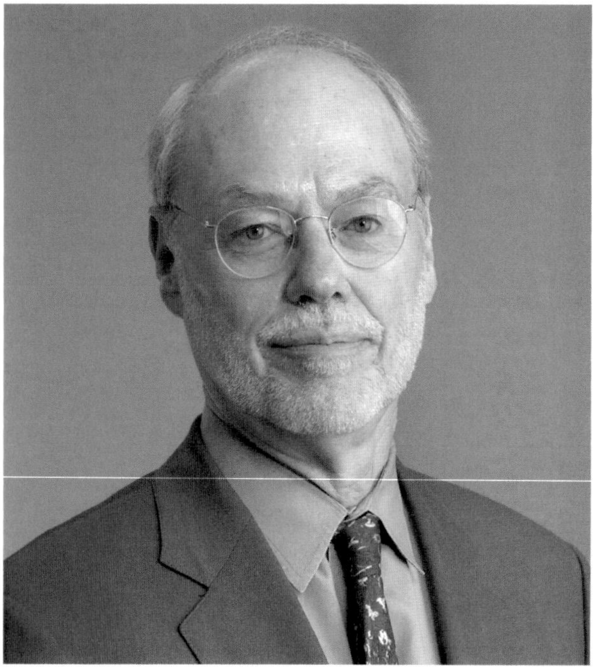

Phillip Sharp, Nobel Prize Winner

Phillip Sharp has devoted his professional life to studying genes as they relate to cancer. In 1993, Sharp shared the Nobel Prize in Physiology or Medicine with Richard Roberts for "their discoveries of split genes." Sharp, a cofounder of Biogen, moved to Newton in 1974 to join MIT's Center for Cancer Research (now the Koch Institute). He ran the institute from 1985 to 1991 and then led MIT's biology department. In 2000, he became director of MIT's McGovern Institute for Brain Research. The author of hundreds of scientific papers, Sharp has received dozens of awards, including the President's National Medal of Honor in 2004. (Courtesy of Phillip Sharp.)

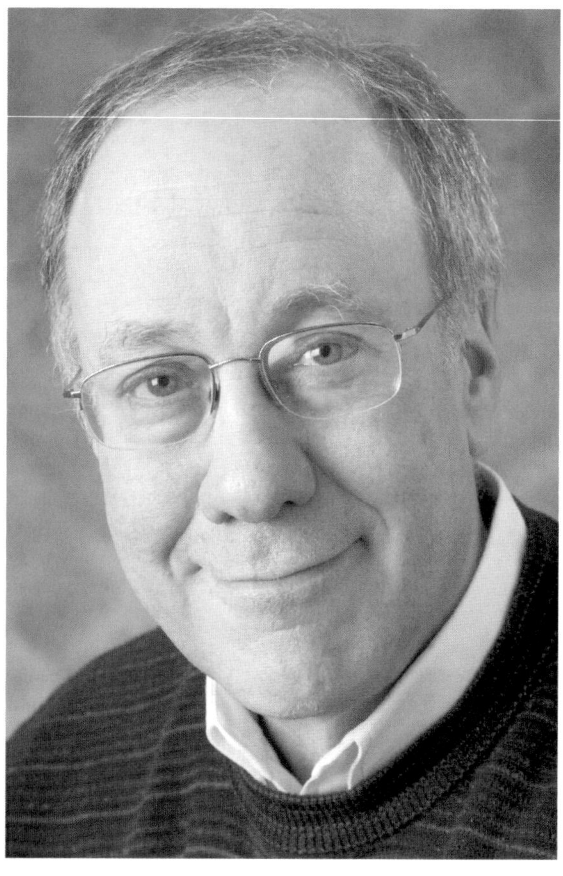

Roger Myerson, Nobel Prize in Economic Sciences

Newton native Roger Myerson shared the Nobel Memorial Prize in Economic Sciences in 2007 for "having laid the foundations of mechanism design theory."

A 1969 graduate of Newton South, Myerson is recognized as an influential contributor to the fields of economics and political science. He is the author of *Game Theory: Analysis of Conflict* and *Probability Models for Economic Decisions*. Myerson, who earned his PhD in applied mathematics from Harvard, taught for 25 years at the School of Management at Northwestern before becoming the Glen A. Lloyd Distinguished Service Professor of Economics at the University of Chicago. (Courtesy of Roger Myerson.)

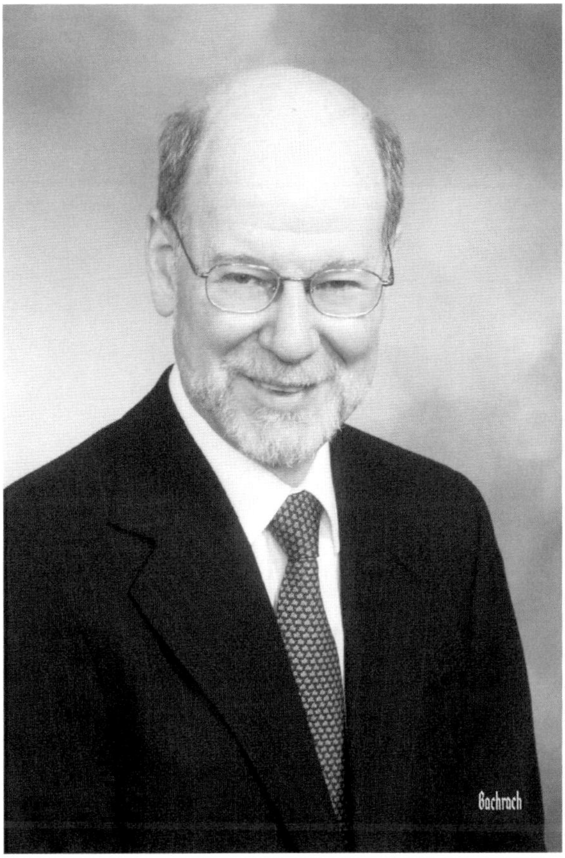

H. Robert Horvitz, Nobel Prize Winner
H. Robert Horvitz lived in Auburndale in 2002 when he and two others won the Nobel Prize in Physiology or Medicine "for their discoveries concerning genetic regulation of organ development and programmed cell death." Horvitz, a founding member of the McGovern Institute for Brain Research at MIT and a faculty member of MIT's biology department since 1978, is an investigator at the Howard Hughes Medical Institute.

He has received numerous awards, including the James R. Killian Faculty Achievement Award, which recognizes extraordinary professional accomplishment by full-time MIT faculty. (Courtesy of Robert Horvitz.)

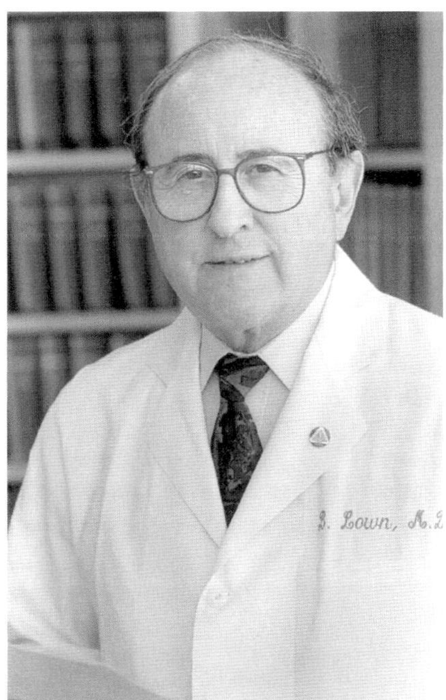

Bernard Lown, Nobel Peace Prize Winner
Considered a pioneer in researching sudden cardiac death, world-renowned cardiologist Bernard Lown invented the direct current defibrillator and cardioverter, instruments that restore the heartbeat to the arrested heart and correct various rhythm disorders, respectively. Lown, who moved to Newton in 1959, has been a leading advocate for peace, justice, and social responsibility. He founded Physicians for Social Responsibility in the 1960s and cofounded International Physicians for the Prevention of Nuclear War with former Soviet premier Leonid Brezhnev's personal physician, Dr. Evgeni Chazov, in the 1980s, an effort that won the men a Nobel Peace Prize in 1985. (Courtesy of Bernard Lown.)

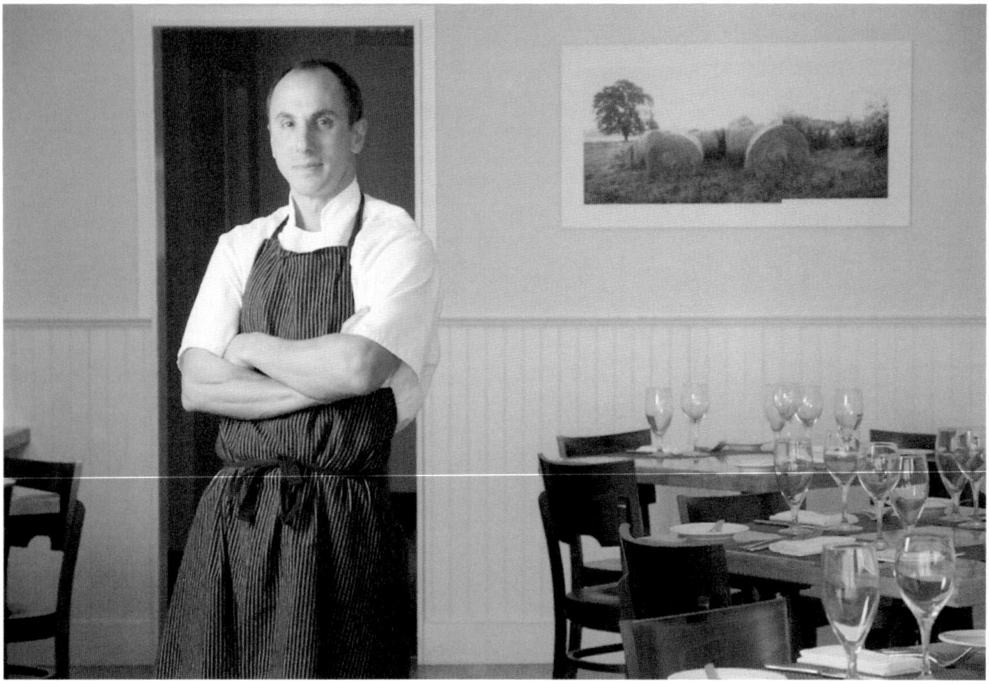

Michael Leviton, Lumiere Owner and Chef
Newton native Michael Leviton expanded fine dining in Newton when he opened French-inspired Lumiere in West Newton Square in 1999. The bistro was an immediate hit, drawing customers from both inside and outside the city's borders. Leviton, who had worked with some of the world's top chefs prior to opening Lumiere, has since won much praise and numerous awards from the culinary world, including seven nominations for "Best Chef: Northeast" from the esteemed James Beard Foundation. He opened Area Four in Cambridge in 2011. (Courtesy of Michael Leviton.)

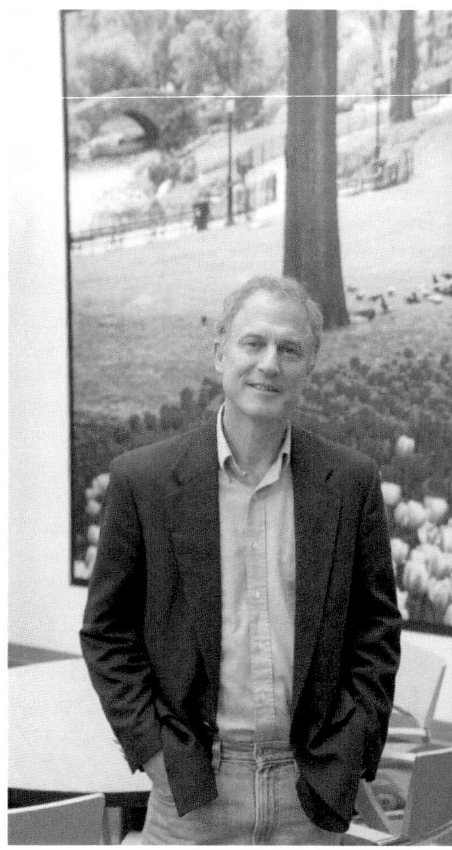

Stephen Kaufer, TripAdvisor Founder and CEO
Frustrated that his Internet search for a vacation spot was only producing marketing materials, Newton resident Stephen Kaufer added advanced Boolean logic into his searches, something the ordinary traveler would not know how to do. The result yielded travelers' photographs depicting settings different from the enticing ones seen on resorts' websites. Soon after, he was doing the same for other travelers, and in 2000, TripAdvisor was born. Kaufer, the winner of the 2005 Ernst & Young Entrepreneur of the Year Award, holds several software patents. The company is headquartered in Newton but plans to move to Needham in 2015. (Courtesy of TripAdvisor.)

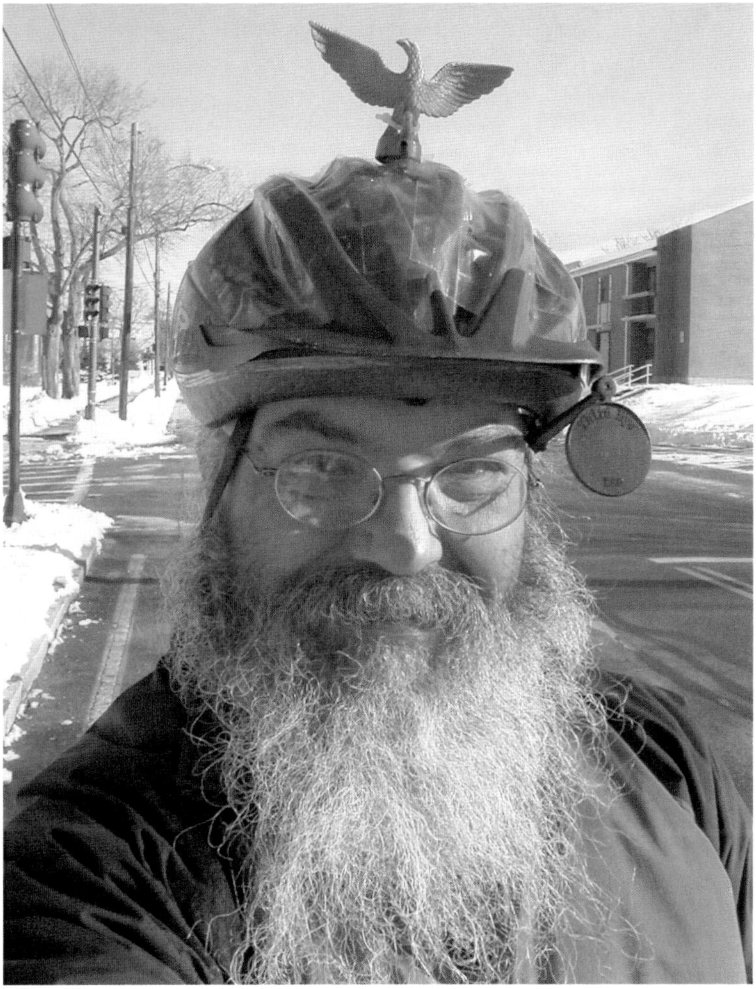

Sheldon Brown, Bicycle Guru

After Sheldon Brown died at age 63 on February 3, 2008, the *London Times* wrote in its obituary of the Newtonville resident, "If Sheldon Brown had been only an excellent bicycle mechanic, the esteem in which he was held, while great, could not have extended much beyond his native Massachusetts. But because of the selfless use to which he put the Internet, regret at his death has been felt across the world."

A self-described compulsive tinkerer who worked at Harris Cyclery in West Newton for 18 years, Brown made extra money as a youngster by building bicycles from discarded parts he found at the town dump. He went on to become one of the industry's most knowledgeable and respected experts on bicycles, particularly classic and vintage bikes. At any given time, Brown owned about 50 different bicycles that he had built or customized for various reasons.

With the advent of the Internet, Brown took on the added role of webmaster for Harris Cyclery, creating for himself a following of devoted fans and, for Harris, a business model that extended well beyond the walls of its Washington Street shop. At *sheldonbrown.com*, a site that is still maintained, Brown captivated cycling enthusiasts with history, technology, travelogues, photography, and general tidbits that reflected his eccentricities and love of life.

Brown was diagnosed with Multiple Sclerosis in August 2007, about one year after his symptoms left him unable to ride a bicycle. After he died of a heart attack in February 2008, several memorial bike rides were held around the world. (Courtesy of Harriet Fell.)

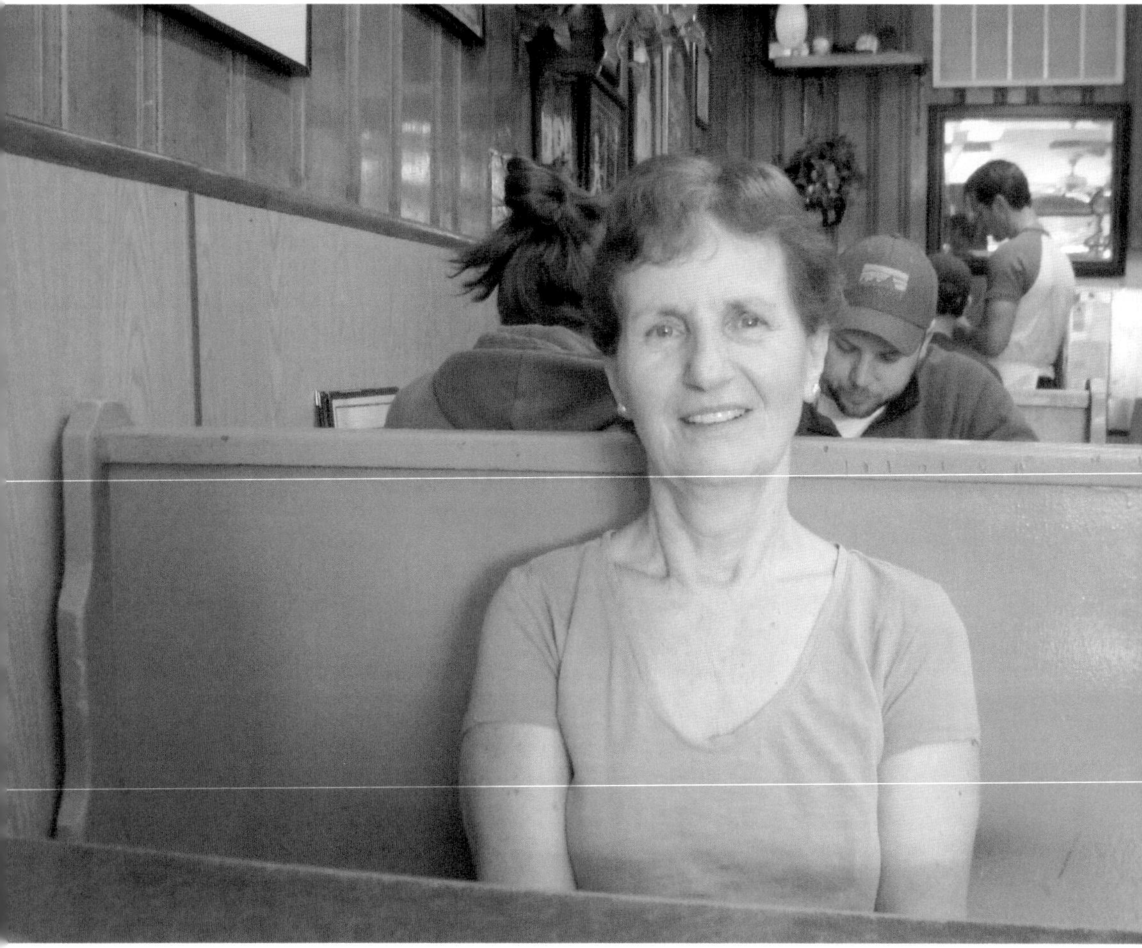

Toula Kourtis, the Face of the Knotty Pine Restaurant

Toula Kourtis was 18 years old when she left her small Greek village for the United States with a husband she had just met. One of seven children living on a farm, with only five years of schooling, she was nervous about life in a foreign country with a groom nine years her senior. It would be five years before she could talk to her mother.

Twenty-five years after that frightening journey, Kourtis, in 1989, bought the Knotty Pine in Auburndale. She had been working in a pizza parlor, saving money and harboring a dream to have her own business. (Photograph by Gail Spector.)

The Knotty Pine on Auburn Street (OPPOSITE PAGE)

Tucked between commercial businesses on Auburn Street, The Knotty Pine is more than 100 years old, and Toula Kourtis is its fourth, but longest-owning, proprietor. Regulars dine at the red formica counter, reading the newspaper and talking about the latest ball game. Photographs of famous patrons plaster the wall. Former Red Sox infielder Kevin Youkilis was a regular when he lived in Auburndale, and Newton natives home for visits often stop in to get their fix of home fries and conversation with Kourtis. (Photograph by Gail Spector.)

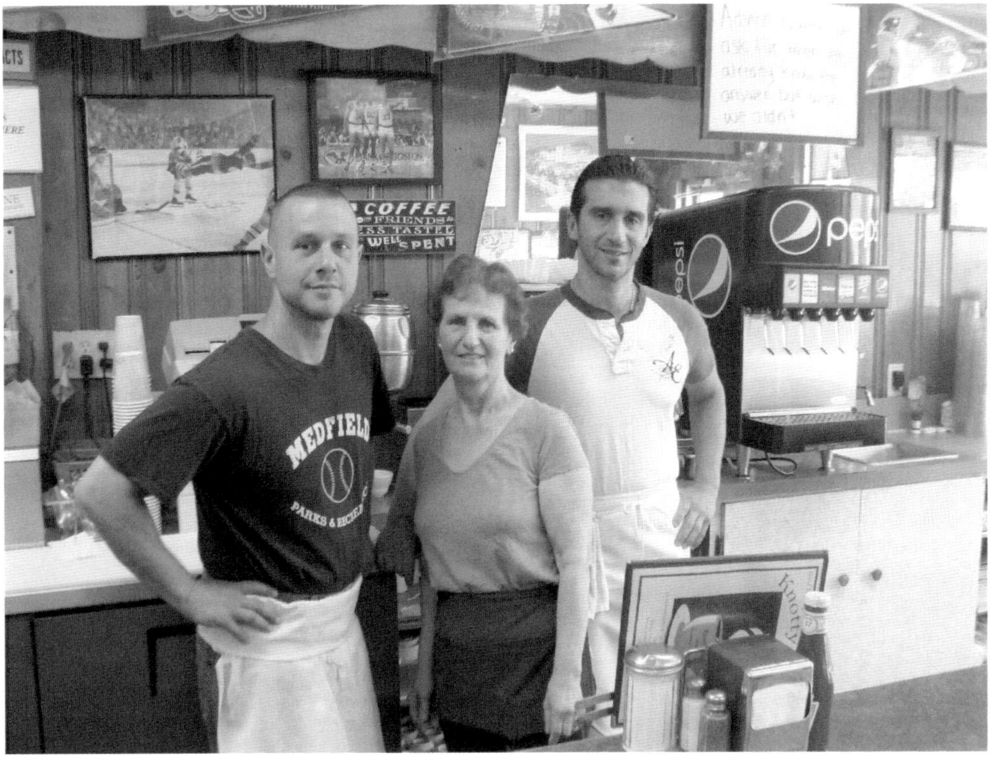

Toula Kourtis with her Sons, Bill (Left) and Nick
Bill and Nick Kourtis are very protective of their mother, Toula. The diminutive mother of three, who turned over the intimate breakfast and lunch shop to her sons in 1996, is the face of the place. Typically with a coffee pot in her hand and a smile on her face, she asks customers about their children, their parents, or why she has not seen them in awhile. (Photograph by Gail Spector.)

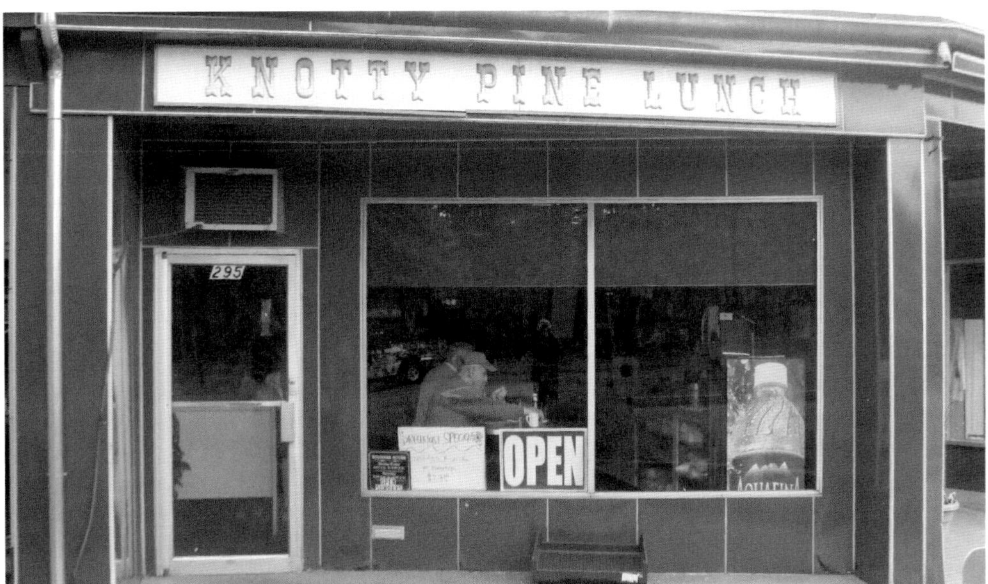

New England Mobile Book Fair

The first retail business on Needham Street, New England Mobile Book Fair is hardly mobile. Located in a one-story, warehouse-like building, the largest independent bookstore in New England was opened in 1957 by Louis Strymish, who then passed it down to his sons. The discounted prices are only part of the appeal. The many rooms make it easy for readers to keep wandering and pulling titles off shelves. In 2011, the bookstore was sold to Tom Lyons, a local businessman. The store remains an icon among Newton businesses. (Photograph by Gail Spector.)

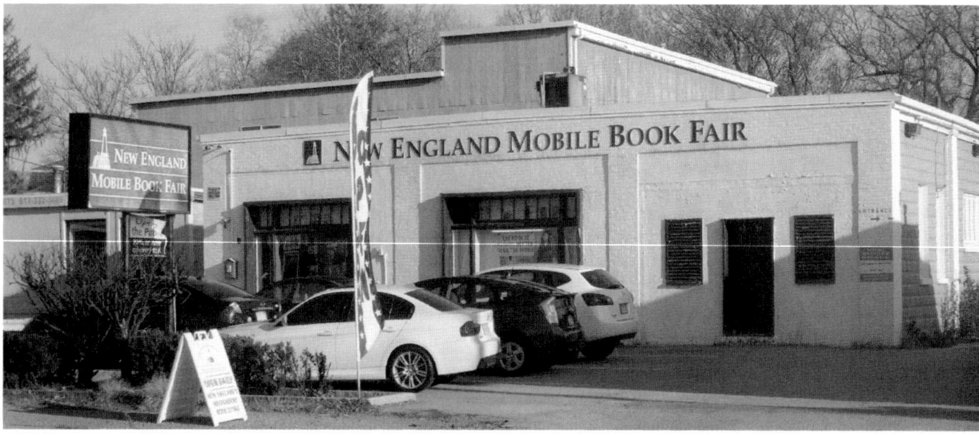

Rene Khachadourian, Antoine's Pastry Shop

Before Jacque Khachadourian, an immigrant from Marseille, France, opened Antoine's Bakery in Nonantum in 1956, there was no place to buy an Italian pastry in Newton. Khachodourian's oldest son, Antoine, was a pastry chef at the Ritz Carlton, and at a time when practically no one had ever tasted a cannoli, the elder Khachadourian decided quickly to bring the North End to Nonantum. Nearly 60 years later, Antoine's is thriving, with Jacque's son Rene at the helm, along with Rene's family. Antoine's specialties include French napoleon, Italian cannoli, and challah. (Photo by Gail Spector.)

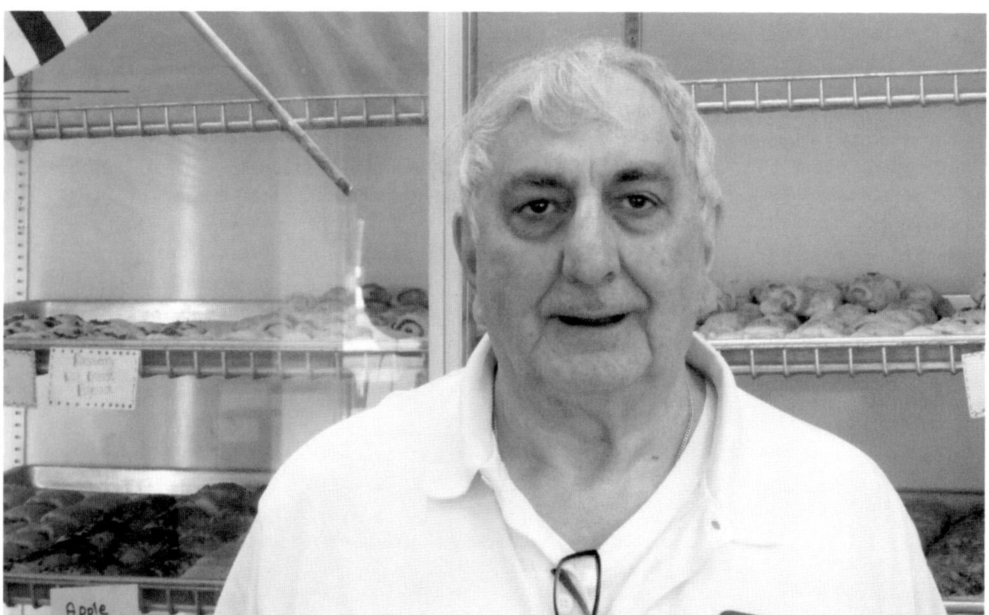

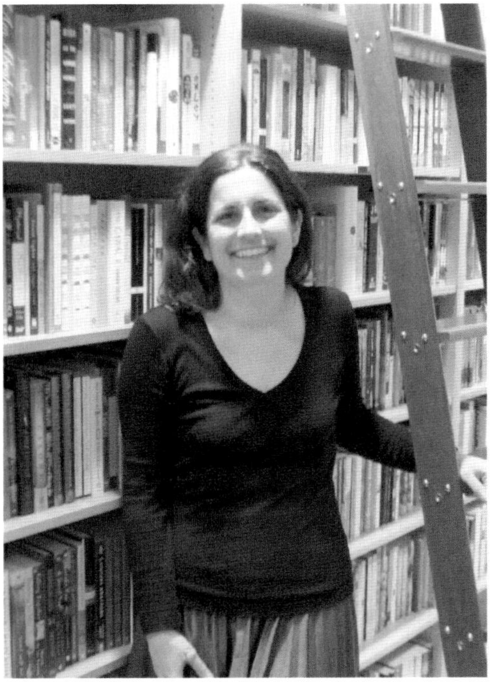

Mary Cotton and Newtonville Books

Husband and wife Jaime Clarke and Mary Cotton met and fell in love in Newtonville Books, well before Newton's second independent bookstore was available for them to acquire. When founder Tim Huggins decided to sell the shop, the couple—who are both published authors—bought the store they couldn't bear to see close, assuming ownership in 2007, preserving the shop's local appeal, and building a loyal customer base.

In 2012, with their lease up, they moved the store out of Newtonville to Newton Centre but kept the Newtonville Books name. (Photograph by Gail Spector.)

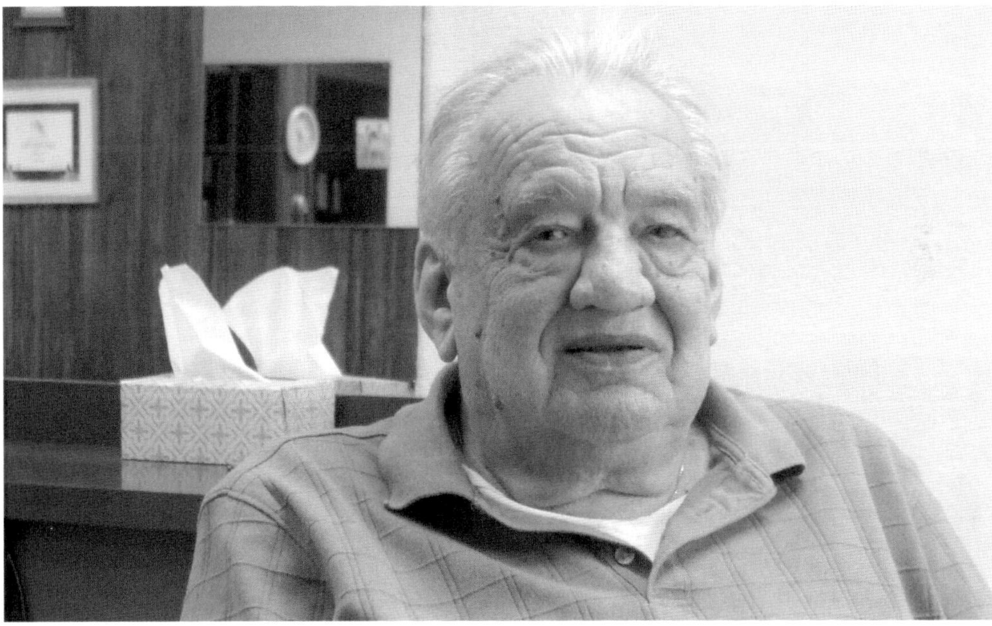

Angelo Ferrera, Angelo's Barber Shop

Angelo Ferrera has spent most of the last six decades cutting hair in a building that's held a barber for at least 100 years. Ferrera, born in 1934 in a family of barbers, bought Angelo's with a partner and then purchased the whole business when the partner hit the lottery. When Ferrara's son Frank turned 20, he joined his dad behind the chair. To keep up with changing times, the elder Ferrera went back to school in 1975, at age 50, and learned how to cut and style long hair, a process that was new to him. (Photograph by Gail Spector.)

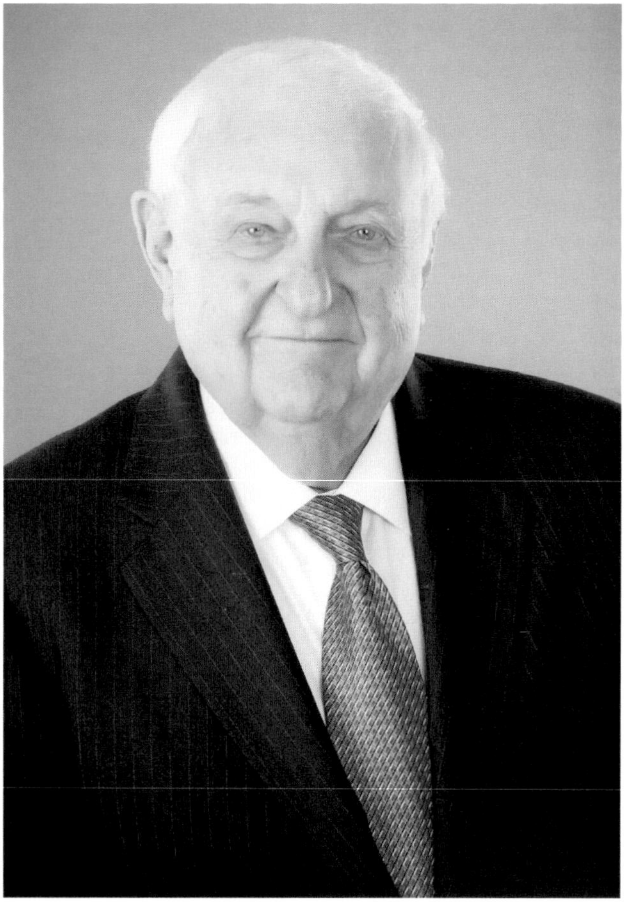

Marshall Sloane, Century Bank Founder

Century Bank and Trust chairman and Chestnut Hill resident Marshall Sloane founded the bank in 1969 in the trailer of a used-car parking lot in Somerville. His purpose then was the same as it is now: to provide banking at the community level, where the big banks usually will not take the risk. Now the fifth-largest community bank in Massachusetts, Century Bank has 26 branches in Eastern Massachusetts, including one in Newton Centre and one in Chestnut Hill.

Sloane, now chairman of the board of Century Bank and Trust, is proud of his bank's flexibility and willingness to help customers solve their problems. Century Bank recently distinguished itself when it agreed to handle the business of a medical marijuana dispensary, taking on a fledgling company in a controversial and uncertain industry.

Known for his philanthropist philosophies and practices, Sloane has been honored multiple times for his dedication to community service. The octogenarian is a lifelong Boy Scout, a leader who vocally advocated for the organization's controversial decision to end its ban on gay troop members, a member of the group's national executive board, and the recipient of the three highest-ranking awards from the Scouts. A World War II Navy veteran, Sloane has been recognized for his scouting service by Jewish, Baptist, Islamic, Catholic, Israeli, and Swedish organizations, among others. He received the Israel Peace Medal for his support for the state of Israel, and in 1994 the Knighthood of St. Gregory the Great was conferred upon him by Paul John Paul II. (Courtesy of Century Bank.)

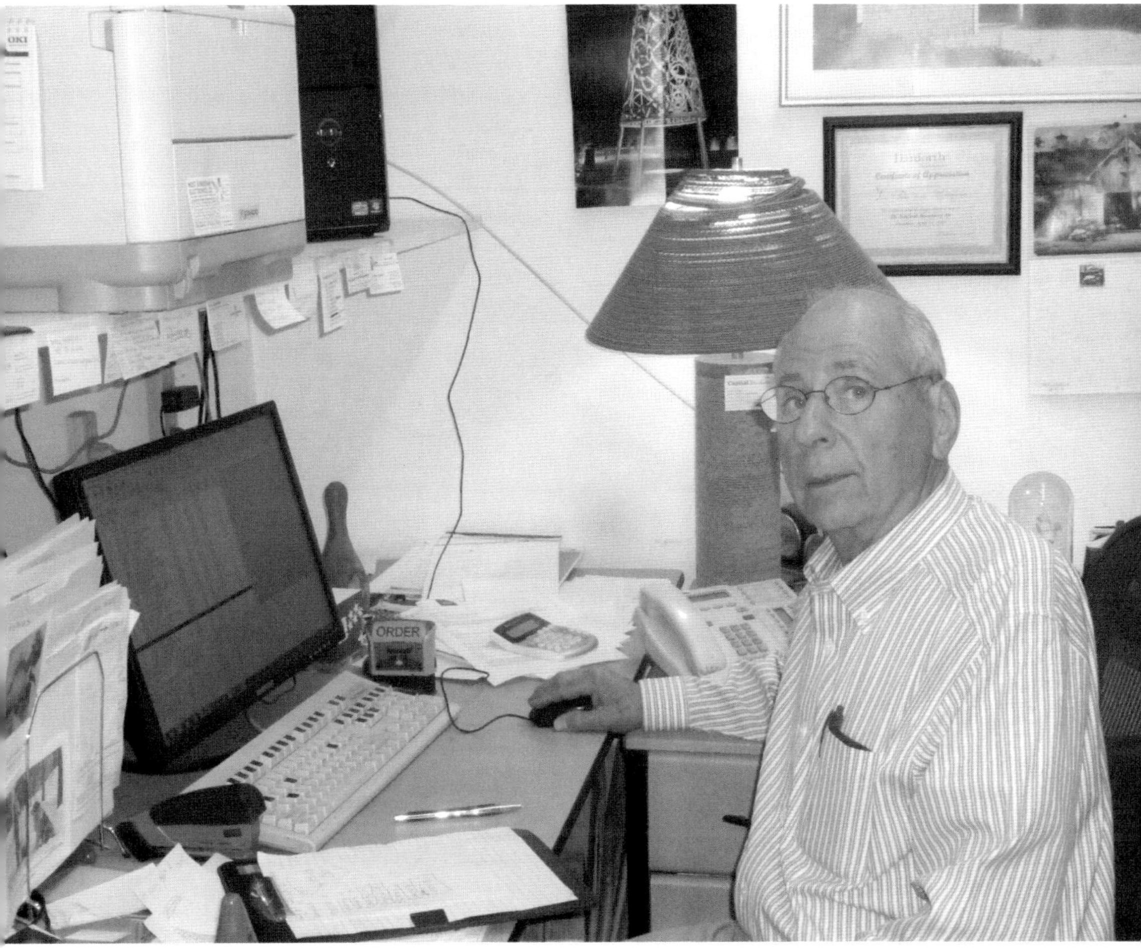

Michael Swartz, Swartz Hardware

When Michael Swartz sold his business in November 2013, he turned over the keys to one of the oldest family-owned businesses in Newton. Swartz's paternal grandparents, Jacob and Julia Swartz, opened the store on Watertown Street in Nonantum in 1890 after emigrating from Germany and Russia. Although it has seen many facelifts, and it moved down the street one block after 10 years, Swartz Hardware has remained at the same Watertown Street location since 1900. The merchandise changed a little over time, but one thing remained consistent: the business's reputation as a hardware store where customer service was top notch.

At age 74 and with children whose careers had taken them in other directions, Swartz decided it was time for a break. Most importantly, for Swartz, he found an experienced hardware store owner and operator to buy the store who he felt confident would continue to care for his customers as well as he and his family had for 123 years. The new owner, Senneth Berrier, has kept the Swartz name for the business. (Courtesy of Mike Swartz.)

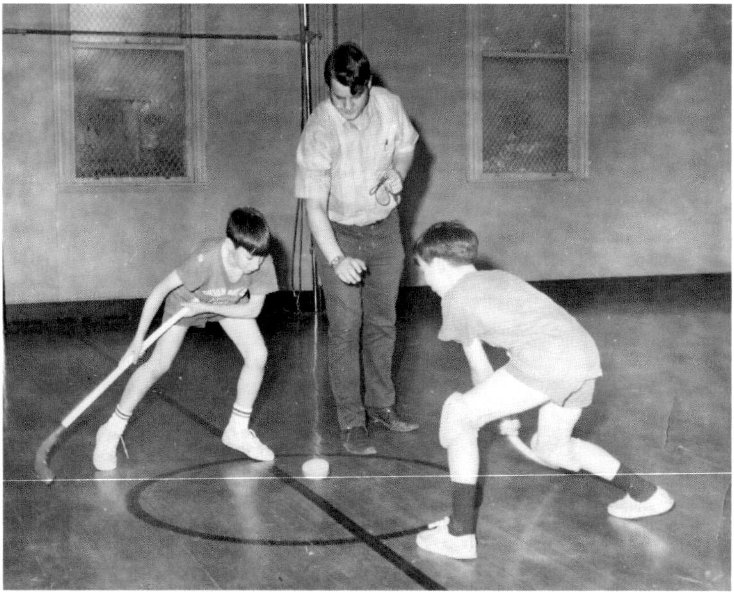

David Sellers Sr., Boys & Girls Club Executive Director

Among the many major decisions David Sellers Sr. made early in his tenure as executive director of the Boys Club of Newton was to include girls in all programs. In 1986, two years after Sellers took over the top job, the Boys Club of Newton became fully coeducational, and in 1988, the name officially changed to the Boys & Girls Club of Newton. Also in 1988, Sellers, recognizing the need for students to receive reading, tutoring and homework help outside school, established the club's Learning Center, making it one of the first youth organizations to offer education services.

During the 1990s, when the club outgrew its small space in a converted church, Sellers led every aspect of the drive for a new facility, including raising $3 million. The John M. Barry Boys & Girls Club opened in 2000 on Watertown Street in Newtonville. During that same time period, membership doubled.

Along with his leadership role, Sellers coached, taught, cleaned, mentored, fundraised, disciplined, played, consoled, and did everything else that only someone with a great love for children will do for 38 years. When Sellers retired in 2008, his son David Sellers Jr. was named executive director. (Both courtesy of the John M. Barry Boys & Girls Club.)

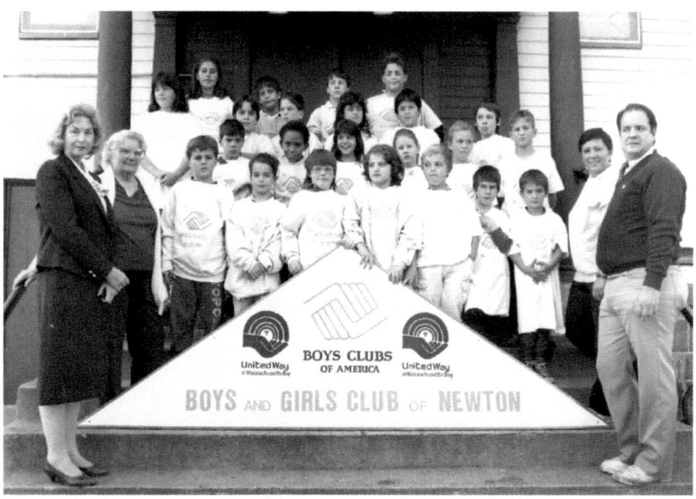

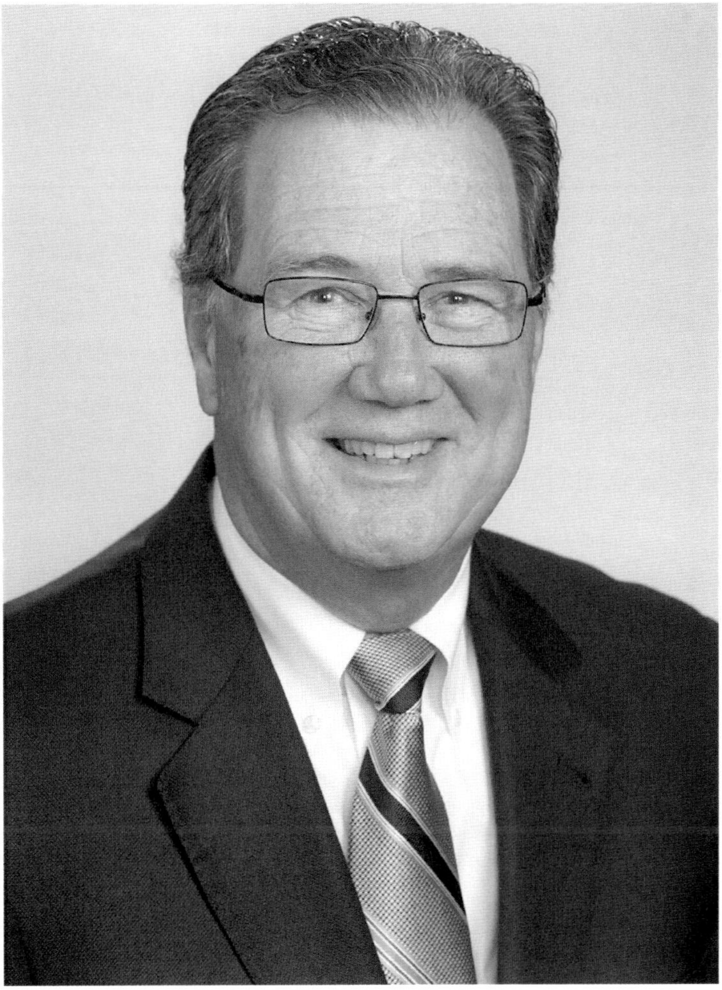

Ken Brennan, Village Bank Helps Raise Community

Ken Brennan has devoted his entire professional career to community banking. He started at a small bank in Waltham and moved to Village Bank in 1983, taking over as president and CEO in 1991. In May 2014, he was appointed chairman of the board.

The Auburndale native, who lives right around the corner from where he grew up, was honored by the Newton Schools Foundation in 2014 for all that the Village Bank has done for the Newton schools under his leadership. Under the reign of Brennan, the bank has also been a partner to the New Philharmonia Orchestra, Good Shepherd Institute, the Newton Food Pantry, Boys & Girls Club, and other Newton nonprofits. In 2013, the Village Bank donated a $25,000, 10-passenger van to the West Suburban YMCA of Newton.

Annually, Village Bank's charitable donations exceed $300,000, not including the bank's Auburndale Community Charitable Foundation, which awards more than $50,000 in college scholarships to graduating high school seniors from Newton and Wayland.

Brennan has served on many Newton committees. He chaired the Newton Childcare Commission board and the board of the Newton-Needham Chamber of Commerce. He served as president of the Woodland Golf Club and he continues to sit on the NewTV board. He was the 2014 recipient of the Newton-Needham Chamber of Commerce's RL Tennant Award for commitment to community, the highest honor awarded by the chamber. (Courtesy of Village Bank.)

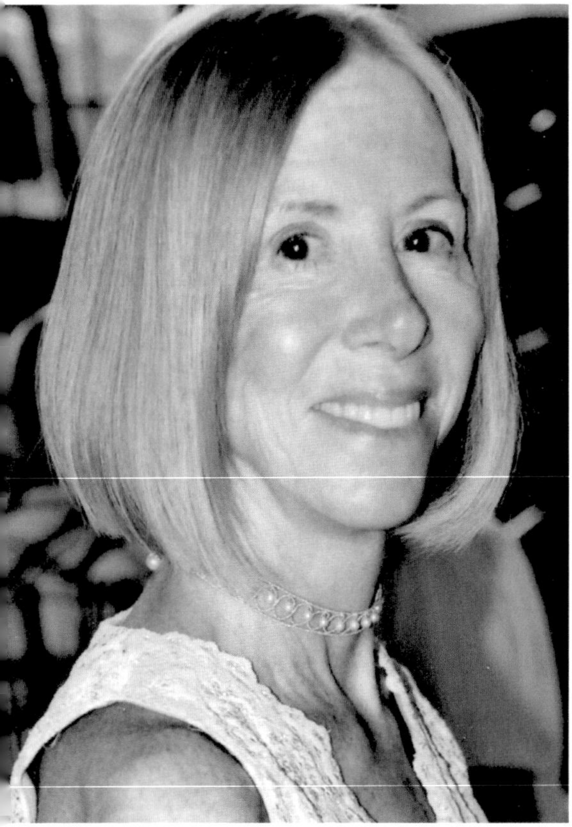

Karen Stives, Owner of the Barn

Karen Stives's father, Russell Wennbergh, did not have a storefront when he started selling shoes. Rather, he launched his business in 1948 selling sneakers out of the trunk of his car. When the trunk was too small, he expanded to rented warehouse bins where shoes were sorted by size instead of style. As sales flourished, he rented the entire warehouse on Kempton Place in West Newton, where The Barn Family Shoe Store remains to this day.

When Wennbergh died in 1964, his wife, Lillian, took over, and in 1995, she turned over the reins to their daughter Karen Stives, who continues to own the store. Stives has since converted The Barn's second and adjacent building, previously used as a sporting goods store, into The Kid's Barn, another popular spot for families.

Stives was not always in the shoe business, though. Considered one of the world's leading equestrians, she represented the United States in international competition from 1980 to 1988 in Three-Day Eventing, among the most challenging disciplines for horses and riders. Stives won Team Gold and Individual Silver Medals in the 1984 Olympics, making history as the first woman to win an Olympic medal in Three-Day Eventing. (Courtesy of Karen Stives.)

Eliot and Barry Tatelman, Jordan's Furniture (OPPOSITE PAGE)

Perhaps the most famous Bay State duo to graduate from Newton's public schools is Barry (right) and Eliot (left) Tatelman. The brothers, who graduated from Newton High School in 1964 and 1968, respectively, introduced themselves and their innovative marketing ideas to Massachusetts when they took over their family's furniture business in the early 1970s. Originally started by their grandfather Samuel Tatelman in 1918, Jordan's Furniture employed just eight people when their father, Edward, handed down the reins to Barry and Eliot.

The pair changed the company's image dramatically. As they opened new stores, they added entertainment to the furniture shopping experience. Two stores feature IMAX theaters; one location was built around a Bourbon Street theme; a trapeze school was added at one store.

Meanwhile, the brothers took to the airwaves with both quirky and entertaining advertising, sealing the connection between the names "Barry and Eliot" and Jordan's Furniture. They took their employees on a surprise trip to Bermuda, and in 2004, they held a special promotion offering a refund if the Red Sox won their first World Series in 86 years. Their insurance furnished a lot of living rooms that year.

The pair has put their notoriety to wider use. They have raised money for and donated to dozens of charities. In recent years, Jordan's Furniture has been a primary partner with the Massachusetts Adoption Resource Exchange and the Department of Children and Families with the goal of finding permanent homes and loving families for children in foster care.

By 1999, when Warren Buffett's investment company Berkshire Hathaway acquired Jordan's, the stores employed 1,200 people. The Tatelman brothers remained in control of operations. In 2006, Barry left to pursue a career as a Broadway producer. Eliot continues to run the business. (Courtesy of Jordan's Furniture.)

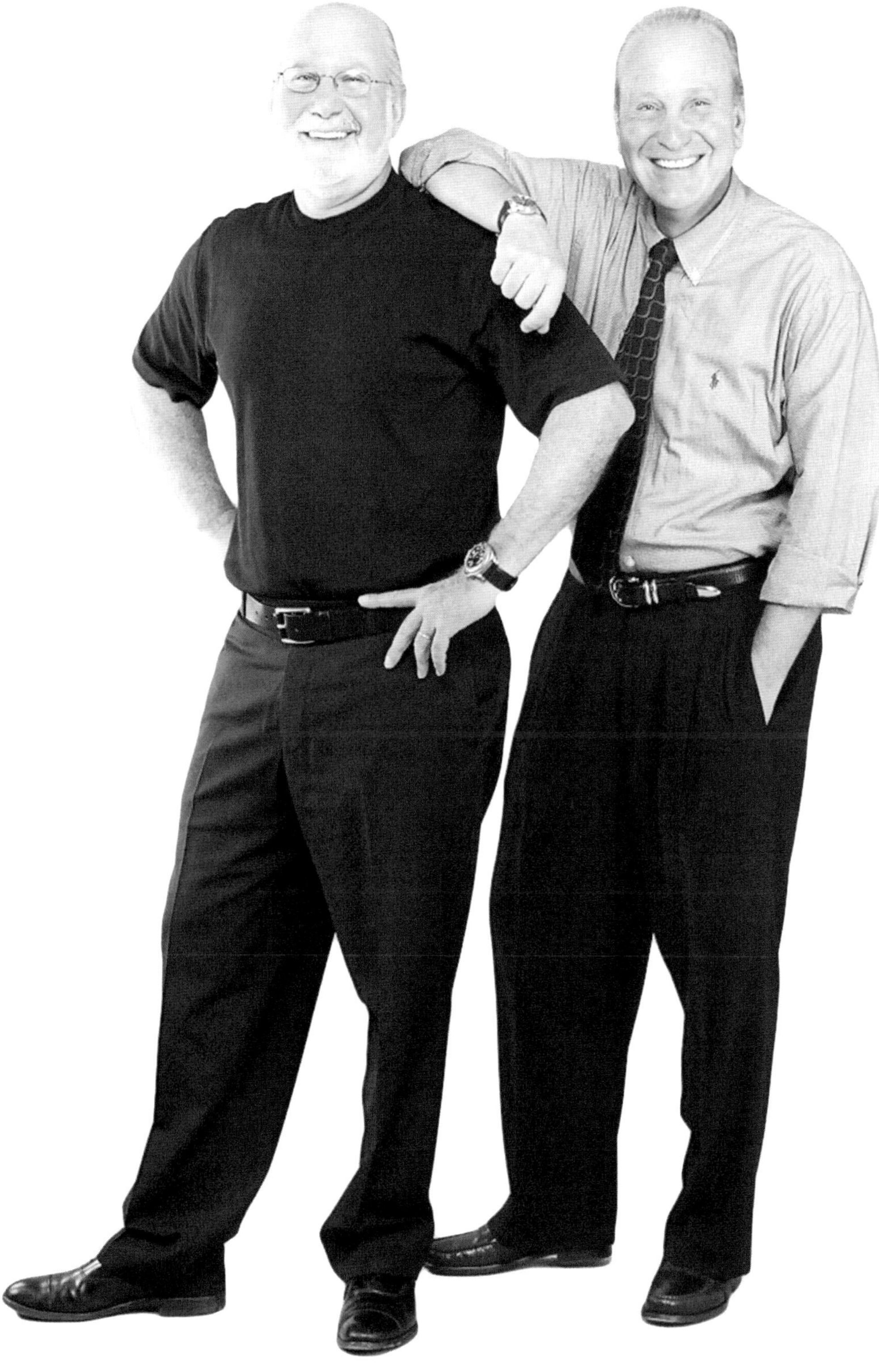

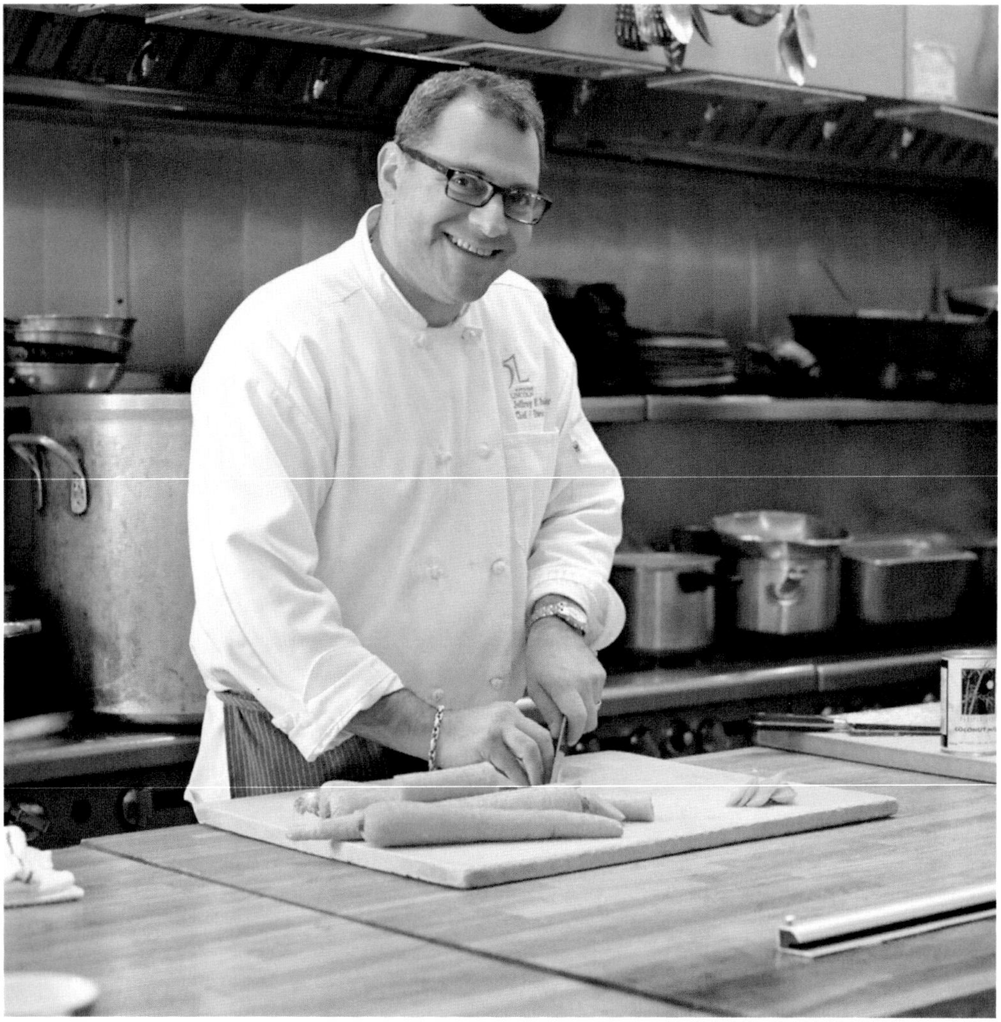

Jeff Fournier, 51 Lincoln and Waban Kitchen Chef/Owner

51 Lincoln's chef-owner Jeff Fournier grew up in a French Armenian home where unusual dishes stretched his palate and drew him to the kitchen at a young age. Upon leaving home, Fournier learned and tested his creativity in some of the finest restaurants on both coasts. In California, he learned the techniques of Austrian Californian cuisine under Chef Hans Rockenwagner, among others.

In Boston, he worked with great chefs like Daniel Baliani and Lydia Shire at such famed restaurants as Pignoli, Locke-Ober, and Excelsior. In 2004, he became executive chef at Sophia's in the Fenway district, where he created a small-plate, Latin-inspired menu, and then moved to the Metropolitan Club in Chestnut Hill where he was also executive chef.

In 2006, Fournier opened his flagship restaurant, 51 Lincoln, in Newton Highlands, bringing together his creativity for food with his other passion—art. Matching the artistry on the plates are walls that are adorned with large, colorful, abstract paintings that are creations of Fournier's, often to the surprise of diners.

51 Lincoln, which features vegetables grown in its rooftop garden, has won many awards, including *Boston* magazine's "Best of Boston" three times and *Improper Bostonian*'s Top 50 restaurants in the city. Fournier, a Newton resident, opened Waban Kitchen, a smaller space with a more casual setting, on Beacon Street in Waban in 2012. (Courtesy of Jeff Fournier.)

CHAPTER FIVE

Religious Leaders and Groups

Faith is and has always been an important part of life in Newton. With dozens of houses of worship celebrating a diverse array of religions, Newton's religious institutions are much more than places to pray. Each one is a community that comes together to learn, to support and to improve the world. And within each community, there are multiple stories of members and leaders past and present who have left a huge imprint, like Father Cuenin at Our Lady Help of Christians Parish who wouldn't tolerate the negligence and insensitivity coming out of the Boston archdiocese when the clergy sex abuse scandal broke in 2002.

Not covered in this chapter but equally heroic is Gregory Ford, who, as a 24-year-old man, showed immeasurable bravery when he shined a light on the sexual abuse and related deceptions that had taken place in the catholic church when he was a boy. Ford's public accusations ultimately led to the imprisonment of the Rev. Paul Shanley. Also missing are Adams Street Shul member Elmer Lippin who maintained the synagogue through its leanest days, and Julian Jaynes who grew the membership and influenced the building of the First Unitarian Society in Newton. Mary Baker Eddy, founder of the Christian Science Church in 1879, lived in a part of Chestnut Hill that is now Brookline, but was then Newton. They couldn't all fit on these pages, but they belong here.

The St. Mary of Carmen Society is included, but profiling all of its colorful legends would require another book.

Rev. Edmund Kelly and the Myrtle Baptist Church

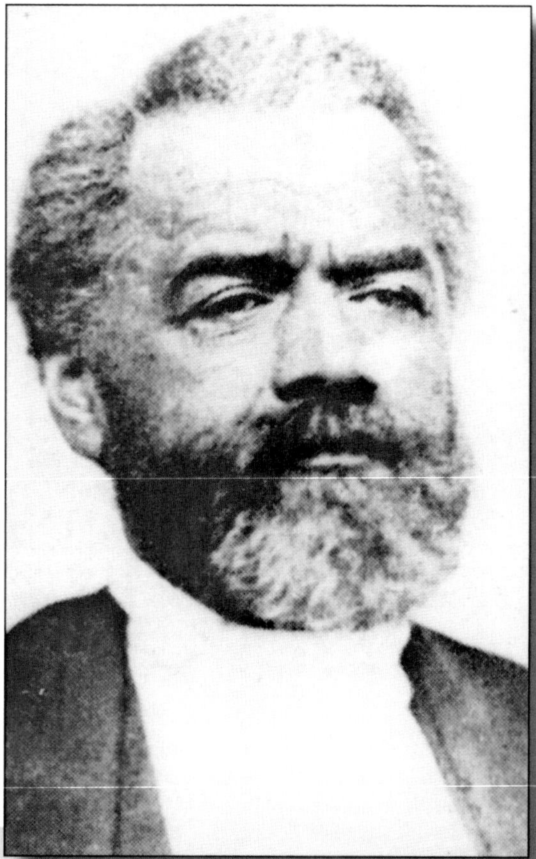

Rev. Edmund Kelley met Deacon Thomas Johnson from Newton at about the same time the city's black community was looking for a place to worship other than First Baptist Church. After Kelley accepted Johnson's invitation to preach to a small group, he organized them into a society and then remained pastor from 1874 to 1876. Kelley was a former slave who had been licensed to preach by the Mission Church of Columbia, Tennessee, in 1842, while he was enslaved. The following year he was ordained as an evangelist, and he organized the First Negro Baptist Church. Upon gaining his freedom, he traveled to several states, including Massachusetts, preaching and organizing churches. After leaving Myrtle Baptist, he played key roles in the National Baptist Convention, the New England Missionary Baptist Convention, and the American Baptist Missionary Convention. The Myrtle Baptist Church, below, opened in the 1870s with a ceremony attended by hundreds of people. (Both courtesy of Myrtle Baptist Church.)

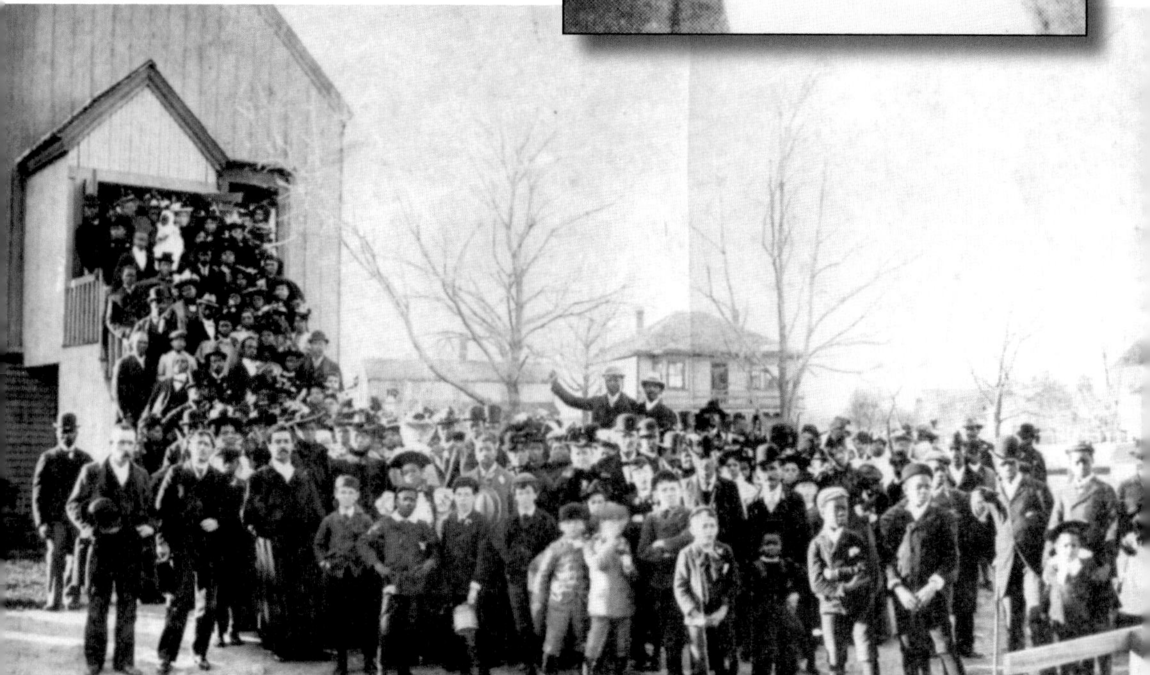

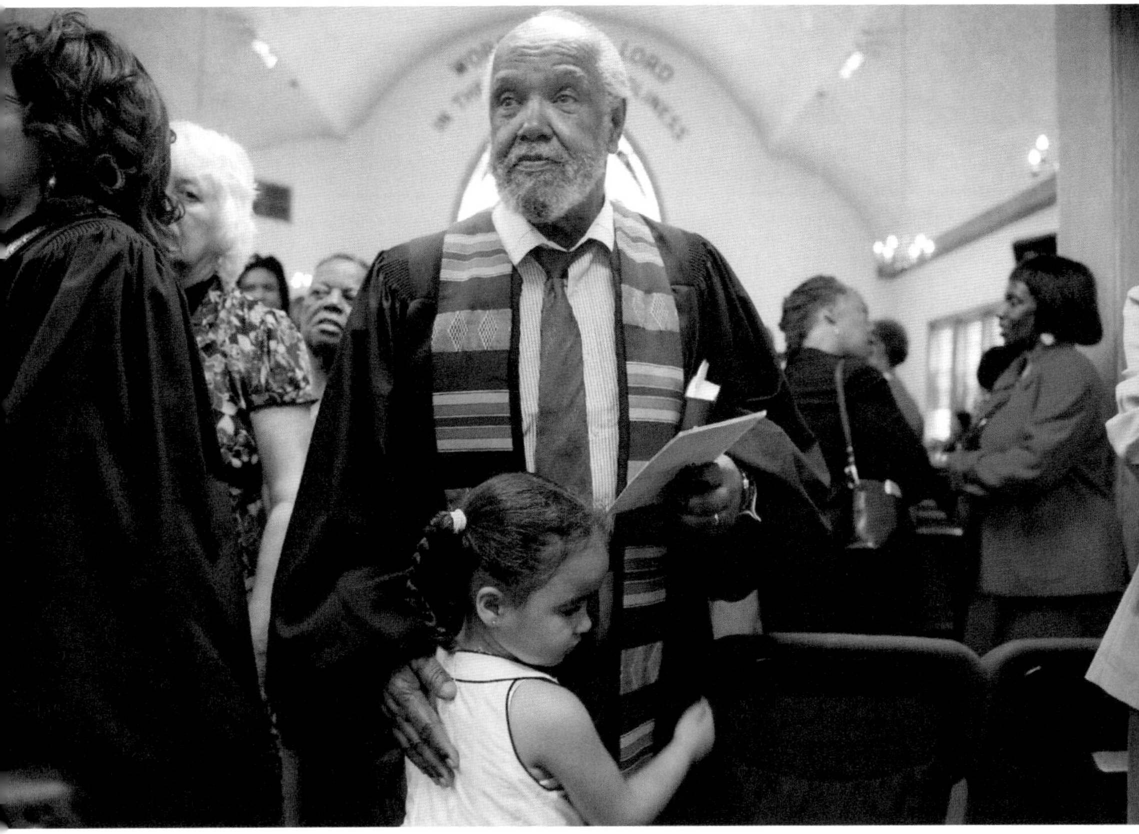

Rev. Howard Haywood, Myrtle Baptist Church
For most of Howard Haywood's early years growing up in Myrtle Baptist Church, he would have been considered an unlikely candidate to become the congregation's beloved pastor for 23 years. Raised with his three siblings by a single mother, Haywood looked for and found trouble often enough that a teacher deemed him least likely to succeed. As he grew older, he struggled with alcoholism.

When he gave up alcohol, he committed his life to God. Four months later, he became interim pastor at Myrtle Baptist, and in June 1985, he was installed as pastor.

Haywood, whose family dates back seven generations in Newton, successfully revived the congregation that had been torn apart during the construction of the Massachusetts Turnpike in the 1960s and the subsequent destruction of many congregants' homes.

Haywood, who maintained a full-time job while serving as pastor, is credited with securing housing for the homeless and meals for the hungry on a regular basis. Former mayor David Cohen said that Haywood did "more to build community in the city of Newton than anyone" he knew. Haywood arranged for trucks of essentials to be sent to New Orleans after Hurricane Katrina; established an international outreach effort with schools in a Nairobi, Kenya, slum; and traveled with fellow congregants to a church in Arkansas after a malicious arson.

Haywood retired in May 2008. (Photograph by David Gordon; courtesy of Wicked Local Newton.)

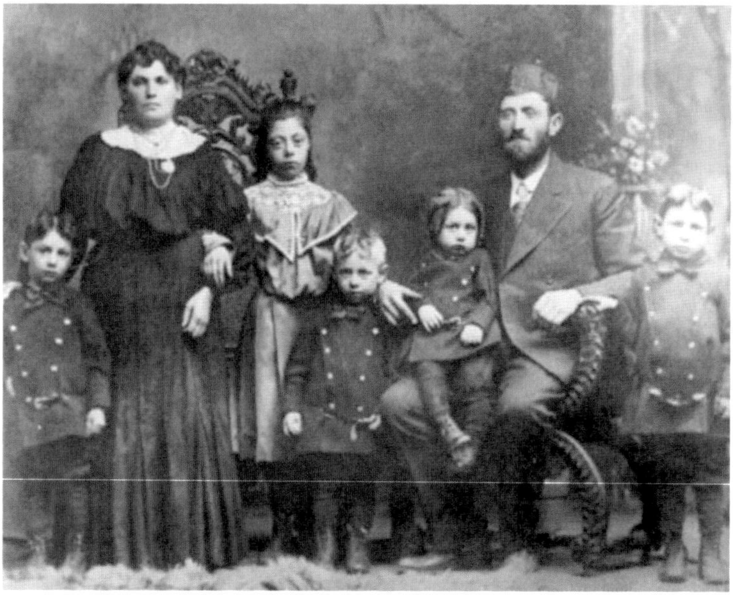

The Gilfix Family, Beri Gilfix, and the Adams Street Shul

Beri Gilfix (below), whose grandfather Benjamin Gilfix (sitting, above), was one of the founders of the Adams Street Shul, knows every nook and cranny of the building's structure and every detail of its history. Her grandfather, an immigrant from Eastern Europe, served as the congregation's first president in 1912, and Beri Gilfix followed in his footsteps several decades later. A member of the board of directors since 1988, she has been a chief fundraiser for the modern orthodox synagogue, which is also known as Congregation Agudas Achim Anshei Sfard.

At the turn of the 20th century, nearly half of Newton's Jewish community lived in Nonantum, and in 1912, the Jewish community decided that it needed a synagogue to call its own. The third-oldest synagogue in New England, the Adams Street Shul is listed in the National Register of Historic Places. (Clockwise from the top, courtesy of Beri Gilfix; photograph by Gail Spector; courtesy of Beri Gilfix.)

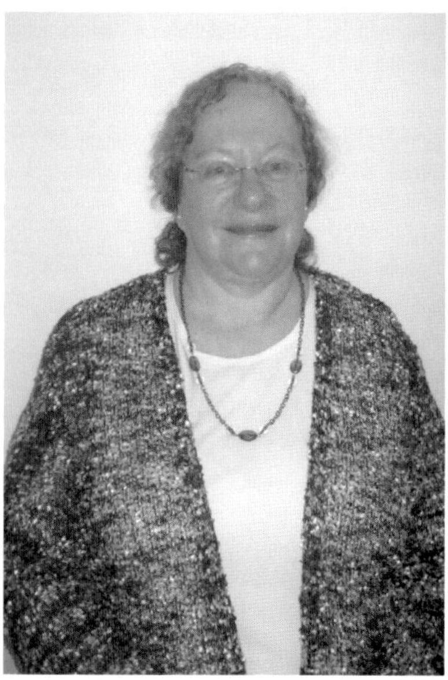

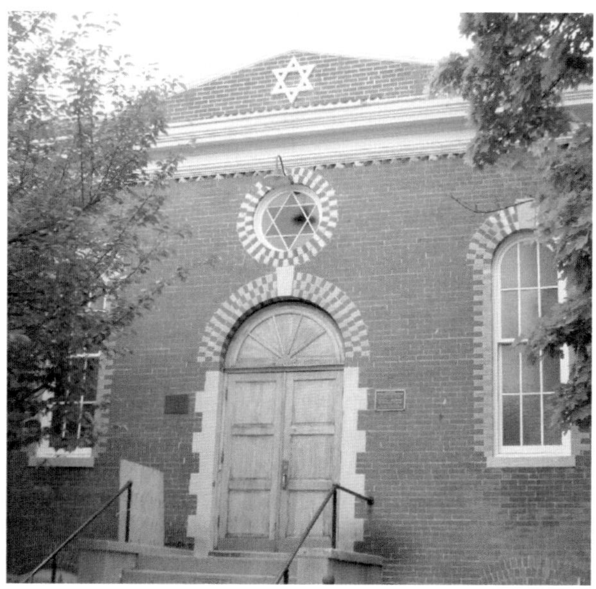

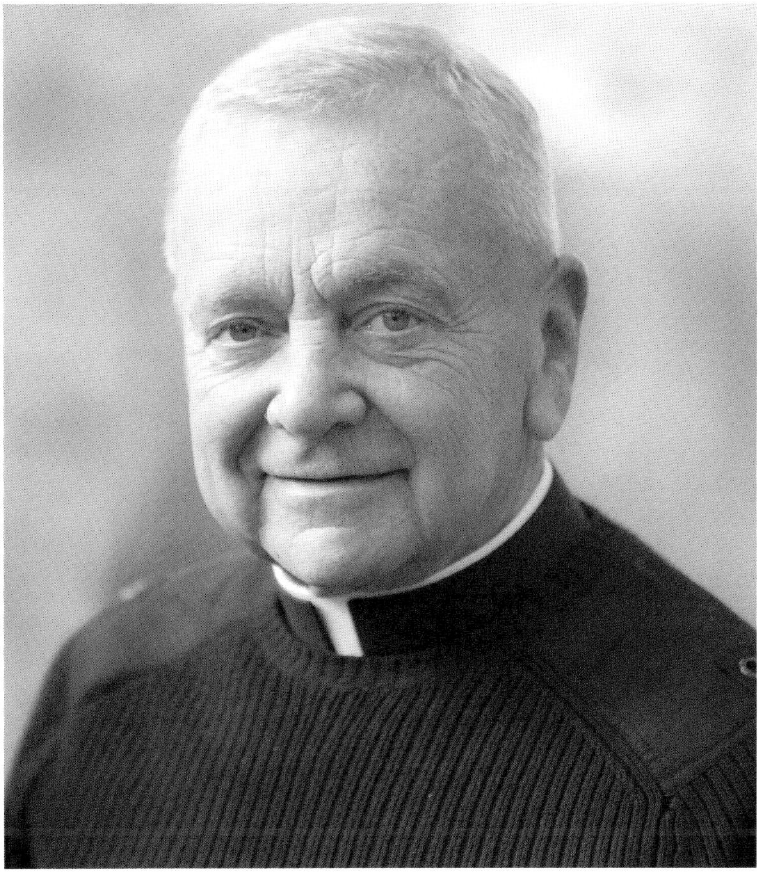

Fr. Walter Cuenin, Beloved Pastor and Leader
Instead of delivering a sermon one August morning in 1997, the Rev. Walter Cuenin appealed to his congregation to show support for a neighboring house of worship. With that, 300 people got out of their seats and marched down Adams Street to the Adams Street Shul, an orthodox synagogue that had been desecrated with several swastikas and Ku Klux Klan symbols two days earlier.

Pastor of Our Lady Help of Christians Parish from 1993 to 2005, Cuenin is revered by both his former parishioners and the Newton community for his leadership, integrity, and broad-mindedness. In addition to rebuilding a struggling parish and making marginalized groups, including gays, feel welcome, Cuenin was an outspoken priest who questioned the archdiocese on its policies regarding gay marriage and the ordination of women as priests. After the shocking news broke that dozens of priests in the archdiocese had been sexually abusing children for decades, Cuenin publicly criticized Cardinal Bernard Law for mishandling the accusations. When those accusations hit close to home, singling out former Newton pastor Fr. Paul Shanley, Cuenin stood firmly on the side of the abused.

Unhappy with how Law continued to react to the clergy sex abuse scandal, he helped organize a group of 58 priests who sent a letter to the cardinal requesting his resignation.

The letter accomplished its mission, but Cuenin paid a price. In 2005, the archdiocese requested his resignation for financial improprieties, even though the congregation had approved his expenses. His parishioners were devastated, and many community members joined them in their beliefs that his dismissal was punishment for his outspokenness.

Cuenin moved to Brandeis University where he became the Catholic chaplain and coordinator of the Multifaith Chaplaincy. He departed Brandeis in 2015 for health reasons. (Courtesy of the Reverend Walter Cuenin.)

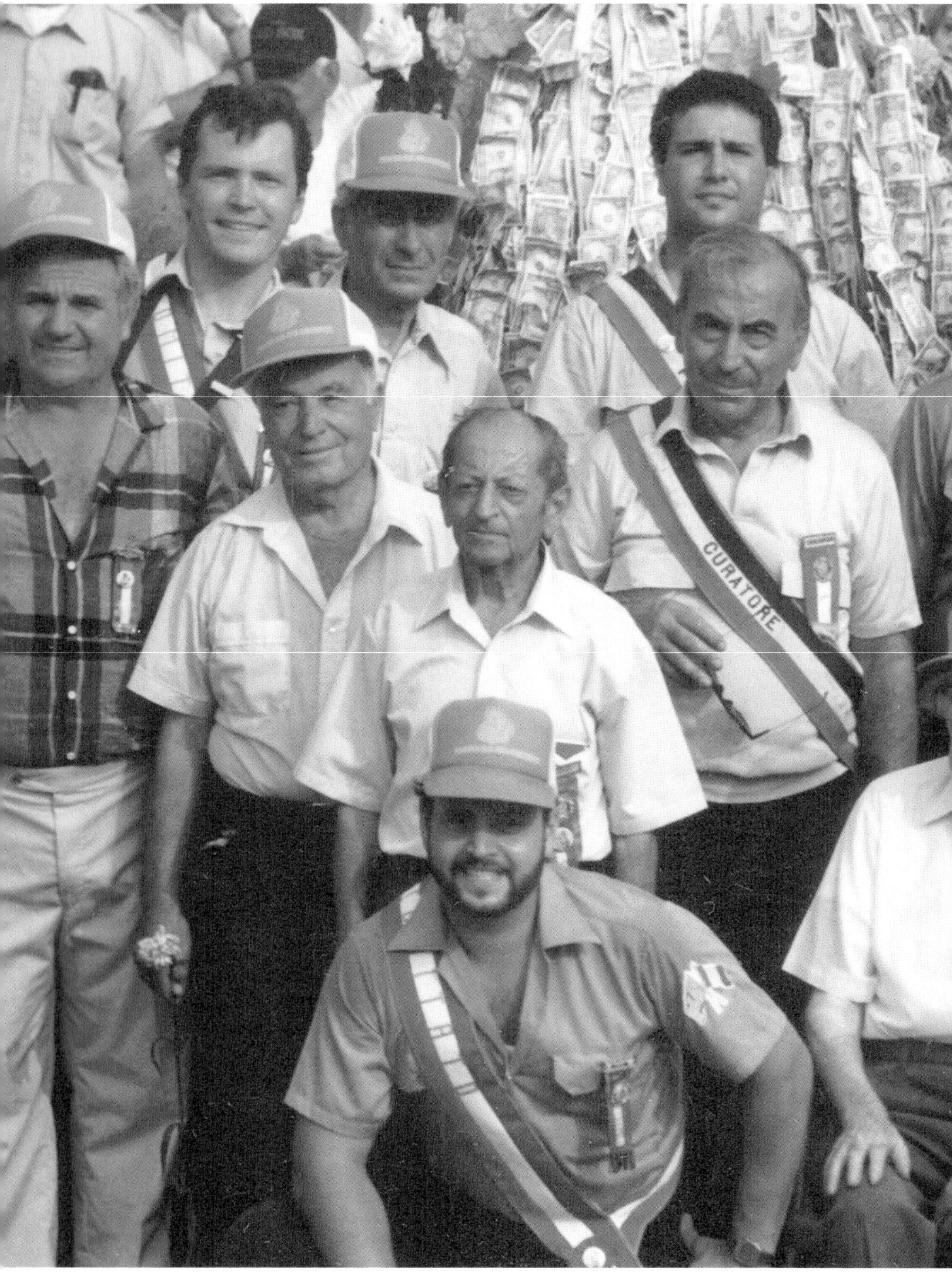
CURATORE

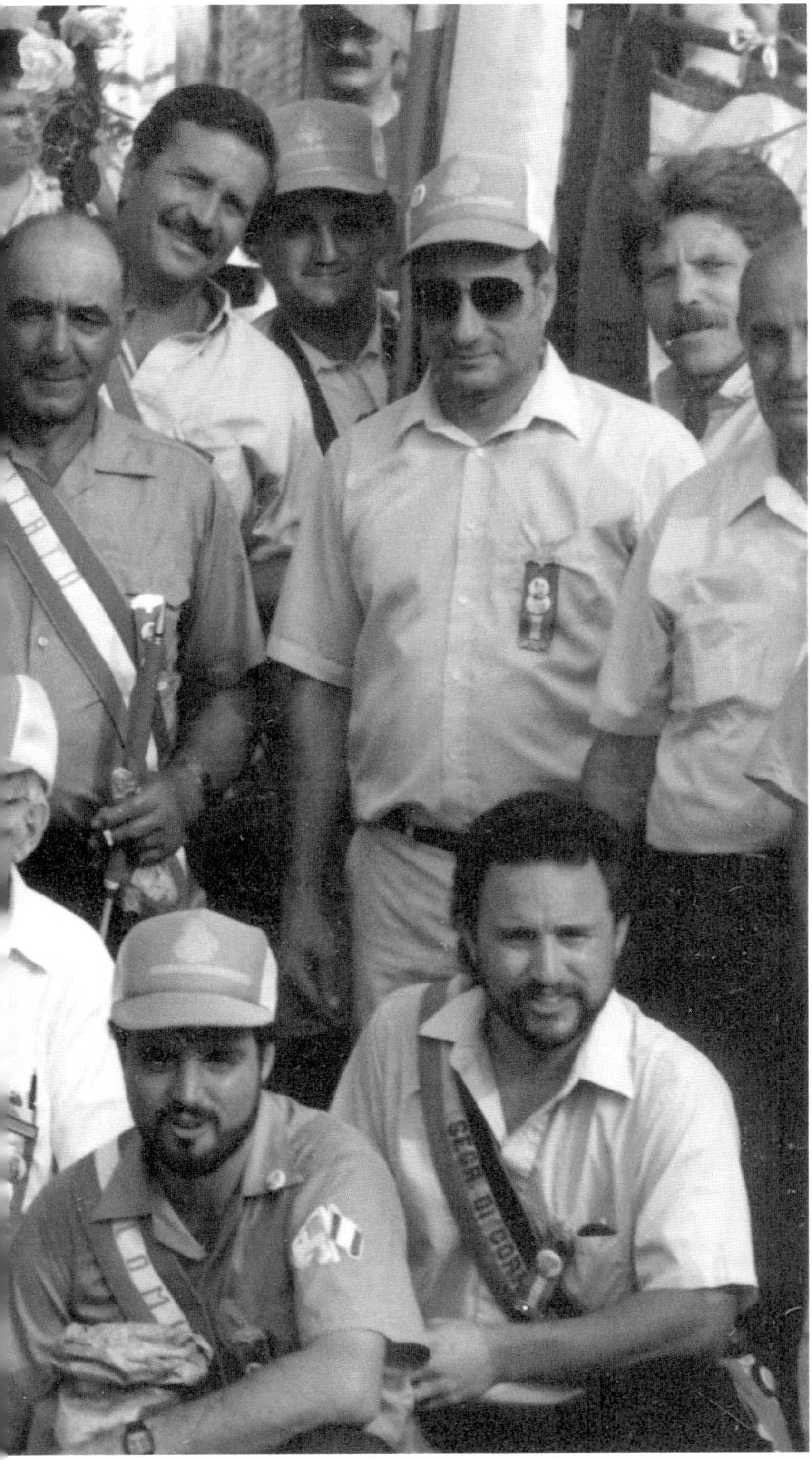

Members of the St. Mary of Carmen Society
Eleven Italian Americans founded the St. Mary of Carmen Society in 1935 to help new immigrants from Italy settle in Nonantum. Sons and grandsons of the original members keep the society alive today.

Every year in July, the society runs the St. Mary of Carmen Society Festival, an event that overtakes Nonantum for five fun-packed days. (Courtesy of the St. Mary of Carmen Society.)

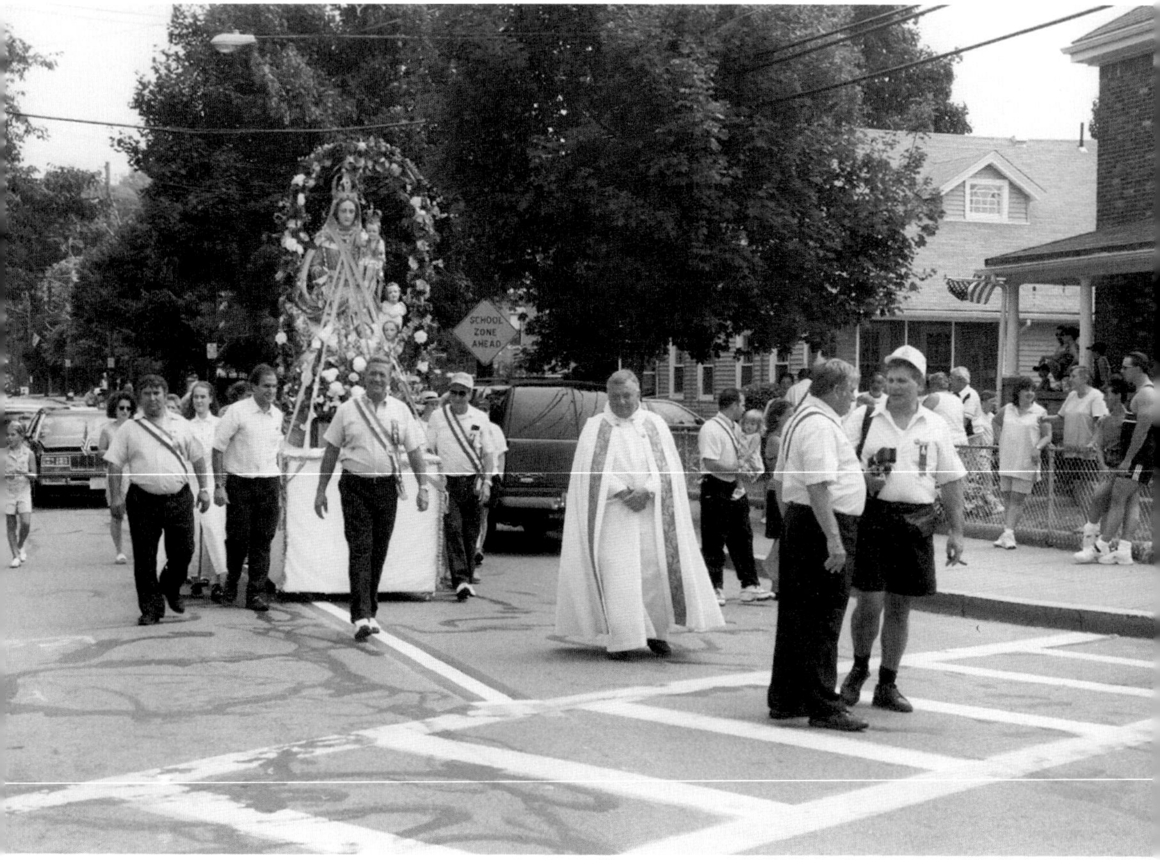

Processional to Our Lady Help of Christians

A religious festival at its heart, the St. Mary of Carmen Society festival always finishes with a procession to Our Lady Help of Christians Parish, with people lining the streets to pin dollar bills on a statue of the Virgin Mary. Father Walter Cuenin from Our Lady Help of Christians Parish led the processional through the streets of Nonantum for many years, as pictured here. (Courtesy of St. Mary of Carmen Society.)

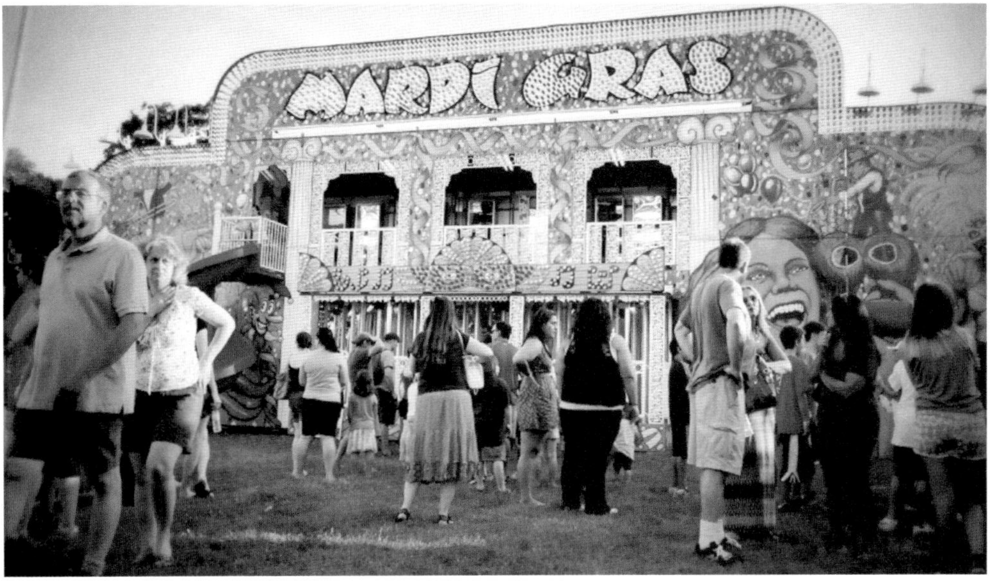

St. Mary of Carmen Society Festival

Started in 1936, the St. Mary of Carmen Festival is a summer highlight in Newton. Eclipsing all other life in Nonantum for five days, "festa" draws people from both inside and far outside the city's borders. The village is painted red, white, and green in honor of its Italian heritage, the streets are filled with hundreds of people spanning generations, nearly every house is teeming with partiers, and backyard fireworks fly above the rooftops regularly. Carnival rides pack Pellegrini Park.

The festival is the creation of the St. Mary of Carmen Society, a group formed in 1935 by 11 Italian Americans trying to build the Italian neighborhood by sponsoring new arrivals to the country and providing health insurance. More recently, the society has provided college scholarships to Newton high school graduates and supported various community organizations. (Both courtesy of the St. Mary of Carmen Society.)

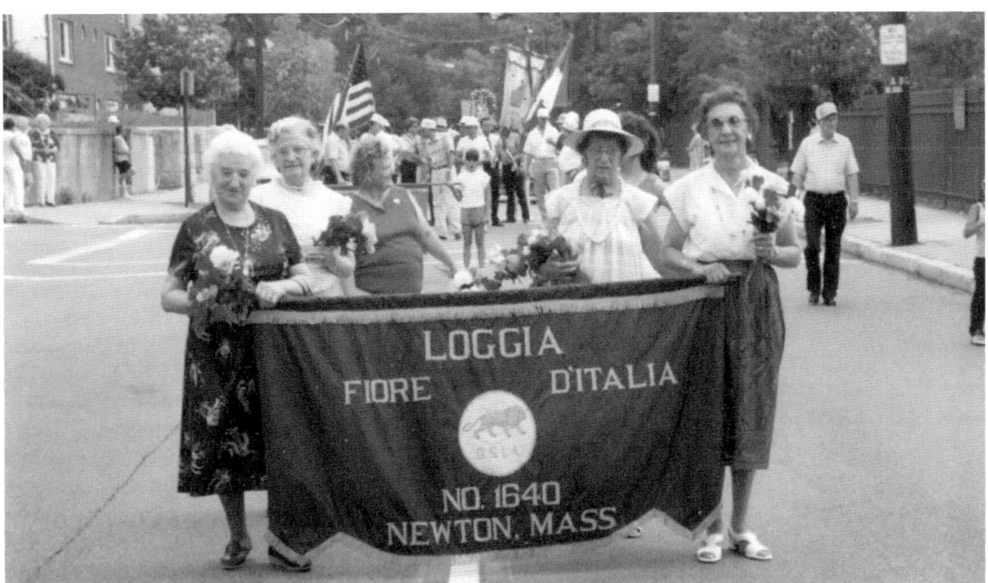

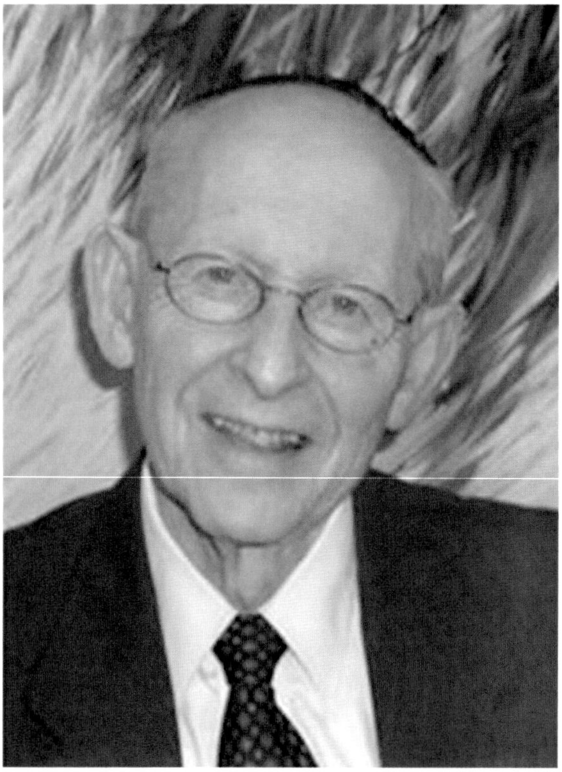

Rabbi Samuel Chiel, Temple Emanuel, 1927–2013

Rabbi Samuel Chiel, Temple Emanuel's beloved rabbi from 1968 to 1995, was described as wise, intellectually and spiritually stimulating, open-minded, and devoted to his community. A strong presence on and off the pulpit, he touched many lives. Scholar-in-residence to both the Combined Jewish Philanthropies and the New England region of the Anti-Defamation League, Chiel worked to forge bonds between the Jewish and Catholic communities in the Boston area. He was also responsible for launching many social action initiatives at Temple Emanuel. Chiel died in 2013. (Courtesy of Janet Chiel.)

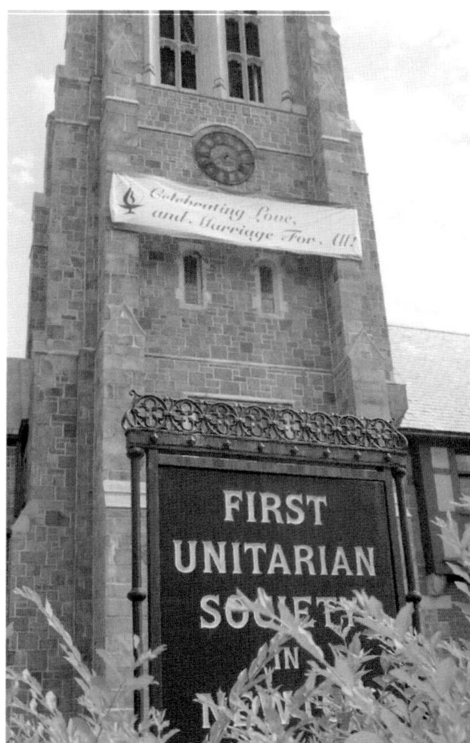

First Unitarian Society in Newton

The First Unitarian Society (FUSN) in Newton, known for its progressive stances and social action programs, was founded in 1848 in West Newton. Horace and Mary Peabody Mann, Nathaniel and Caroline Bassett Allen, and Caroline Wells Healey Dall were among the founders who touted progressive ideals like women's rights, education reform, and abolition. FUSN carried its liberal values into the 20th century by advocating for black empowerment, resistance to the Vietnam War, and nuclear disarmament. Today, it continues fighting for same-sex marriage, economic and racial justice, a humane criminal justice system, and other human rights issues. FUSN is housed on Washington Street in an American Gothic structure, built in 1906, with a square bell tower. (Photograph by John Ruttenberg.)

CHAPTER SIX

Protectors

In 1776, more than 218 volunteers from Newton, a town of just 1,400, marched to the first battles of the American Revolution in Lexington and Concord. Their ranks included many older men who were exempt but were determined to serve their country. Noah Wiswall, 76, and Joshua Fuller, 72, walked 28 miles to Lexington on that fateful day in 1776.

In the civil war, 61 Newton men—whose names are engraved on the Newton Soldiers' Monument in the Newton Cemetery—lost their lives. In the 20th century, 3,760 Newton men served in World War I, 9,422 served in World War II, and 2,240 served in Korean War. More than 20 died in Vietnam. Currently, there are about 2,000 veterans living in the city.

Protecting our homes and our safety are the Newton Police and Fire Departments, groups that are rich with legendary locals. Many Newton natives speak fondly of Charlie Feeley, the police sergeant who taught bicycle safety to just about every student who attended a Newton public school. Fire chief Henry Bixby died in a collision in 1894, when he was thrown from his buggy on his way to a fire. In this chapter, readers will learn about the heroics of Sgt. Dominic Marrocco, firefighter Ray McNamara, patrolman Lawrence Murphy, and others.

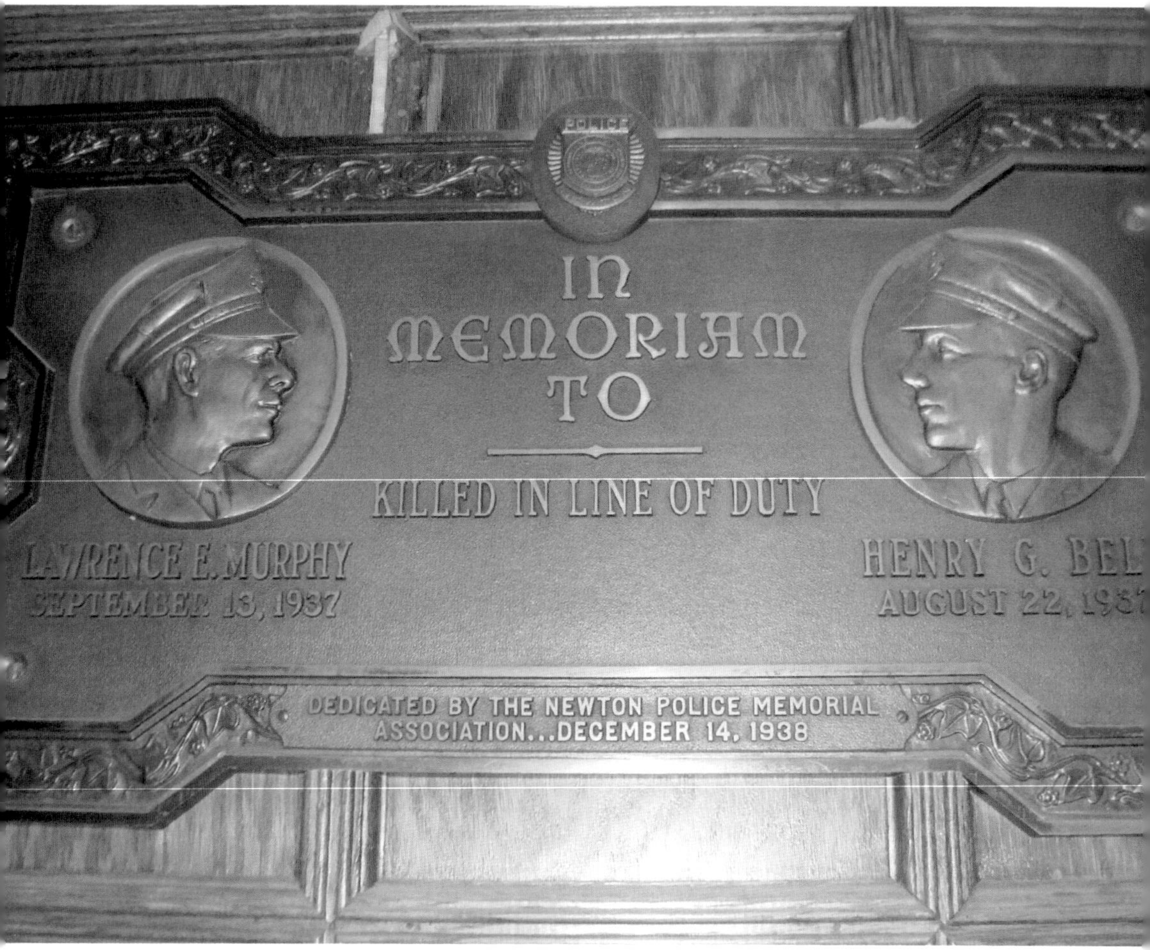

Patrolmen Henry Bell and Lawrence Murphy

While on duty on August 22, 1937, patrolman Henry Bell and his partner stopped a car that matched the description of a getaway car used in a recent robbery. Because they were suspicious after questioning the occupants of the car, Bell stayed with the car and his partner drove the patrol car to the nearest call box to check with headquarters on the registration.

Patrolman Lawrence Murphy was sent to the scene on his motorcycle. By the time he arrived, the female driver of the vehicle had disarmed Bell and passed the gun to the male passenger, Edward Simpson, a known criminal and jail breaker, who put the gun against Bell's back, ordering him to drive. Murphy overtook the car and forced it to stop. The suspect fired shots at Murphy, striking him. The suspect then shot Bell twice in his right side and fled. Murphy, though seriously injured, fired at the fleeing suspect, hitting him at least once.

Bell died at the scene. Murphy was taken to the hospital where he remained until his death from his wounds the following month.

The female suspect was captured at the scene. A week later, Simpson was caught in a Dorchester apartment in a raid led by Newton police chief Michael Hughes. Simpson was found guilty of murder and executed.

Murphy had served with the Newton Police Department for two years. He was survived by his wife and four children.

Bell had been with the police force for just eight months. (Photograph by Gail Spector.)

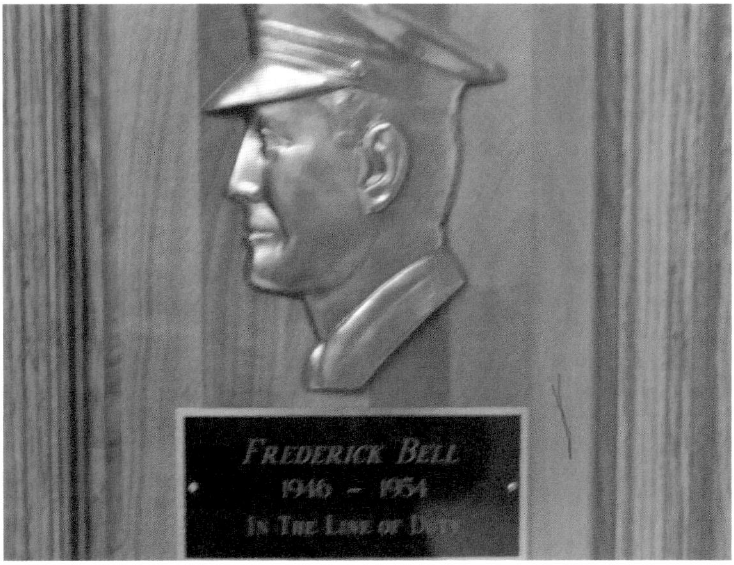

Officer Frederick Bell, Brothers Down
While escorting an ambulance to a local hospital in 1954, Ofc. Frederick Bell's patrol car collided with a lumber truck, throwing the World War II veteran from his vehicle. At first Bell's injuries were not thought to be life threatening, but four months after the accident, he died from brain injuries sustained in the collision.

Bell's brother patrolman Henry Bell had also been killed in the line of duty when a robbery suspect shot him in 1937.

Frederick Bell had been with the Newton Police department for eight years. He was survived by his wife, son, daughter, three brothers, and three sisters. (Photographs by Gail Spector.)

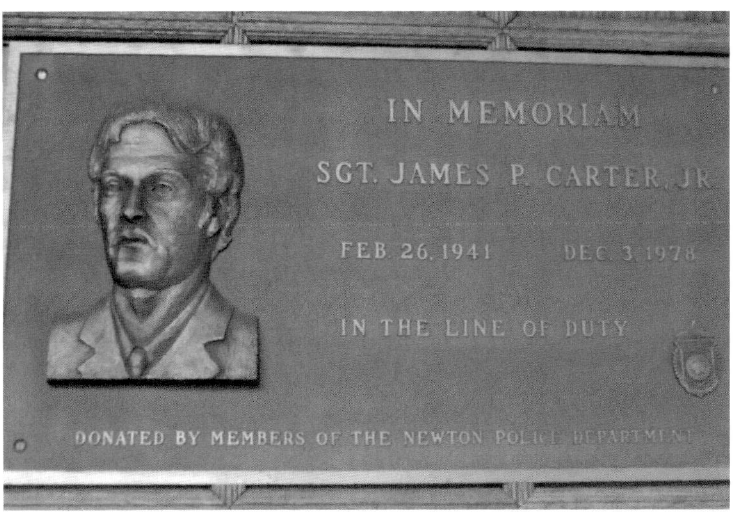

James P. Carter Jr., Officer Down
Sergeant Carter, who had served with the Newton Police Department for 11 years at the time of his death, was struck and killed by a drunk driver who was fleeing the scene of a robbery in Auburndale in 1978. The driver was sentenced to 17 years but released after 18 months. Carter was survived by his three children. (Photograph by Gail Spector.)

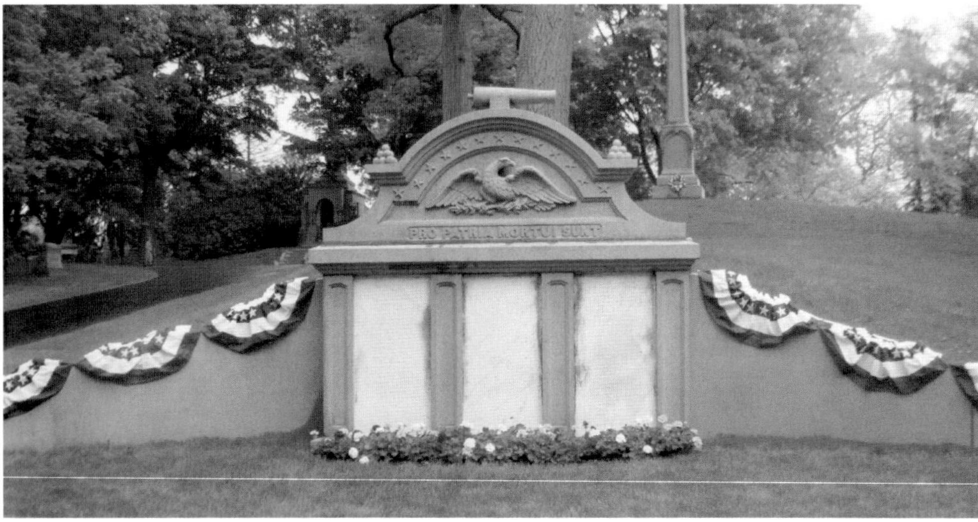

Elliot Littlefield, Civil War POW

Elliot Littlefield left a wife and three children when he died in prison on January 23, 1864, at Belle Isle in Virginia. The 38-year-old carpenter, originally from Holliston, enlisted as a private in the cavalry in the Massachusetts 1st Regiment, Company G, in September 1861. Four other Newton men served in this regiment along with Littlefield.

Historic Newton reports that Littlefield's widow, Martha Winslow Littlefield, lived on Elliot Street and, later, moved to Richardson Street. (Photograph by Gail Spector.)

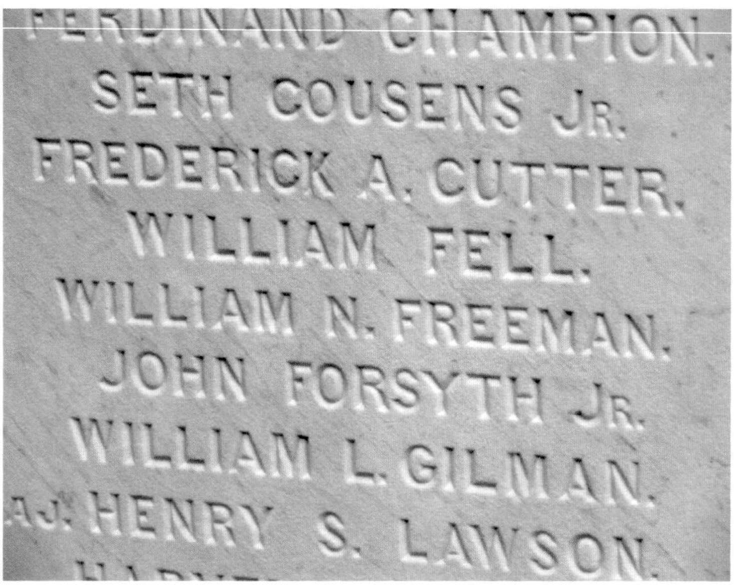

William Fell, One of Newton's Oldest Civil War Soldiers

At 44, William Fell was one of Newton's oldest-serving soldiers during the Civil War. Born in England, he lived with his wife and three children on Chestnut Street in Upper Falls where he worked as a knitter. Fell enlisted as a private in the Massachusetts 32nd, Company K, infantry along with the 22 other Newton men. He was one of at least four men from Upper Falls. Less than a year after enlisting, Fell died of disease. He is buried in South Burying Ground on Winchester Street. (Photograph by Gail Spector.)

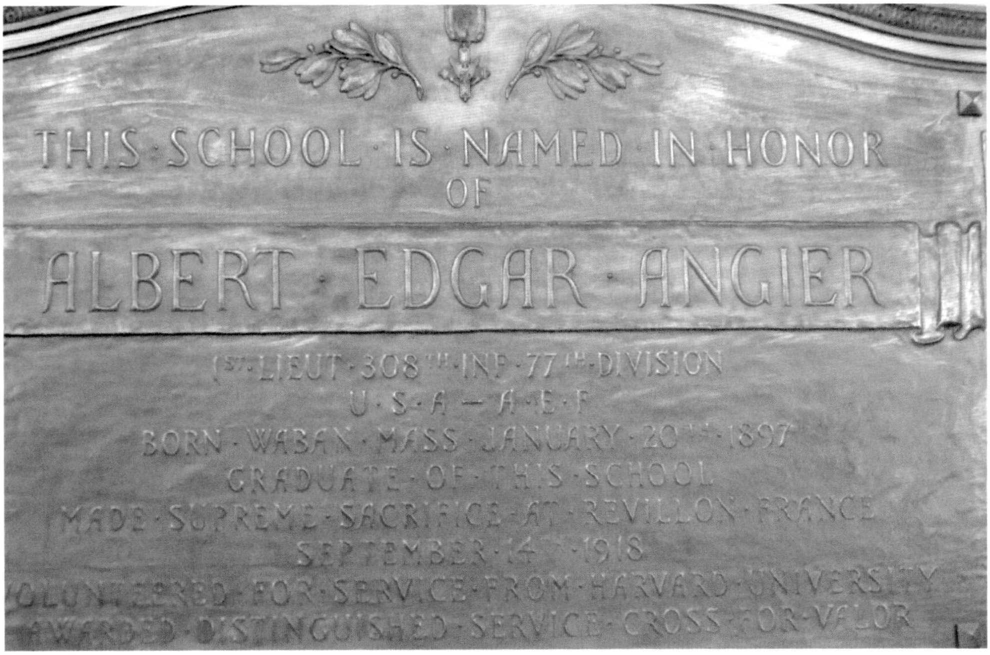

Albert Angier, World War I Hero Never Returned
Albert Angier, a 1914 graduate of Newton High School, was the only one of 44 World War I soldiers from Waban who never returned home. The young man, for whom Angier Elementary School is named, loved the outdoors but struggled with his studies. According to his relatives, he would likely be identified as a student with special needs in modern times.

In April 1918, Angier joined the war. By July, he was a second lieutenant in a regiment that was on the battlefield in France most of the time. By September, he was a first lieutenant commanding a platoon in France.

Lieutenant Angier was injured in battle when he was cut down by German gunfire. When one of his soldiers tried to tend an injured lieutenant's wounds, Angier ordered the sergeant to take care of the other men instead. Angier died not long after on September 14, 1918, at age 21. Angier was awarded the Distinguished Service Cross for his heroism. (Photograph by Gail Spector.)

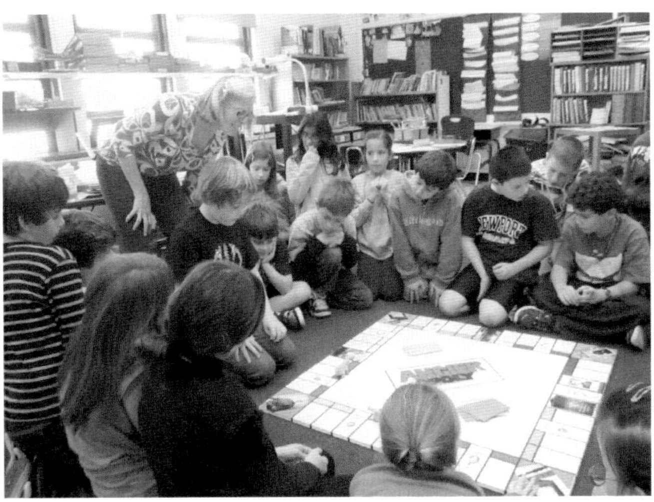

Students Playing Angier-opoly
Students learn history by playing Angier-opoly, a teacher-designed board game including palm-sized pieces such as Angier's horse, a pup tent, a cannon, and a doughboy helmet. (Courtesy of Lauren Comando.)

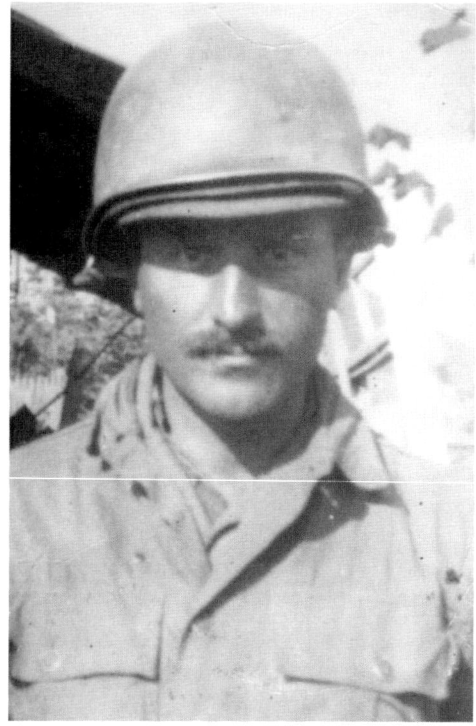

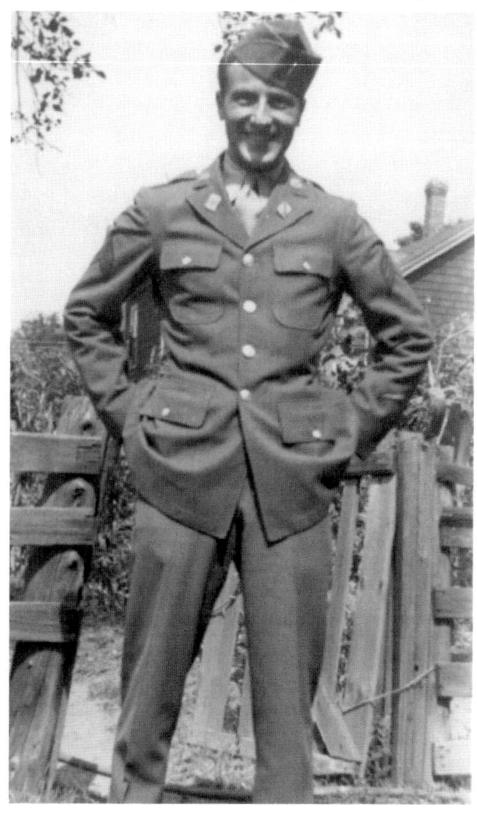

Sgt. Dominic Marrocco, Killed in Action, Korea

It was not enough for Dominic Marrocco to have served his country in World War II. A soldier whose commanding officer was the renowned Gen. George Patton, Marrocco spent much of his time during World War II in gruesome battles, including the Normandy invasion and the Battle of the Bulge. He was taken prisoner in Germany on a mission behind enemy lines. When he was liberated, he returned to Nonantum where he reunited with his two brothers and two brothers-in-law, all of whom had served overseas. Still, he stayed in the Army.

He turned down a position as a weapons instructor at West Point in order to lead his men into battle in Korea. Eight months later, in April 1951—just days after he had written his family to tell them he would be on his way home soon—Marrocco, 33 years old, was killed in action in Chunchon, South Korea, when his battalion was overpowered. (Both courtesy of Roger Marrocco.)

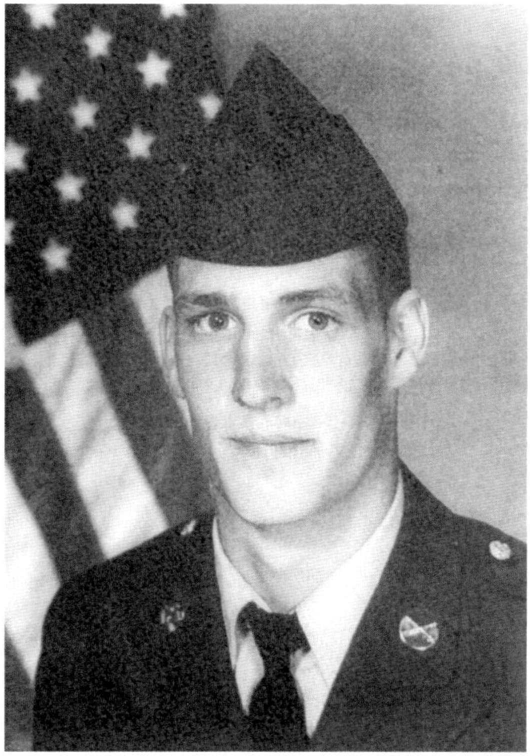

Richard Likely,
Killed in Action, Vietnam
Richard Likely went to Vietnam when his wife was just two months pregnant. The 1968 graduate of Newton High School had enlisted in the Army at age 19. He died at age 20 when he helped another soldier into a medical tent and then offered to replace him on patrol. A booby trap exploded, hitting him in the right temple, killing him instantly. He never met his daughter, who was born shortly after his death. A bridge in Auburndale is named in his honor. (Courtesy of Nikki Likely.)

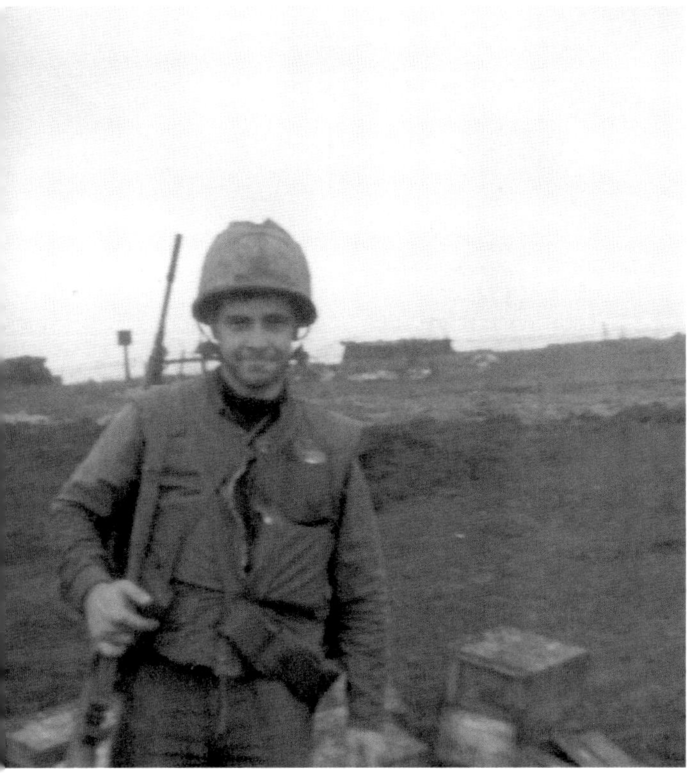

James Rice,
Killed in Action, Vietnam
Newtonville resident Jim Rice was 21 when he joined the Marines. Both his father and his uncle for whom he was named had served in World War II.
Rice never returned to Newton. On February 7, 1968, three days before he was scheduled to leave Vietnam, he was shot and killed by a sniper when he ran out to an open field to retrieve two wounded soldiers.

Rice was awarded the Bronze Star posthumously. His younger brother John is currently an alderman from Ward 5. (Courtesy of John Rice.)

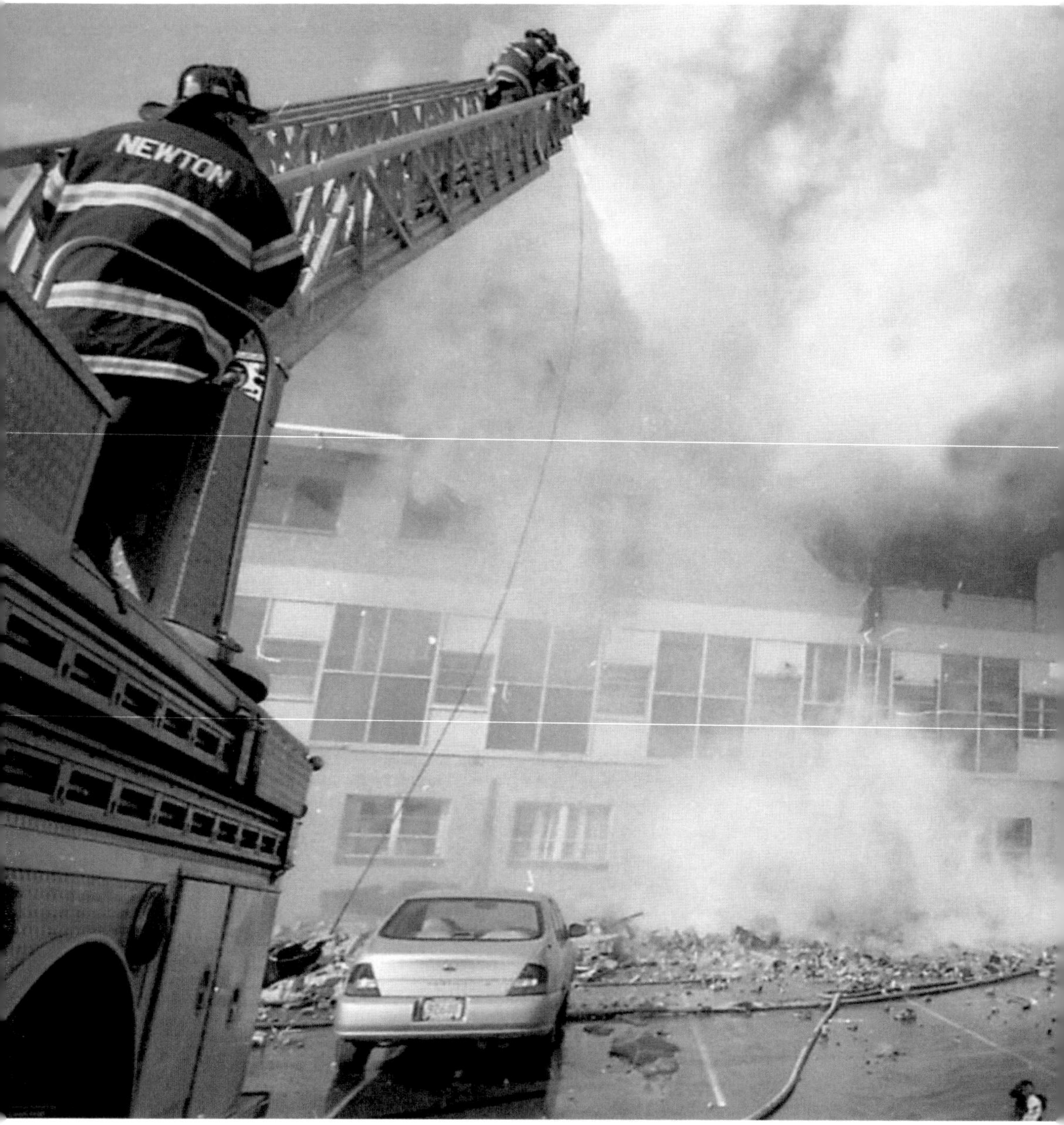

Newton Firefighters

Perhaps no stronger legends exist in Newton than the stories about firefighters running into burning buildings, ready to sacrifice their own lives in order to save those of Newton citizens.

And perhaps no fires better demonstrated that devotion to their mission than the HC Starck chemical company fire on October 25, 1993, and the Route 9 fire on February 9, 2000 (above).

A fire was already burning when a chemical explosion at HC Starck blew firefighters off their feet and burned their skin through their melting fire gear. Among the 12 injured firefighters was Ray McNamara, a 23-year veteran of the fire department. McNamara, who had been thrown against a wall, left the building hanging on the arm of another firefighter, his features torn from his face. He was burned on more than 90 percent of his body.

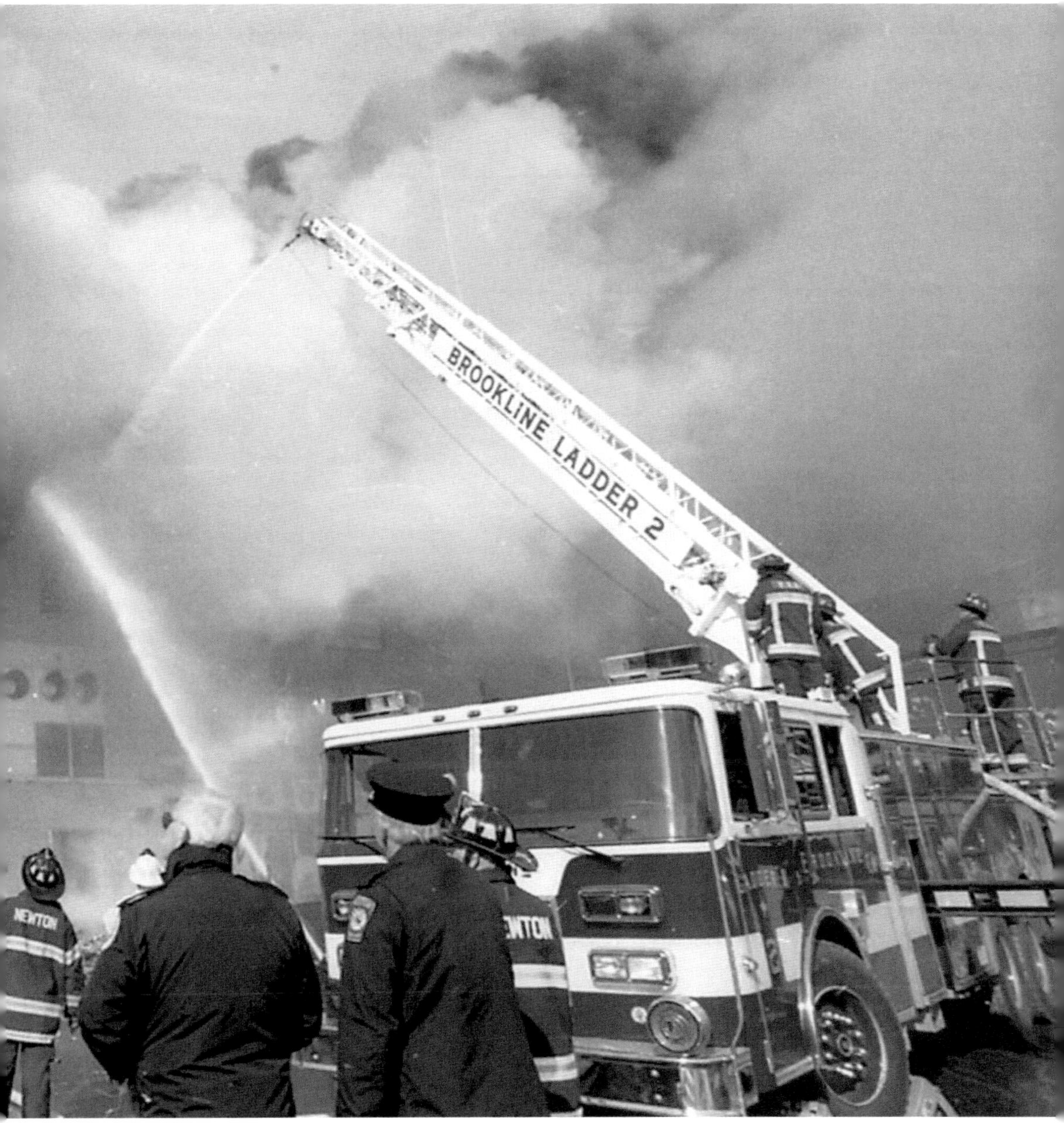

Despite doctors' prognoses to the contrary, McNamara survived. While some of his injured colleagues recovered, McNamara spent eight months in a medically induced coma while undergoing close to 30 operations. Firefighters gave blood, raised money, visited, and maintained his house. McNamara and other injured firefighters stopped fighting fires, but they kept hanging out with their firefighting buddies.

Nearly 17 years later, in a devastating fire that some called the worst in the Boston area in 25 years, Newton firefighters climbed ladders to pull more than a dozen people from a window ledge as fire ripped through a Route 9 office complex. Firefighters searched for four days to recover the remains of the five victims, all who worked at the office building at 200 Boylston Street. The deceased were Gerald Kaplan, mother and son Virginia and Robert Lewis, all of Newton; David Stulin, a Newton native who lived in Sharon; and Lynne Brady of Tewksbury. (Photograph by Keith E. Jacobson.)

Tyrone Powell, 41-Year Newton Police Officer

Newton Police officer Tyrone Powell was stationed at the corner of Franklin and Main Streets in Watertown, guarding the sealed-off area when SWAT teams were hunting for alleged Boston Marathon bomber Dzhokhar Tsarnaev on April 19, 2013. A 40-year veteran of the Newton Police Department, Powell stood tall and large in his six-feet, four-inch, bulky frame, arms crossed and face stern. Neither spectator nor media member dared defy his order that no one enter the crime scene.

Suddenly, his phone started buzzing at an uncharacteristic rate. Only later would he find out that, in the course of one hour, friends and family had left 138 voice mail messages and 200 texts, many suggesting that he smile—because his face was spreading across the Internet as the meme of the hunt for the marathon bombing suspect. Powell did smile spontaneously for the cameras awhile later, and again his image traveled fast, upon hearing that Tsarnaev had been caught alive. Powell's jubilant face appeared on the Jumbotrons at Fenway Park and the *Boston Garden* and in the morning newspapers.

Powell is Newton's longest-serving police officer. (Photograph by Gail Spector.)

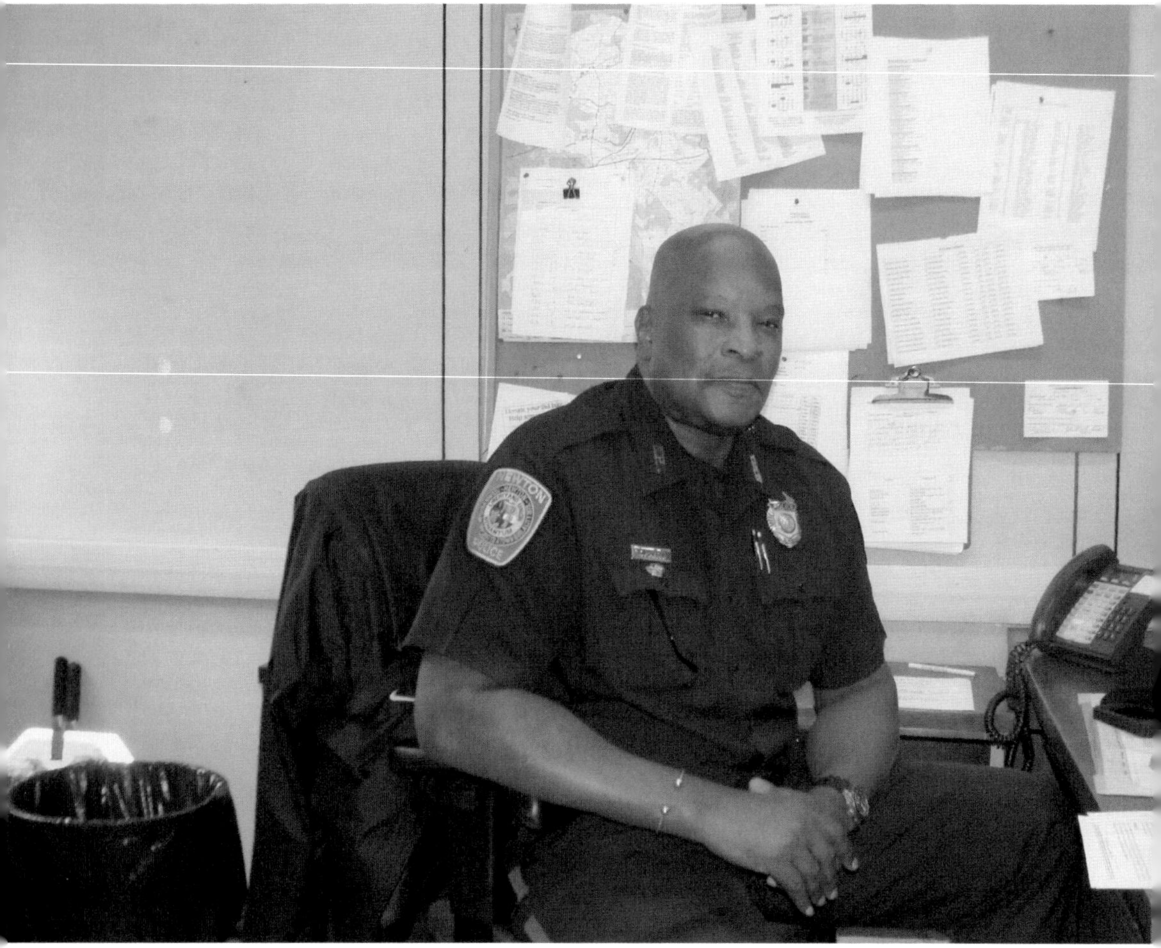

CHAPTER SEVEN

Athletes

Newton's proximity and easy access to Boston make it an appealing place to live for professional athletes, particularly those employed at Fenway Park. Like almost everybody in the Boston area, Newtonians love their Red Sox players and are delighted when zip codes overlap. The best hitter in Red Sox history, Ted Williams, lived in Upper Falls. Dom DiMaggio, a solid ballplayer nicknamed the "Little Professor" who was overshadowed by his big brother Joe, lived and died in the city. More recently, Jason Varitek, David Ortiz, and Kevin Youkilis have been some of our most famous neighbors.

But Newton's athletes go beyond the ballpark. Tenley Albright, who skated on Crystal Lake, was the first American woman to win an Olympic Gold Medal in figure skating in 1956. Figure skater and 2014 US national champion Gracie Gold, who competed for the United States at the 2014 Winter Olympics, was born here. NASCAR racer Pete Hamilton, winner of the 1970 Daytona 500, grew up in Newton. Yet another professional athlete who chose Newton as his home was New England Revolution striker Taylor Twellman, founder of the ThinkTaylor Foundation, whose vision is to create social change relating to traumatic brain injuries.

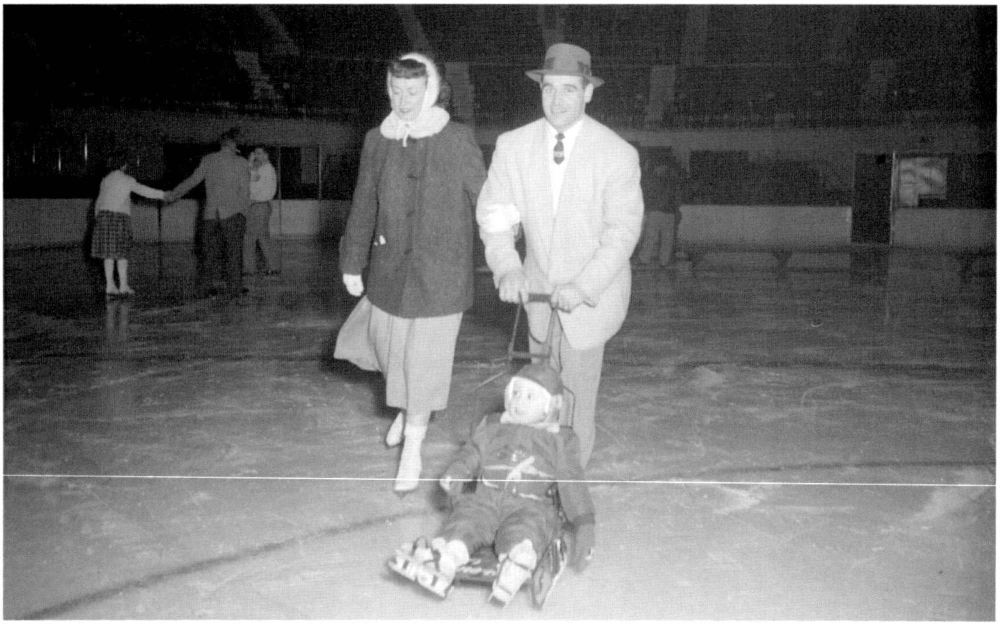

Bruins Defenseman Leo Boivin

Defenseman Leo Boivin played in the National Hockey League for 19 years, 12 of them with the Boston Bruins, and lived in Newton for some of those years. Legend has it that the city flooded the tennis courts at the Newton Highlands Park in the winter so Boivin could teach hockey to children. The Hall of Fame player was captain of the Bruins for 4 of his 12 seasons with the team. (Courtesy of the Boston Public Library/Leslie Jones Collection.)

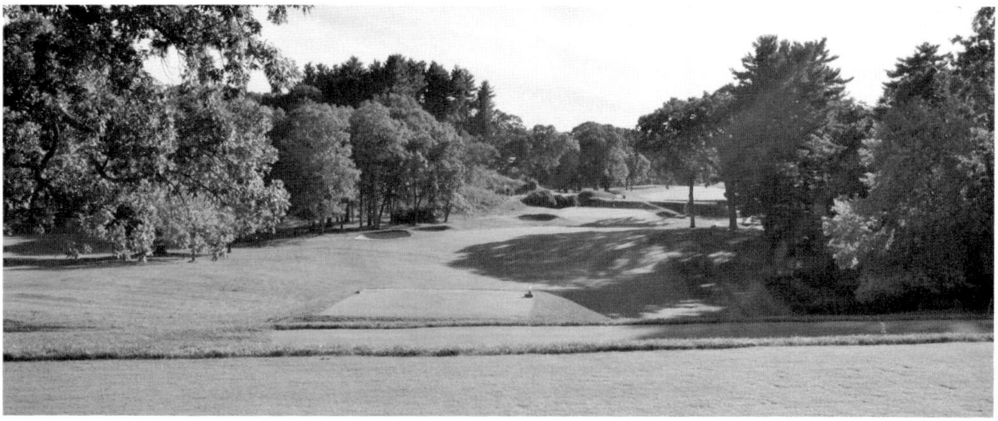

Donald Ross, Designer of Golf Courses, Including Brae Burn

Donald Ross's fans do not consider his golf courses merely a place to play a few rounds. Rather, they believe that his golf courses are works of art that require precise preservation.

Ross, a talented golfer and groundskeeper originally from Scotland, came to America in 1899 to help build and run Watertown's Oakley Golf Club. He went on to design 413 courses in the country, 100 of which have hosted national championships. He designed three in Newton alone: Brae Burn, Charles River Country Club, and Commonwealth Golf Course.

Ross lived in Newton Centre and is buried in the Newton Cemetery. (Courtesy of Brae Burn Country Club.)

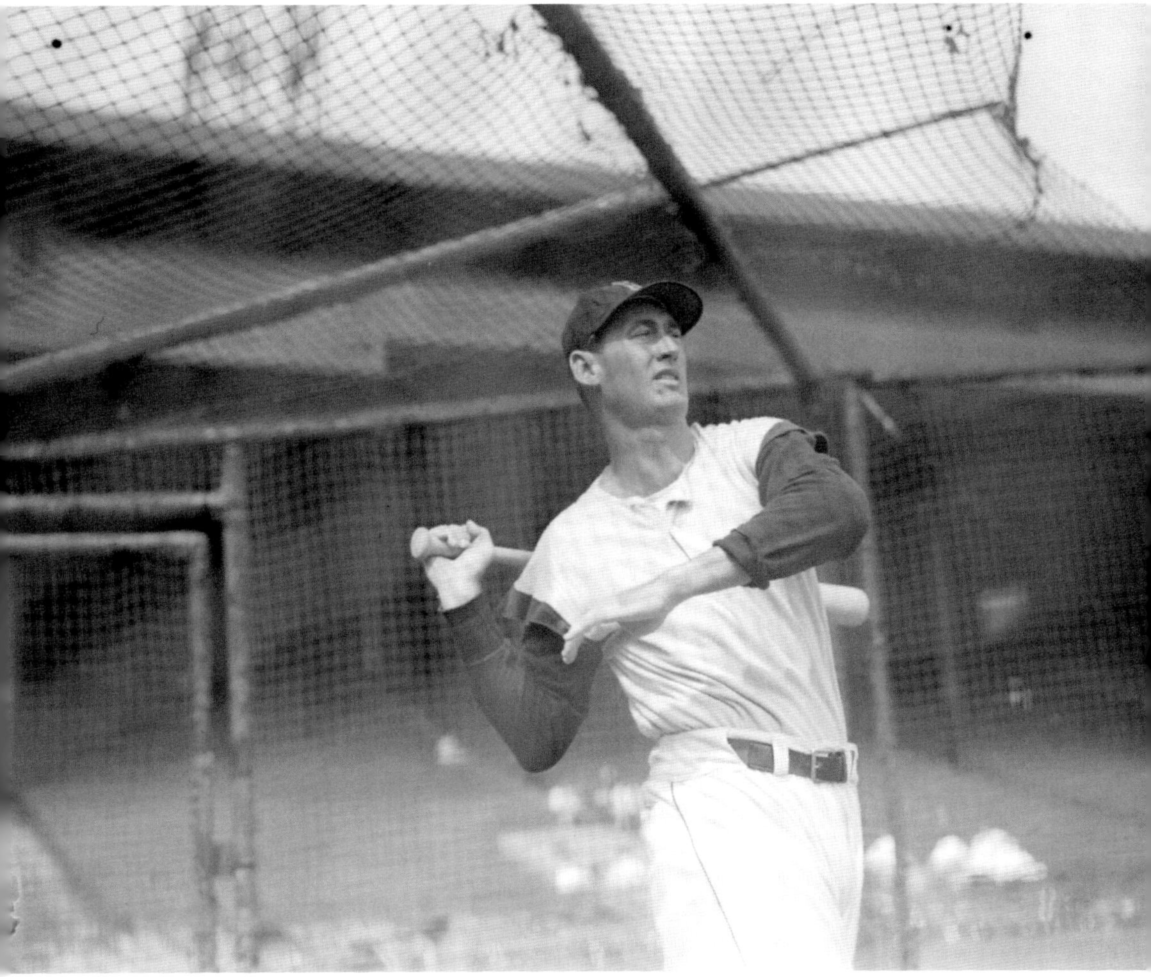

Ted "The Kid" Williams, 1918–2002
Many Boston Red Sox players have lived in Newton over the years, but arguably, no greater ballplayer has ever resided in the Garden City than Ted Williams.

Williams moved within Newton during his Red Sox days, and Newtonians remember him living in both Waban and Newton Upper Falls. Some Newton residents recount childhood stories of visiting Williams and his young family on Lucille Place in Upper Falls to request an autograph with varying degrees of success.

Regarded as the greatest hitter ever, Williams, or "Teddy Ballgame," played left field for the Red Sox for his entire 19-year major league baseball career. In 1941, his third season with the Red Sox, he batted .406, making him the last MLB player to bat over .400 in a season. The six-time batting champion and two-time Triple Crown winner finished his career with a .344 battling average, 521 home runs and a .482 on-base percentage, a record that still stands today. He was inducted into the Baseball Hall of Fame in 1966.

In 1988, Newton legislators filed a bill that named a section of Route 9 from Framingham to Newton—just before the Centre Street underpass—the Ted Williams Highway. (Courtesy of the Boston Public Library/Leslie Jones Collection.)

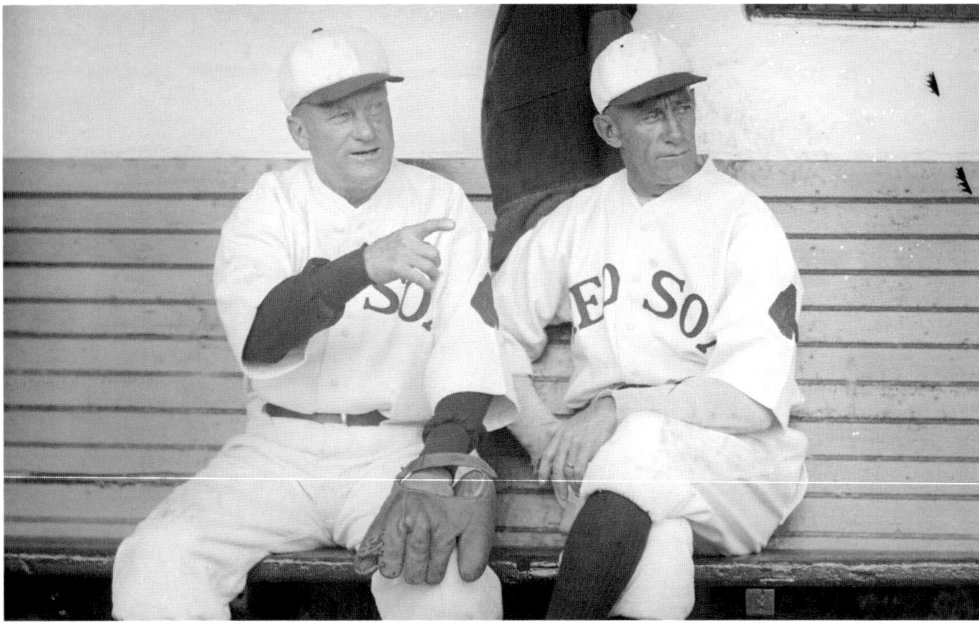

Shano Collins (Left), Red Sox Outfielder and Manager

John Collins, also known as Shano, never won any titles, but the five-year Red Sox outfielder and Newton resident still received one vote for entry into the Hall of Fame in 1937.

Some baseball historians speculate that the one vote was a reward for his honesty during the 1919 World Series. While a member of the infamous Chicago Black Sox squad that threw the series, Collins played a clean game. Collins managed the Red Sox in 1931 and part of 1932. After retiring from baseball, he opened Collins Bar and Grill on Needham Street. He lived in Newton until his death in 1955. (Courtesy of the Boston Public Library/Leslie Jones Collection.)

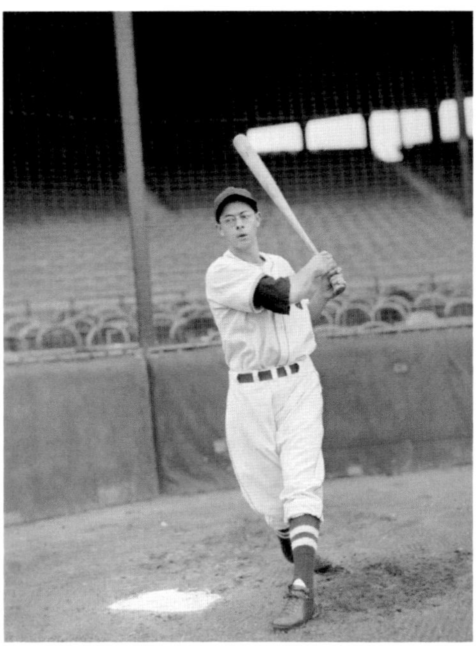

Dominic DiMaggio, Red Sox Centerfielder

Although Dom DiMaggio (1917–2009) had a lifetime batting average of .298 over his 11 years with the Boston Red Sox, he is often overlooked because his older brother Joe was one of the greatest players of all time. Dom DiMaggio, however, made his own contributions to major league baseball. The seven-time All-Star still holds the 34-game hitting streak he set in 1949. The streak ended when his brother caught a sinking liner on August 9, 1949.

DiMaggio is buried in the Newton Cemetery. (Courtesy of the Boston Public Library/Leslie Jones Collection.)

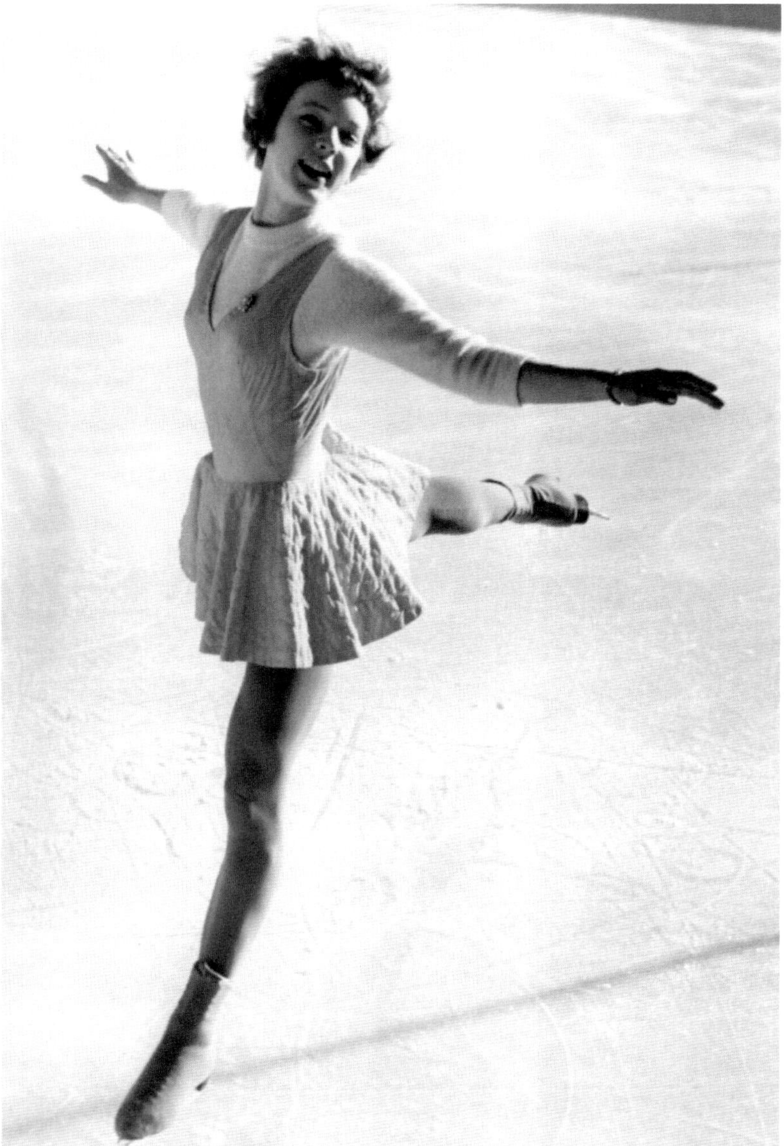

Tenley Albright, Gold Medal Skater

At age 11, polio struck Tenley Albright, leaving her bedridden and unable to use her legs. Yet as soon as the determined young athlete gained enough strength, she donned her ice skates and glided onto one of her favorite training settings, Crystal Lake in Newton Centre. Four months later, she won the Eastern United States Junior Ladies Figure Skating competition.

Albright, who was born and grew up in Newton Centre, went on to become the first American woman to win a gold medal in Olympic figure skating, in 1956. She was also the first American woman to win the World Figure Skating Championships.

The city of Newton threw her a 39-float parade when she won her gold medal. According to newspaper reports, nearly 50,000 people lined the parade route.

After retiring from figure skating, Albright went to Harvard Medical School and became a surgeon. (Courtesy of US Figure Skating.)

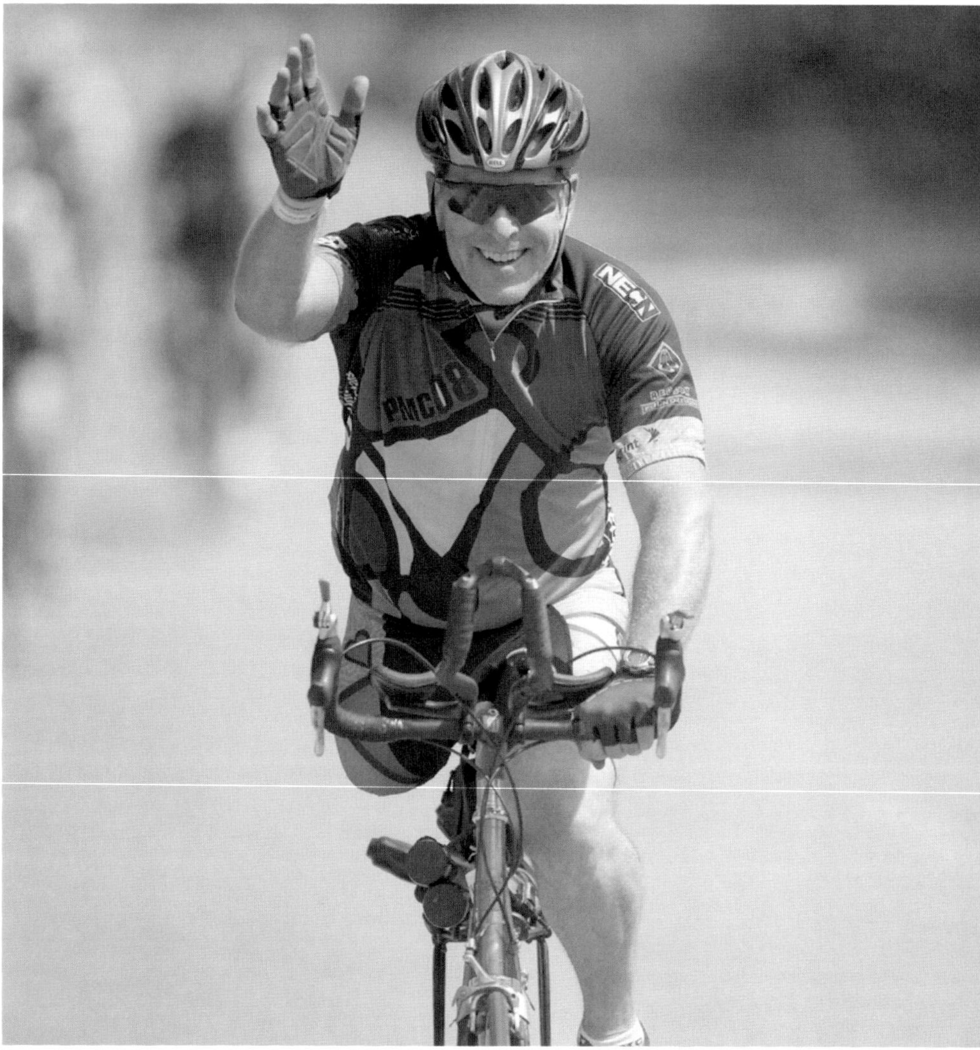

Jothy Rosenberg, Amputee Cannot Be Stopped
Few communities are as well represented as Newton at the Pan Mass Challenge bicycle ride, where thousands of cyclists ride anywhere from 25 to 190 miles to raise money for cancer research. And few cyclists are as awe-inspiring as Jothy Rosenberg.

The extreme athlete, who lived in Newton for 16 years, has cycled the two-day route from either Wellesley, but more often, Sturbridge, to Provincetown a dozen times, raising nearly $100,000. With just one leg and one lung, however, Rosenberg is hardly the typical cyclist. The cancer survivor rides without a prosthetic on a bike with just one pedal. He also raises money for cancer research by swimming from Alcatraz to San Francisco every summer.

Rosenberg's prowess is not limited to athletics, though. With his doctorate from Duke in computer science, he has founded eight high-tech companies, written three technology books, and authored *Who Says I Can't*, a memoir that recounts how he defied doctors' death sentence as a teenager, using extreme sports to recover from two bouts of cancer, a leg amputation, and the removal of a lung. Rosenberg has also created the Who Says I Can't Foundation to help people with disabilities succeed at high-challenge activities they love. Its initial focus is to help Boston Marathon bombing victim Roseann Sdoia, who lost her right leg above the knee. (All courtesy of Jothy Rosenberg.)

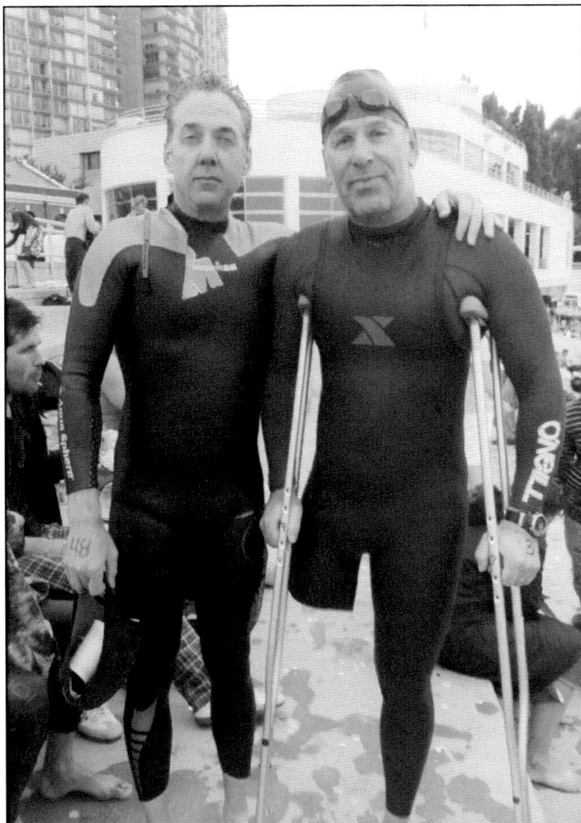

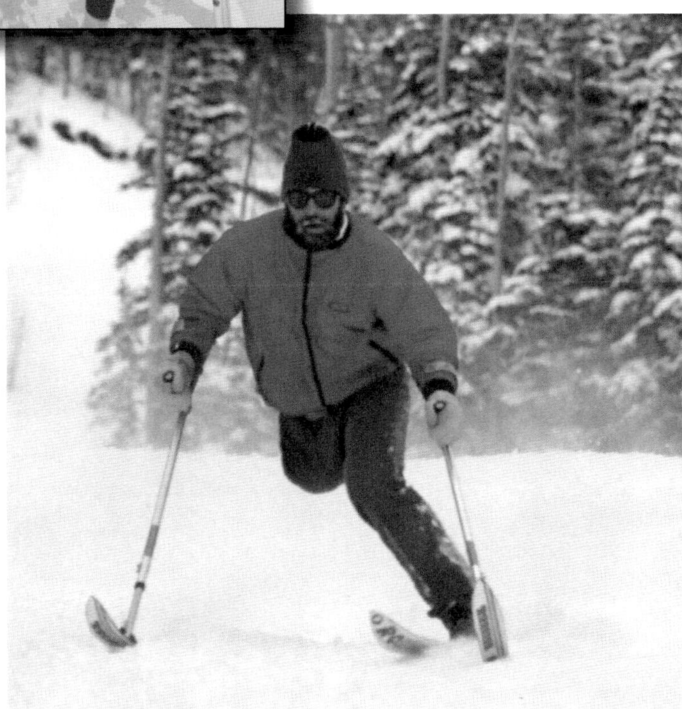

Jason Varitek, Red Sox Catcher

Red Sox catcher Jason Varitek spent his entire 15-year career in Boston, the last seven of them as team captain. He was with the team in 2004 when it won its first World Series in 86 years, and again for its repeat victory in 2007. A Gold Glove winner, "Tek" was a favorite among pitchers for his strength at calling a game.

Tek was not just a great baseball player, though. He was also a Waban resident. Thrilling adults and children alike, on Halloween 2007, the frequent diner at Barry's Deli pulled up a chair to the top of his driveway and signed his autograph on anything trick-or-treaters handed him.

Varitek retired in 2012 and was named special assistant to the general manager later that year. (Courtesy of Boston Red Sox.)

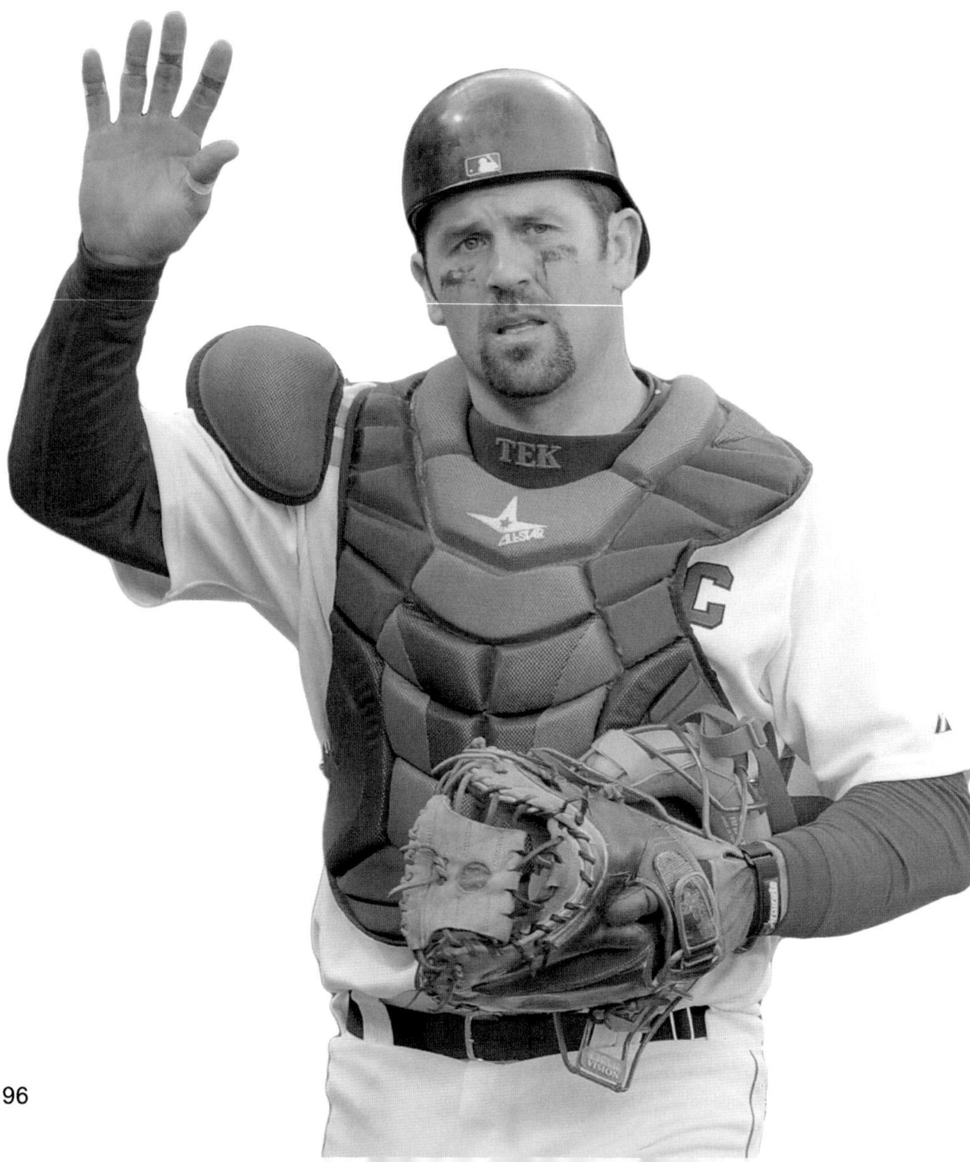

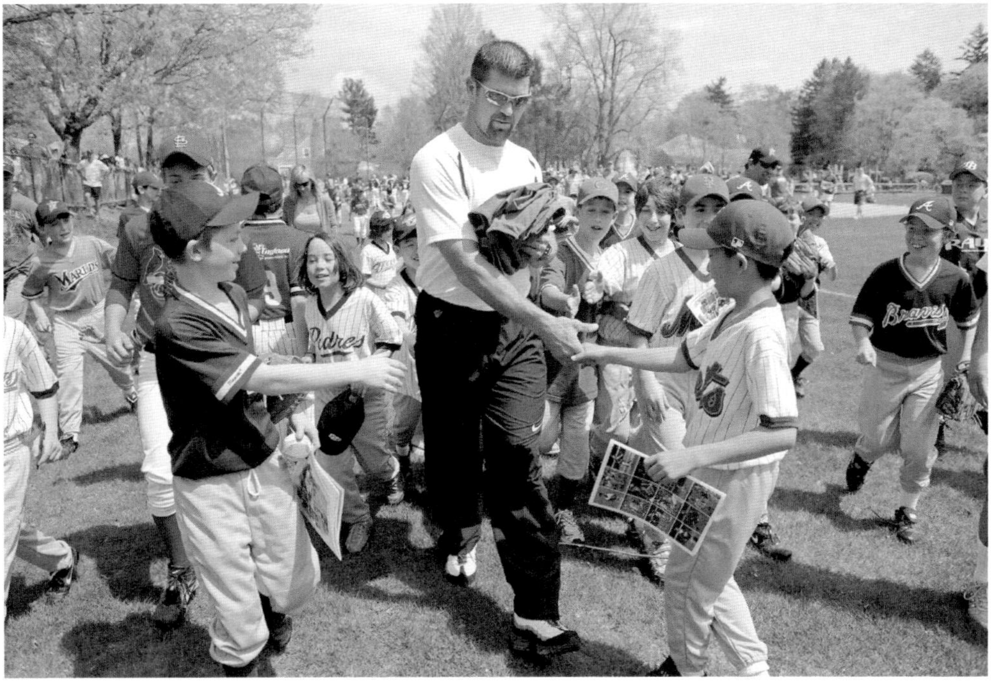

Jason Varitek Greets Newton South Little Leaguers
Jason Varitek delighted Newton South Little Leaguers and their parents when he threw out the first pitch in 2009 to open the season. (Courtesy of Wicked Local Newton.)

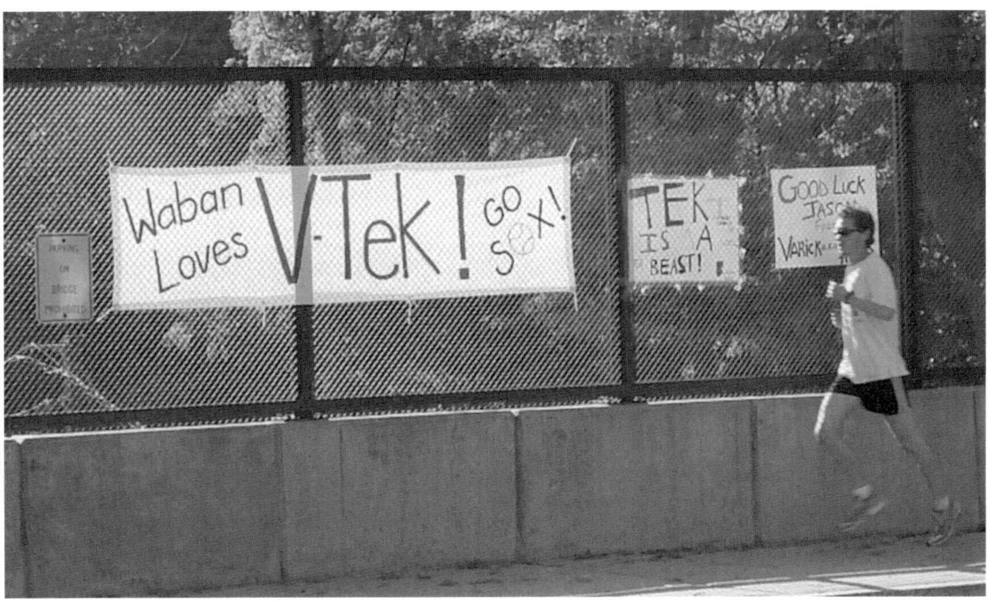

Jason Varitek Fans Show Their Support
Newton residents were very supportive when Jason Varitek, a favorite Red Sox player, lived in their city. For many years, the street sign for Varick Road in Waban was informally changed to Varitek Road. (Photograph by Lorianne DiSabato.)

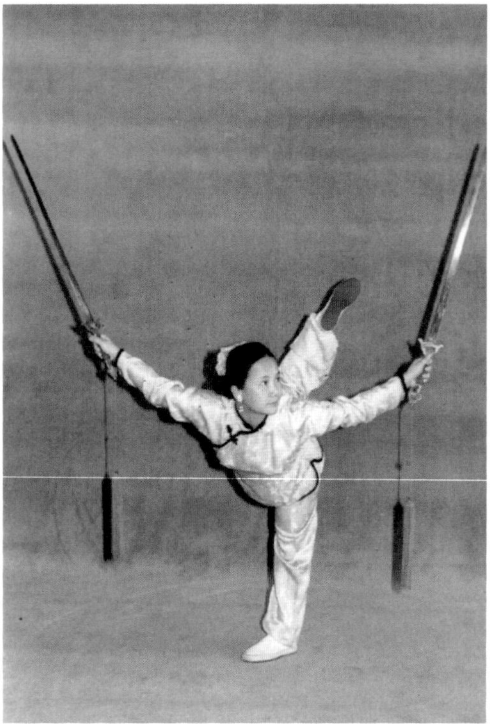

Bow Sim Mark, Wushu Master

Bow Sim Mark is credited with introducing Wushu—a form of contemporary Chinese martial arts that blends elements of performance and martial application—to this country.

A rare female master, Mark, called Sifu (meaning teacher or master in Cantonese) by her students, is especially known for her mastery of Wudang Sword techniques. In 1976, she founded the Chinese Wushu Research Institute in Boston. *Black Belt* magazine named her one of the most influential martial arts masters of the 20th century, and *Inside Kung-Fu* magazine called her one of the most influential masters of the last millennium. (Courtesy of Chinese Wushu Research Institute in Boston.)

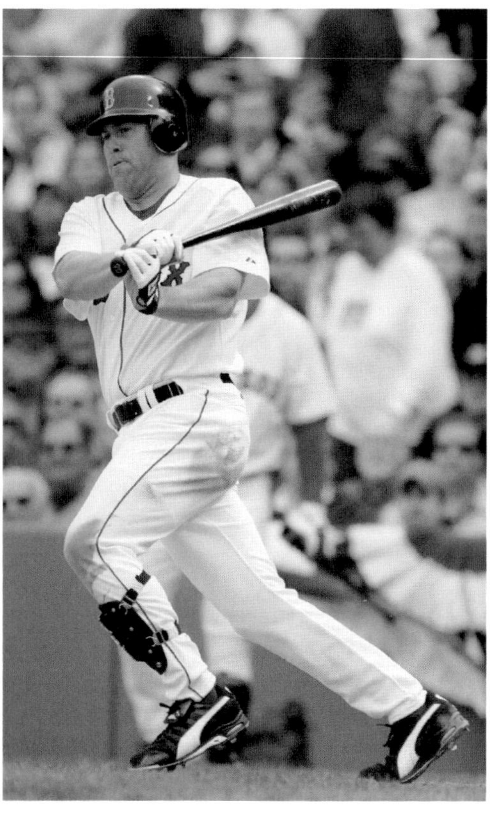

Kevin Youkilis, Red Sox Infielder

Former Red Sox infielder and Gold Glove winner Kevin Youkilis lived in Auburndale for some of his eight-plus years with the team. During that time, "Youk" partnered with the New England Mobile Book Fair in the creation of "Youk's Kids Reading Group," to stress the values of reading and literacy. As part of the program, participants wrote essays about the importance of reading, with the winners earning lunch with the slugger. Youkilis, who was traded to the Chicago White Sox in 2012, retired in 2014. (Courtesy of Boston Red Sox.)

CHAPTER EIGHT

Actors, Entertainers, and Musicians

Newton residents are proud of the many actors and entertainers the city has produced over the years. Among them are Jack Lemmon, who spent the early years of his childhood in Newton schools, and actor Matt Damon, who, as a young boy, lived next door to activist Howard Zinn (page 32). Actor, comedian, and producer Louis C.K. attended Newton North High School, as did *Friends* costar and native of The Lake, Matt LeBlanc. Little League teammates and Newton South graduates John Krasinski and B.J. Novak coincidentally ended up on the same hit series, *The Office*. Hollywood director William "Wild Bill" Wellman, who grew up in Newton Highlands and attended Newton public schools, directed *Wings*, the first movie to win an Academy Award. Robert Preston, who played Harold Hill in the movie *The Music Man*, was yet another Newton native. Film star Bette Davis attended Newton High School.

Famous composer and conductor Leonard Bernstein spent a handful of years in Newton as a youngster. To his father, owning a home in Newton was the ultimate sign of success.

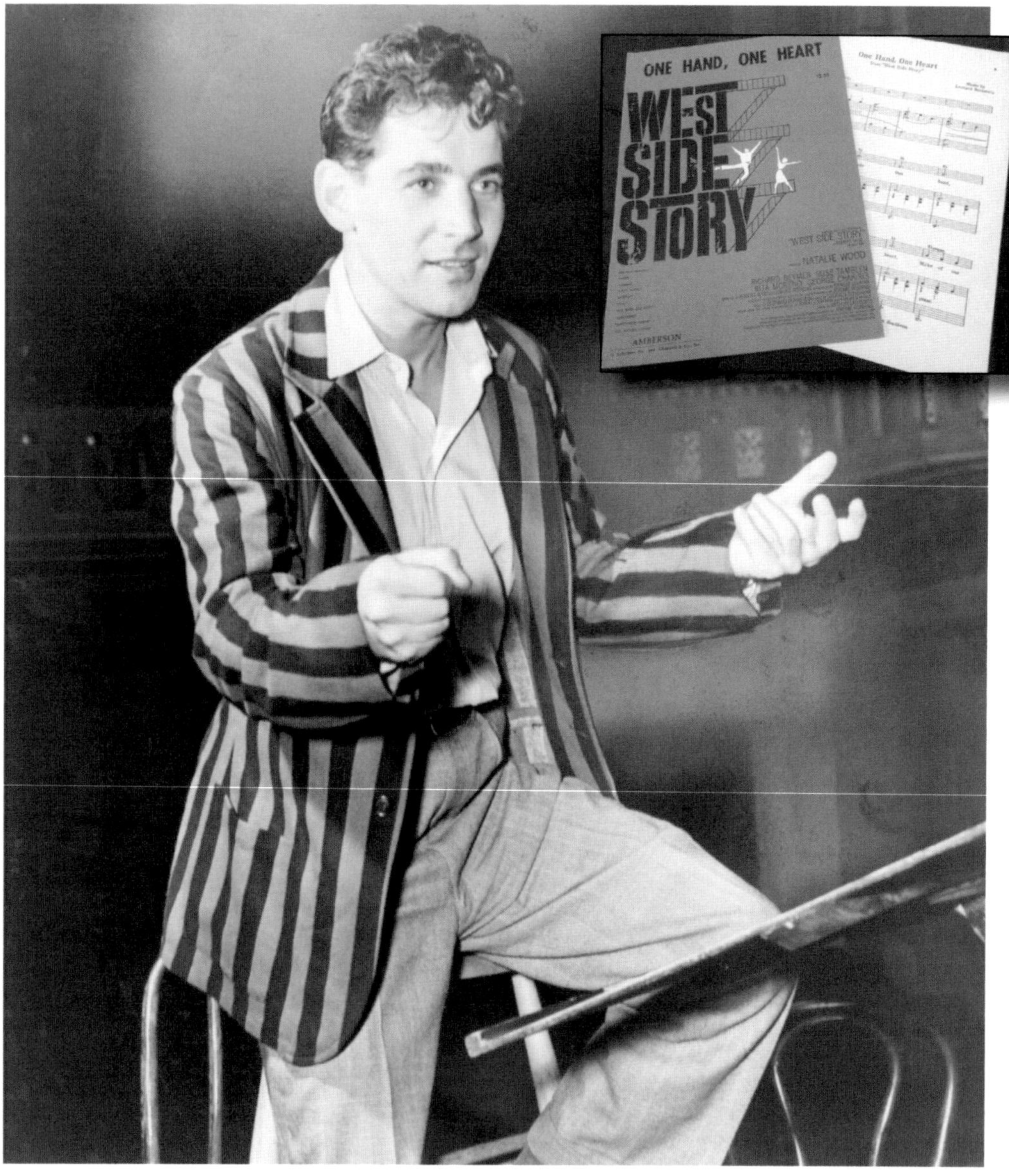

Leonard Bernstein, Conductor, Composer, Maestro

Leonard Bernstein, longtime music director of the New York Philharmonic and among the first American composers to gain worldwide fame, spent most of his adult life in New York City. But the maestro was born in Lawrence, Massachusetts, and, later, moved around the Boston area with his family. It was the family's second home at 85 Park Avenue in Newton that represented what Bernstein's father Sam considered a sign of success.

Leonard's mother, Jennie, told one Bernstein biographer that neighbors used to call on the phone complaining about her son's piano playing, saying that they could not sleep. She would respond to them, "Some day, you're going to pay to hear him!" Proving his mother prophetic, people worldwide paid to hear Bernstein play, conduct, or direct or to see one of the many Broadway shows he composed. Leonard Bernstein wrote the music for *West Side Story*, an American musical that debuted on Broadway in 1957. (Above, courtesy of Library of Congress; inset, photograph by Lisa Spector.)

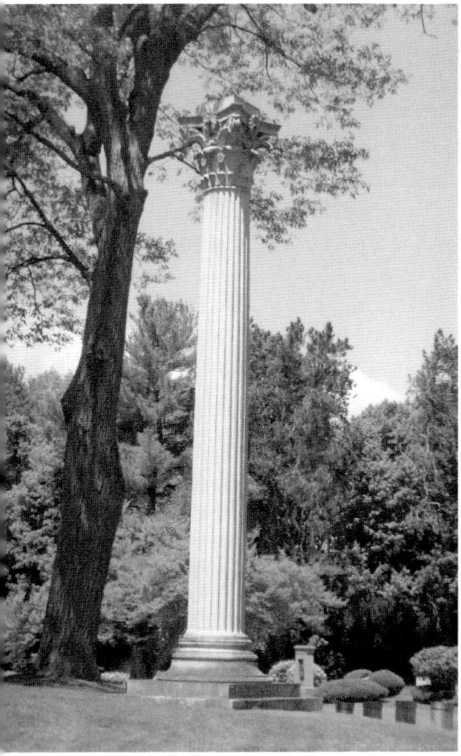

Benjamin Franklin Keith, Father of Vaudeville

B.F. Keith (1846–1914), considered the father of American vaudeville, is buried in one of the most impressive mausoleums in the Newton Cemetery in a lot that was owned by his son Paul, a Newton resident. The one-time barker for P.T. Barnum's circus opened B.F. Keith's New Theatre in Boston in 1894 and with Edward Franklin Albee II, the grandfather of legendary playwright Edward Franklin Albee III, cofounded the Boston Bijou Theatre in 1895. There, they ran a continuous variety show program all day, a format that came to be known as vaudeville. (Photograph by Gail Spector.)

Josephine Hull, Actress

Born Josephine Sherwood in Newtonville in 1877, Hull was an Academy Award–winning film, stage actress, and film director. She is most remembered for two Broadway performances that she later reprised in film: Abby Brewster in *Arsenic and Old Lace*, and Veta Louise Simmons, the sister of Elwood Dowd in *Harvey*. Hull won an Oscar for Best Supporting Actress in *Harvey*, a movie that costarred Jimmy Stewart. Hull, who has a star on the Hollywood Walk of Fame, died in 1957. She is buried in the Newton Cemetery. (Photograph by Gail Spector.)

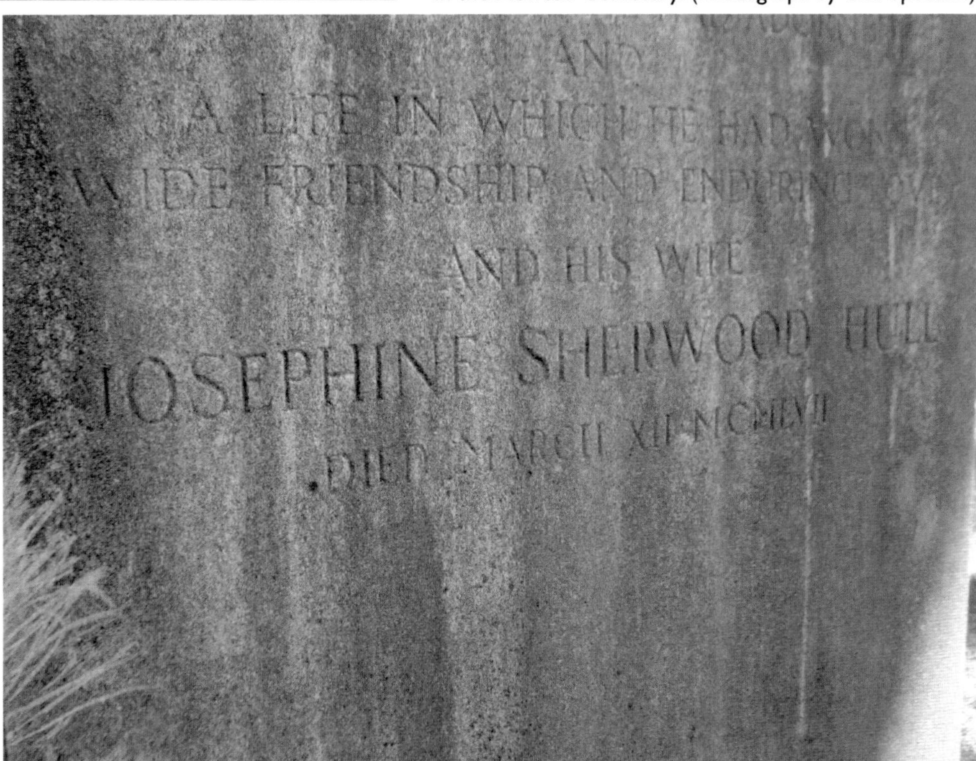

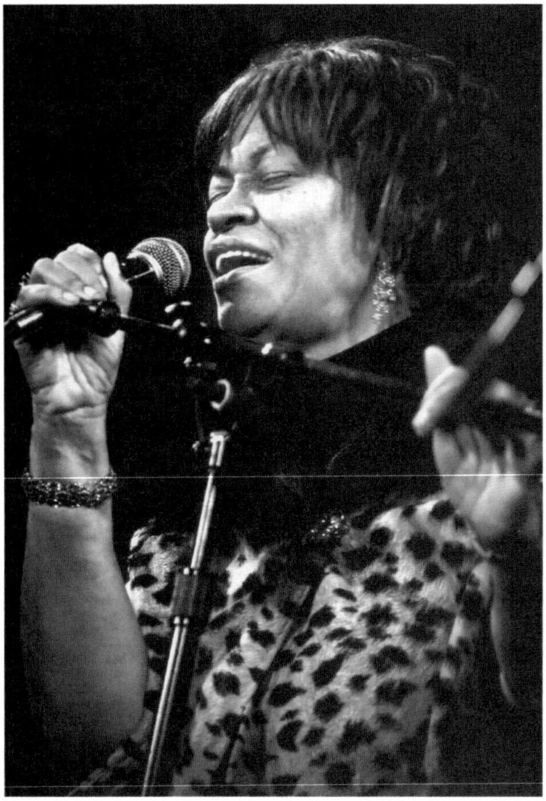

Shirley Lewis, Regal Queen of Blues

When Shirley Lewis (1937–2013) was four years old, the youngest of 12 children joined her father, who was a vaudeville performer, and brothers singing and tap dancing at fairs, ball games, and saloons in New Jersey. By the time she reached adulthood, Lewis had become a force in the blues scene, frequently opening for big names like B.B. King, Ike and Tina Turner, Wilson Pickett, and Ray Charles.

In 1987, Lewis moved to Newton, where a *Boston Globe* music critic dubbed her the "Regal Queen of the Blues," because of her dazzling hat and gown ensembles. In 2001, she received the Blues Trust Lifetime Achievement Award, and she was nominated twice for outstanding blues act at the Boston Music Awards. (Courtesy of Angela Warner.)

Jack Lemmon, Hollywood Star

Movie star Jack Lemmon (1925–2001) was born in an elevator at Newton-Wellesley Hospital. He lived in Newton as a child, attending Ward Elementary School before transferring to a private school. The actor, known for playing affable but down-on-their-luck characters, performed in more than 50 movies, with two of them earning him Academy Awards; he was named best actor in *Save the Tiger* and best supporting actor in *Mister Roberts*. (Courtesy of Alan Light.)

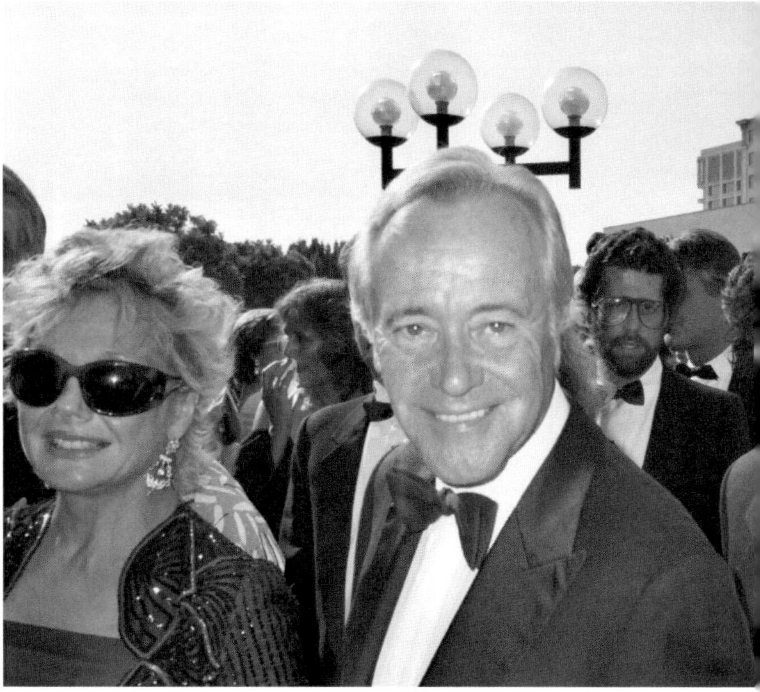

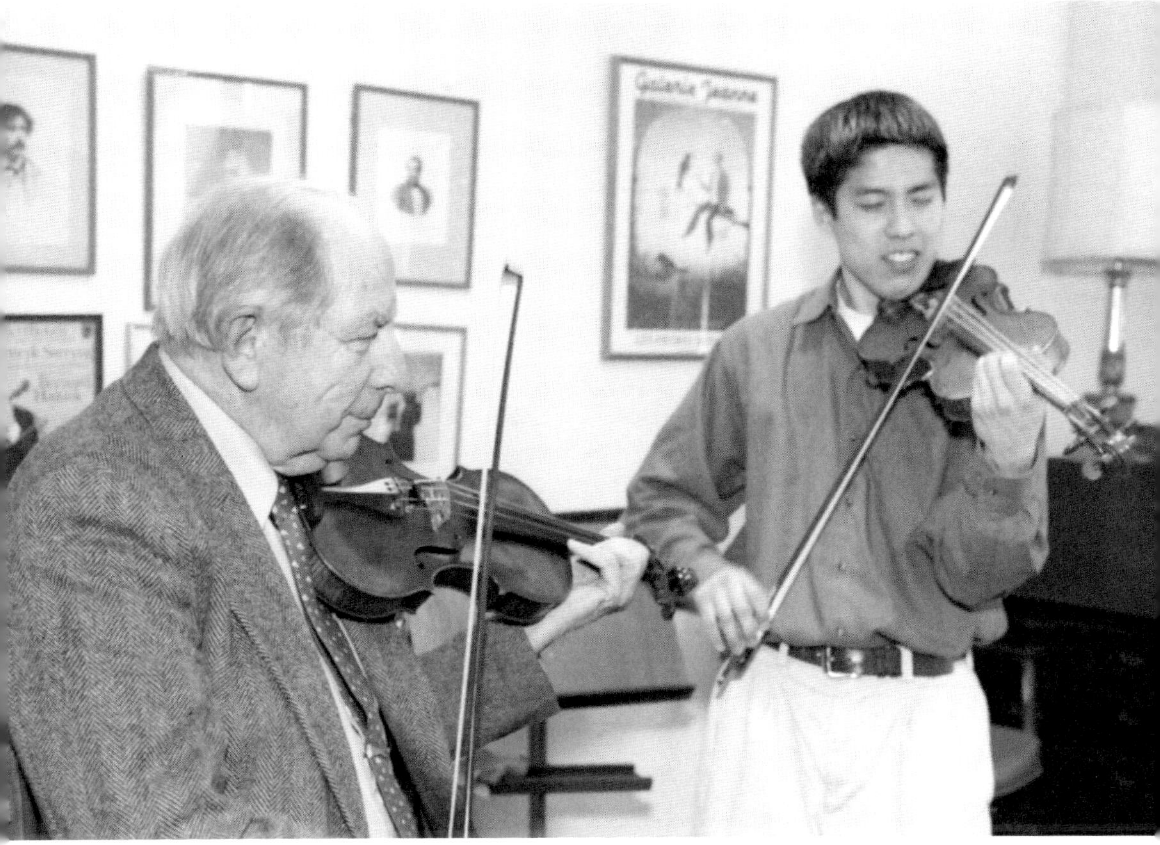

Roman Totenberg, Master Violinist and Teacher

Roman Totenberg, world-renowned virtuoso violinist, delighted in teaching violin as much as he loved playing it. In the days before he died in 2012 at age 101, many former students traveled to his bedside for one last lesson with their beloved teacher. He listened to them play, waving his arm as he kept them on tempo, and instructed them on fingering, pitch, and tone.

Totenberg (1911–2012) was born in Lodz, Poland, and made his debut with the Warsaw Philharmonic at age 11. He won several prestigious awards and performed with practically every major orchestra in the United States and Europe.

A faculty member at Boston University (BU) for more than 50 years, Totenberg chaired the strings department from 1961 to 1978 and cochaired again in 1994 after serving as director of the Longy School of Music in Cambridge, Massachusetts. In 1983, the man who gave his first violin lesson when he was nine years old was named Artist Teacher of the Year by the American String Teachers Association, and in 1996, he received BU's Metcalf Prize for outstanding teacher of the year.

Totenberg also recorded with all the major record labels during his career. His daughter Nina is an award-winning journalist for National Public Radio. (Photograph by Fred Sway for Boston University.)

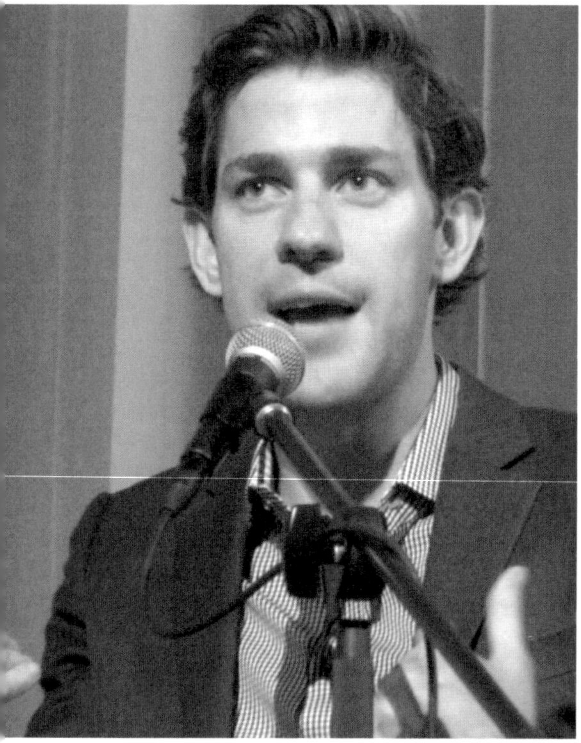

John Krasinski (Left) and B.J. Novak, Classmates and Costars

B.J. Novak gave John Krasinski his first acting break. Even though Krasinski had never acted, Novak cast him as the lead in the senior show at Newton South High School. The Little League teammates parted ways at graduation, only bumping into each other occasionally when back in Newton. Then, coincidentally, they both landed roles in *The Office*, a mockumentary of modern American office life that starred Steve Carrell.

Since then, Krasinski has appeared in several movies, including *It's Complicated*, *License to Wed*, and *Leatherheads*.

Novak, who was also a writer and coexecutive producer for *The Office*, is also known for his stand-up comedy. He has written and appeared in the comedy *The Mindy Project* and appeared in *Inglorious Bastards* and *Saving Mr. Banks*. He is the author of *One More Thing: Stories and Other Stories* and *The Book With No Pictures*. (Krasinski photograph by Kirk Kittell; Novak photograph by Gail Spector.)

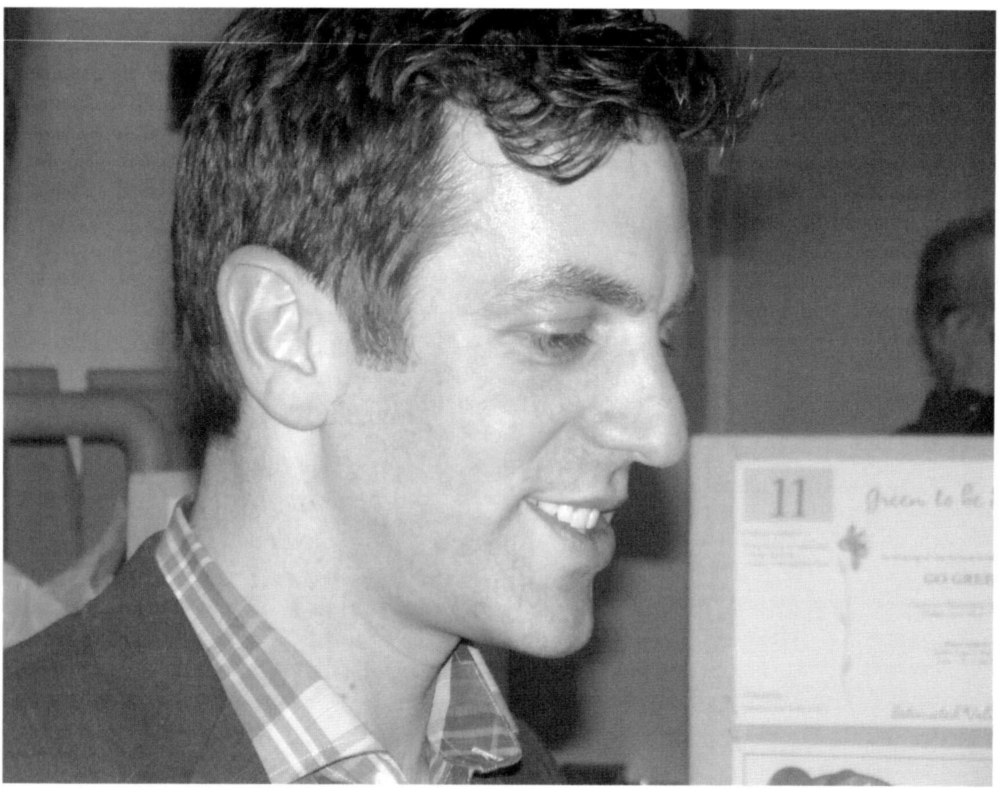

Matt LeBlanc, Famous TV Friend

Matt LeBlanc, a 1985 graduate of Newton North High School, gained fame along with his five costars in the award-winning sitcom *Friends*, which ran on NBC from 1994 to 2004. LeBlanc, who did not act in high school, has described those years as the best in his life.

Coming from a blue-collar family in Nonantum, LeBlanc was a carpentry major in high school who went to college for one semester as a building construction technology major. When that did not work, he moved to New York City to study acting and became a successful commercial actor. His first big break was starring in a Heinz Ketchup commercial that won an award at the Cannes Film Festival.

After the finale of *Friends*, LeBlanc kept his role alive in the two-season series *Joey*. In 2011, he returned as a fictional version of himself in *Episodes*.

In a 2014 appearance on *Conan*, LeBlanc divulged the secret code of his home village when he spoke to host Conan O'Brien in the dialect local to Nonantum, or more specifically, "The Lake." (Photograph by Joe Wolf.)

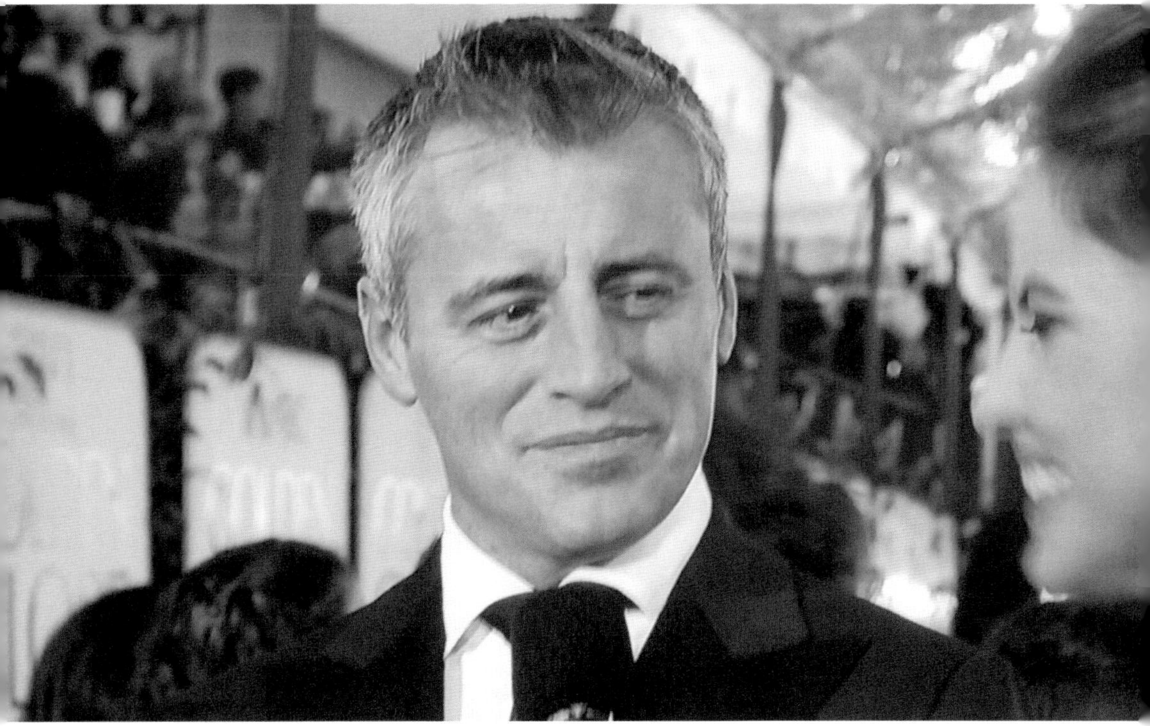

Mark Sandman, Indie Rock Icon

Mark Sandman, lead singer and slide bass player of the alternative rock band Morphine, was just 46 years old when he collapsed on stage in Italy while performing with his band. The cause of death was a heart attack, attributed to smoking cigarettes, heavy stress, and high temperatures on the night of his death. Sandman, who grew up in Newton, was well known in the Boston/Cambridge music scene. Morphine disbanded after Sandman's death on July 3, 1999. (Courtesy of Erik Gamlem.)

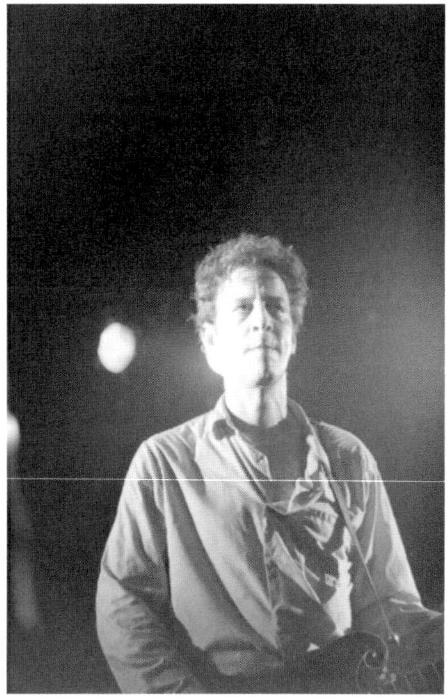

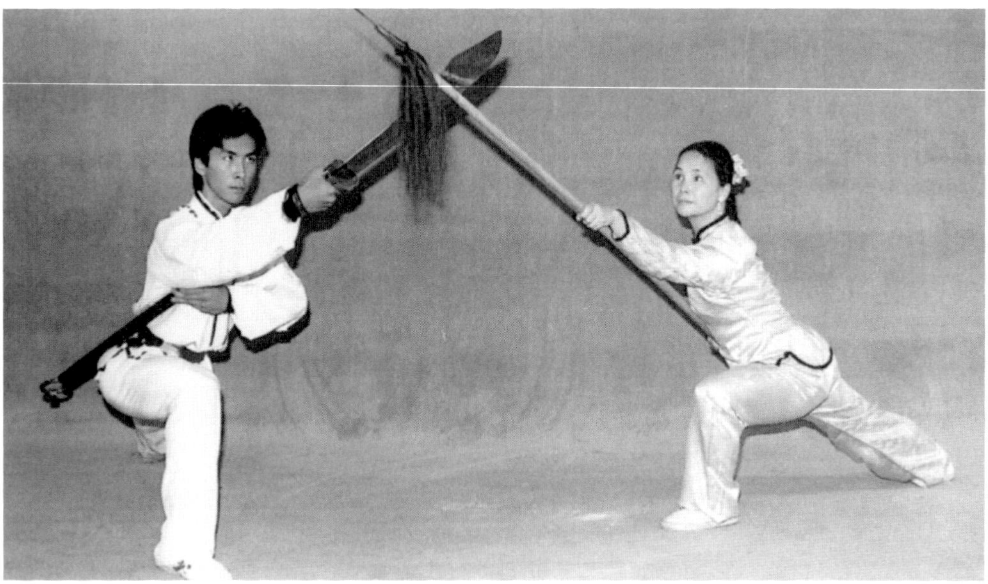

Donnie Yen, Martial Arts Action Star

Donnie Yen (left), the son of martial arts master Bow Sim Mark (right and page 98), had been studying martial arts for seven years when he moved to Newton from Canton, China, at age 11 in 1974. By the time he was 16, he was fighting so much that his parents removed him from Newton North and sent him overseas for intensive martial arts training. A screen test in Hong Kong a few years later led to a stunt role in a movie. He starred in his first movie, *Drunken Tai Chi,* at age 19. By the late 1980s, he had a movie contract and numerous fans, and today he enjoys a reputation as a formidable action movie performer. (Courtesy of Chinese Wushu Research Institute.)

CHAPTER NINE

Artists, Writers, and Media

From Frank Avruch, the nation's first syndicated Bozo the Clown, to Tom Ashbrook, the National Public Radio host of *On Point*, to sculptor Nancy Schön, Newton is teeming with people who are willing to share their talents. Public art enthusiast Robert Guillemin, who was better known as Sidewalk Sam, the artist who reproduced masterpieces on sidewalks in the Boston area, lived in Newton and ran a public art foundation. Playwright, author, and screenwriter David Mamet was a West Newton resident for several years. Popular science fiction author Isaac Asimov lived and wrote in Newton for 14 years. Nathaniel Hawthorne wrote *The Blithedale Romance* in Newton. Ralph Waldo Emerson lived on Woodward Street in the 1830s.

Long before Newtonian and media mogul Russel Pergament founded the TAB Newspapers and BostonNow, a Newton resident purchased the *Boston Herald*. Edwin B. Haskell edited the *Herald* for 21 years after buying it with two others in 1865.

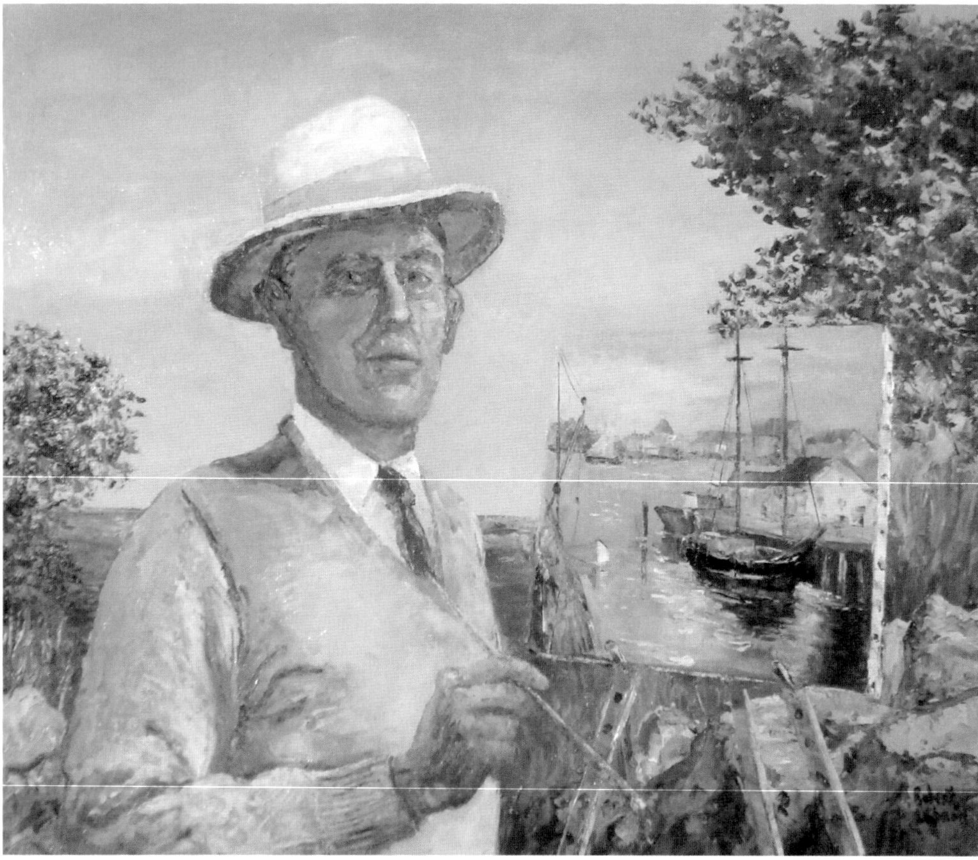

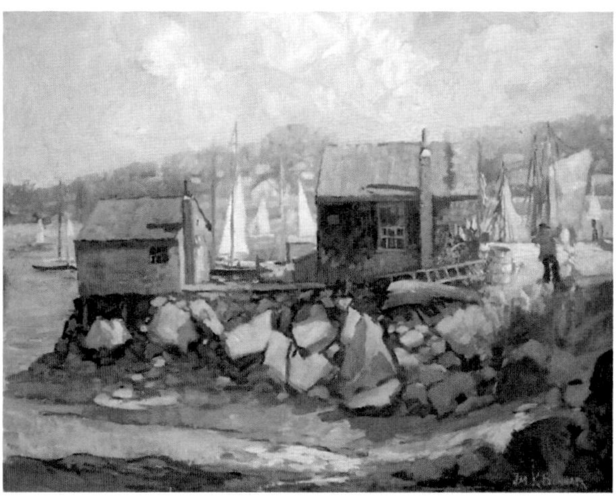

Portrait of James King Bonnar, American Artist

Artist and teacher James King Bonnar, shown above in a portrait painted by his friend Robert Lebrón, was born in North Adams in 1883, but he lived in Newtonville when he founded the Newton Art Association in 1949. Within just a couple of years of its founding, the association had 200 members.

Already active in the prestigious Copley Watercolor Society and well respected for his open-air paintings, particularly of seascapes and Vermont, Bonnar started the Newton Art Association because he was a strong believer in bringing art to more people. Bonnar, who spent summers on Cape Ann with many well-known artists, was a member of both the Rockport and Gloucester Art Associations. Because he believed that there was much to be gained from gathering together to create art and that everyone had an inner artist, he spent a great deal of time encouraging others. His work is also represented in several private collections in the United States. In honor of Bonnar, who died in 1961, his family in 2003 established the annual James King Bonnar Award for artistic achievement. (Both courtesy of David Bonnar.)

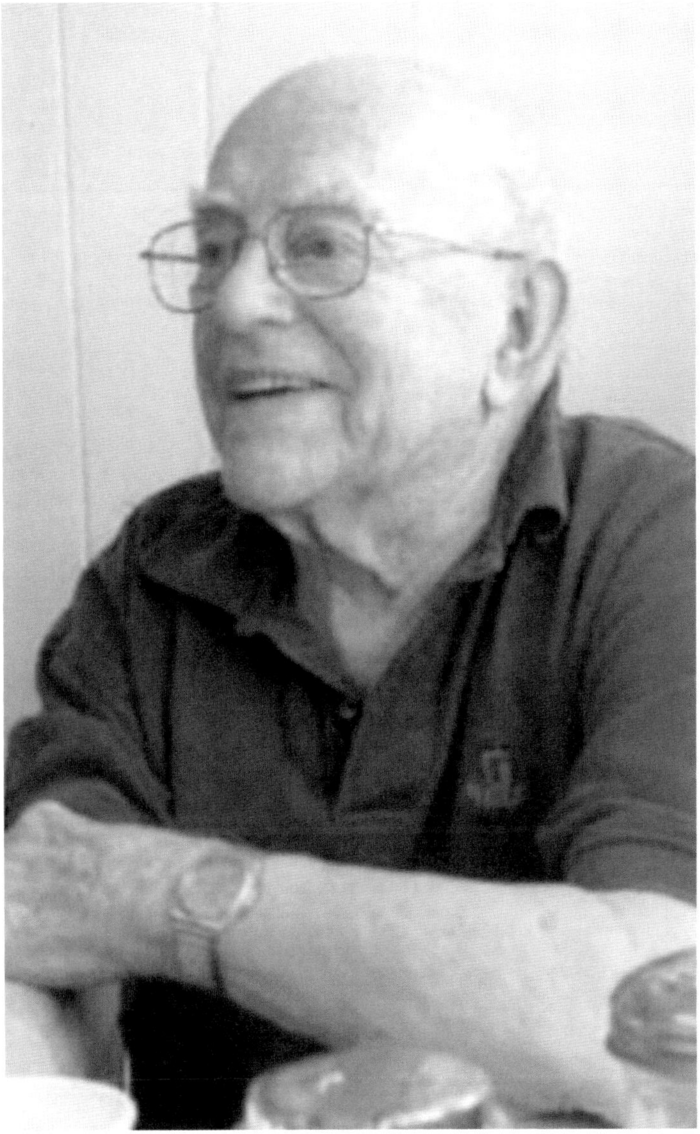

Milton Levy, Poet and Sailor

Milton Levy (1915–2006) could seemingly make any words rhyme to fit his topic. A film production audio-visual producer professionally, Levy had a knack—and passion—for poetry. Informally dubbed the "Poet Laureate of Newton," Levy started writing poetry for the *Newton Graphic* in the late 1980s and continued when it was rolled into the *Newton TAB* in 1997. Weekly, he opined poetically about topics that included food, sailing, politics, parking in Newton Centre, and anything else that was on his mind.

One such poem, "Newton Centre is Making Me Sick to My Stomach," included the following refrain: "I don't mean to complain, but it gives me a pain / While at heart I am not a dissenter. / The facts are quite stark. There is no place to park / If you have to drive into the Centre!"

A US Navy veteran who served in both Europe and the Pacific from 1941 to 1945, Levy's interest in poetry was topped only by his love for sailing. The 50-year Newton resident and father of three daughters stopped writing for the *TAB* when he had a stroke in 2003. Many readers sent him cards and notes wishing him well and letting him know how much they missed him. (Courtesy of the Levy family.)

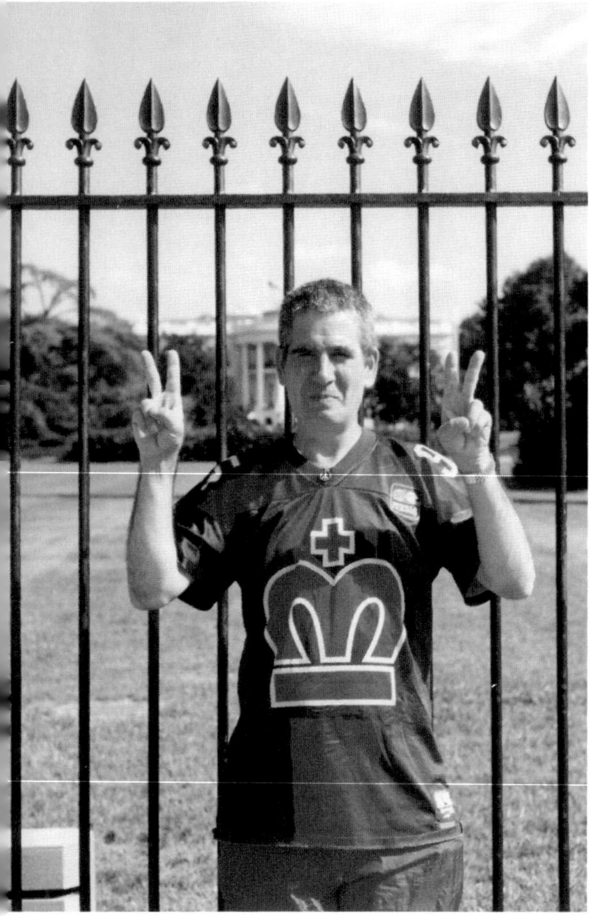

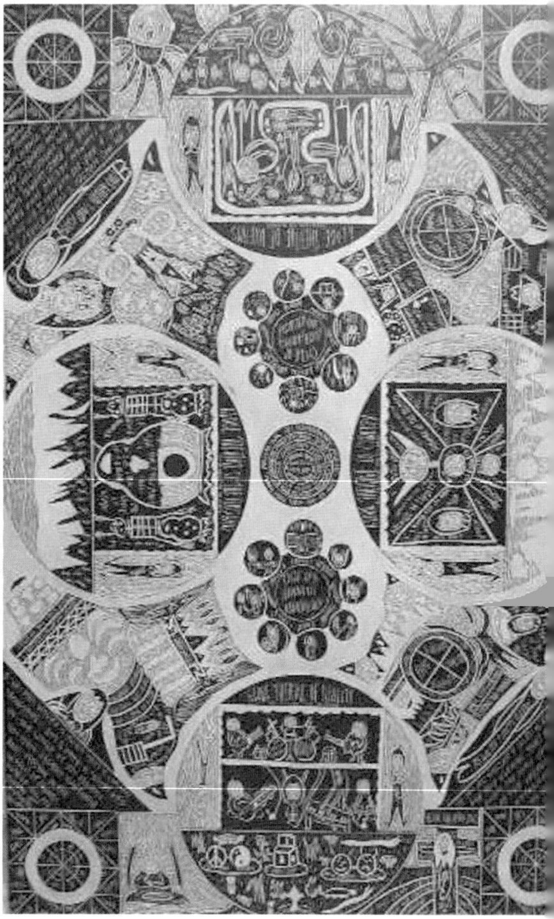

Sanford Winslow, Artist with Limitless Creativity

Sandy Winslow (1950–2002) was all about expressing his creativity. A Newton native and a 1968 graduate of Newton High School, Winslow was overcome by mental illness that started during his junior year at Boston University and would continue for the rest of his life. While spending years in psychiatric hospitals and halfway houses, he developed his own style of art. As his life progressed, he painted, photographed, created scratchboards, sculpted wire and clay, danced, wrote, and played guitar and keyboards.

Winslow worked at Corners on Needham Street for more than 12 years and was a familiar face to many. His art has been shown in Newton's New Art Center and in cities around the country. He was said to be as proud to have been included in the Museum of Bad Art as a catalogue from the American Visionary Art Museum. Winslow died in 2002 after a brief battle with cancer. (Courtesy of Julie Bernson.)

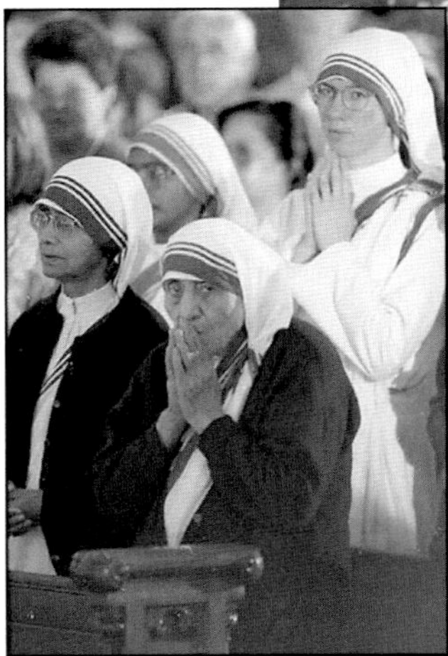

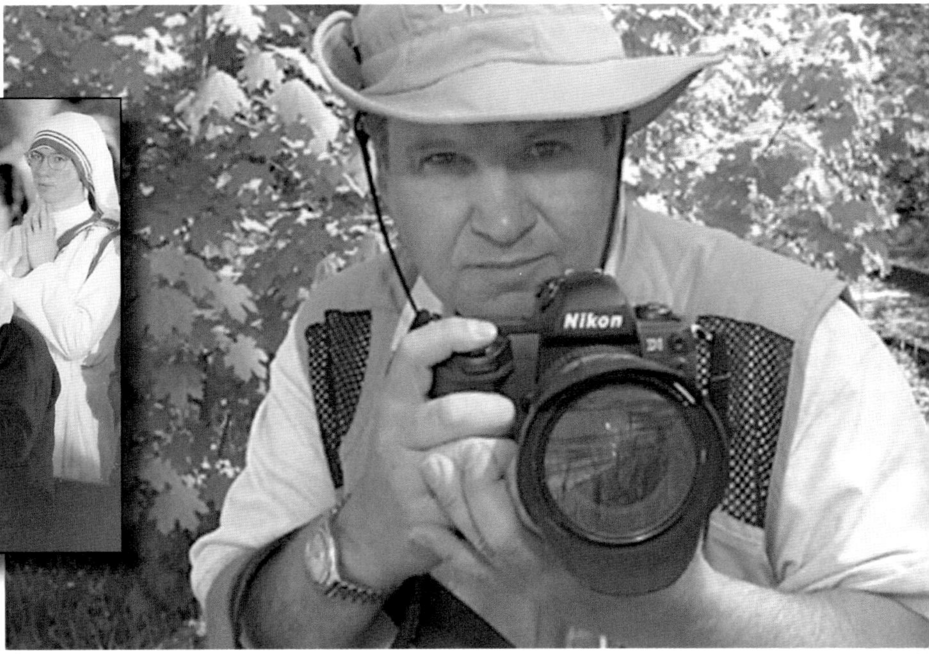

Keith Jacobson, TAB Photographer

Keith Jacobson knows Newton. The retired Newton TAB photographer spent 34 years behind the lens, capturing Newton at its finest and saddest moments, getting to know city leaders and unsung heroes, finding stories and making friends in the most unlikely places. The Newton native, who was the first full-time photographer hired by TAB founder Russel Pergament, chronicled some of Newton's most memorable moments, including Mother Teresa's visit to Our Lady Help of Christians Parish on June 15, 1995 (pictured here). Jacobson, who won several awards for his photographs, retired in 2013. (Both courtesy of Keith E. Jacobson.)

Ken Newcomb,
Author of *The Makers of the Mold*

Ken Newcomb was a railroad worker and neighborhood leader who devoted 20 years to researching the history of Newton Upper Falls. Upon completion, he unsuccessfully tried to find a publisher. In response to his fear that he would die without seeing the book in print, the Friends of Hemlock Gorge printed the book online. About a decade after Newcomb died, in 2011, a newcomer to Upper Falls, Jerry Reilly, found the book while researching his new community. He engaged members of Friends of Hemlock Gorge, and together, they published *The Makers of the Mold*, which is sold in stores throughout Newton. (Photograph by Gail Spector.)

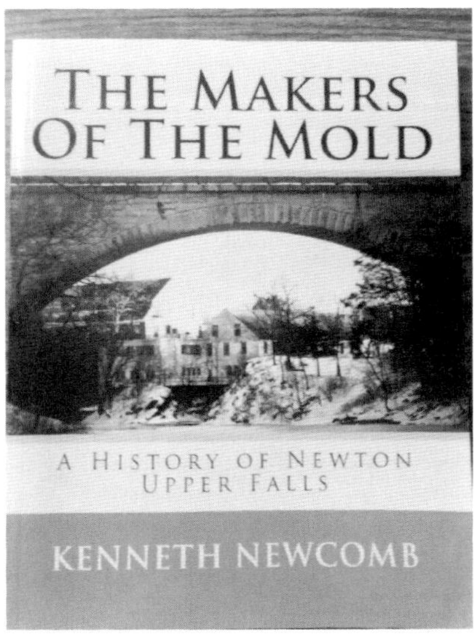

Frank Avruch, Bozo the Clown

After a long stint playing the famous clown on local television, Frank Avruch became the first Bozo the Clown to enter living rooms all across the United States. Avruch, the first nationally syndicated Bozo in the country, traveled around the world as Bozo on behalf of the United Nations Children Fund, giving performances that would result in a series of documentaries for UNICEF.

However, Boston-area television viewers are far more likely to recognize Avruch as the host of the 18-year classic film series, *The Great Entertainment*. Dubbed "Man about Town" and "Goodwill Ambassador" by Boston's ABC-TV affiliate, Avruch represents the station at cultural and community events.

Avruch's commendations include a United Nations award for his work with children, two Emmy Awards, and a Man of the Year Award citing his tireless work for charities of all kinds. He was inducted into the Massachusetts Broadcasters Hall of Fame in 2007. (Both courtesy of Frank Avruch.)

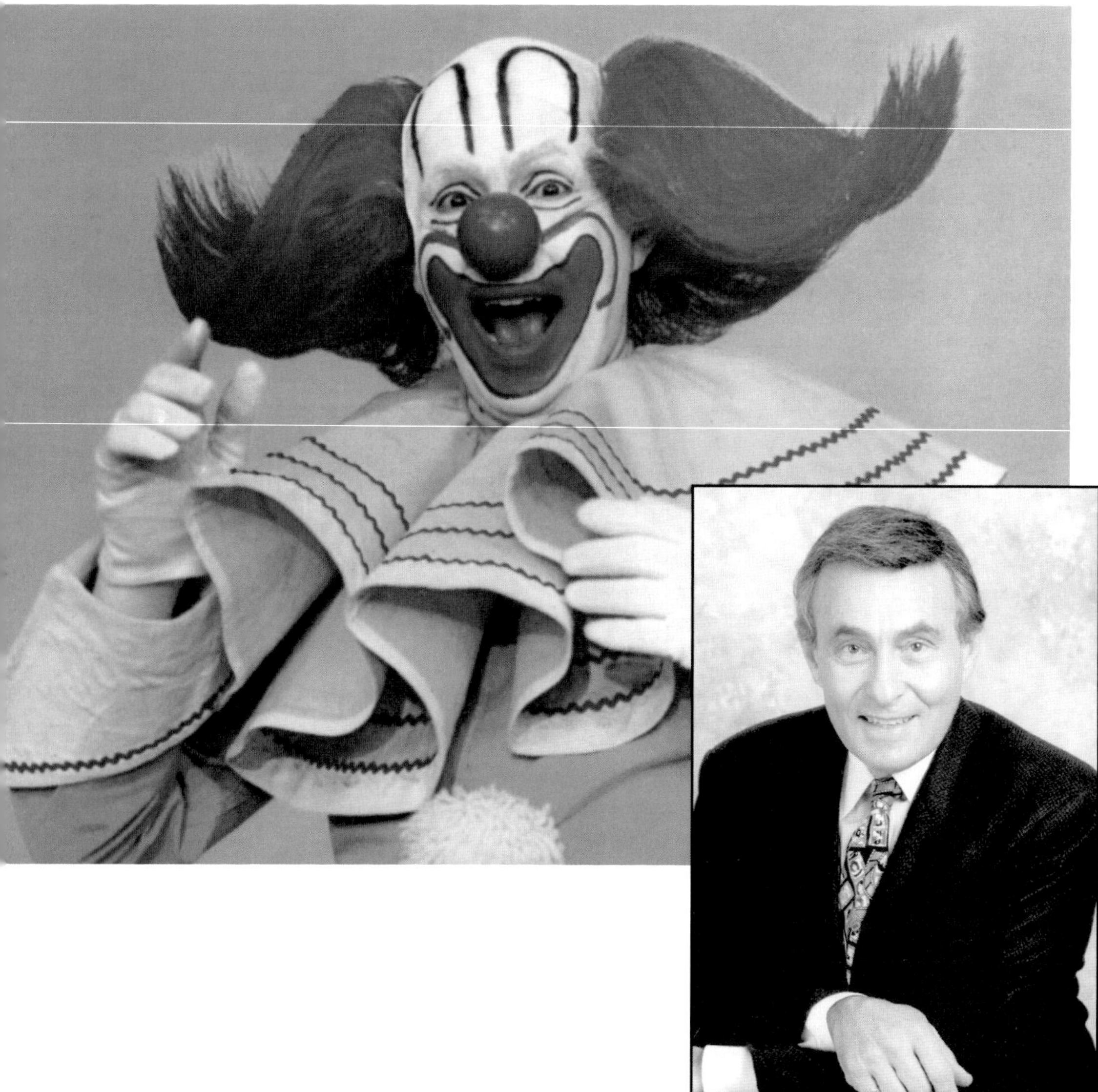

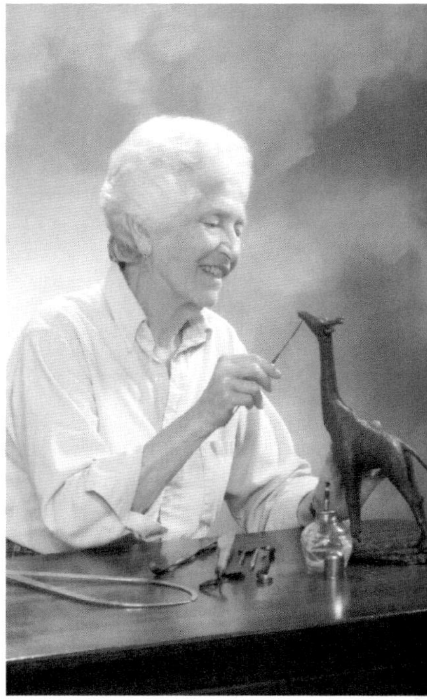

Nancy Schön, Sculptor

Nancy Schön's first sculpture was crafted from a stick of chewing gum. As a young child attending a Halloween party, she was told to chew a piece of gum and make something. She made a teacup and saucer and won first prize.

Since then, the Newton native has worked with much more sophisticated media. A prominent name in the sculpting world, she is the sculptor behind the famous bronze sculptures, *Make Way for Ducklings*, in the Boston Public Garden. Identical pieces were commissioned by former first lady Barbara Bush as a gift to Raisa Gorbachev in 1991 as part of the START treaty.

Closer to home, children delight in the sculpture *Eeyore* Schön created from *Winnie-the-Pooh* for the Newton Free Library in 1991 in memory of a four-year-old boy. Schön added *Winnie-the-Pooh and Hunny Pot* and then *Piglet* in 2013.

The octogenarian also created *Tortoise and Hare* in Boston's Copley Square, in honor of the Boston Marathon's 100th running, and several other pieces of public art. She is a strong advocate for a Charles River Skate Park, a cause she adopted upon realizing that youth were skateboarding on her sculptures because they had no place else to skate. (Both courtesy of Nancy Schön.)

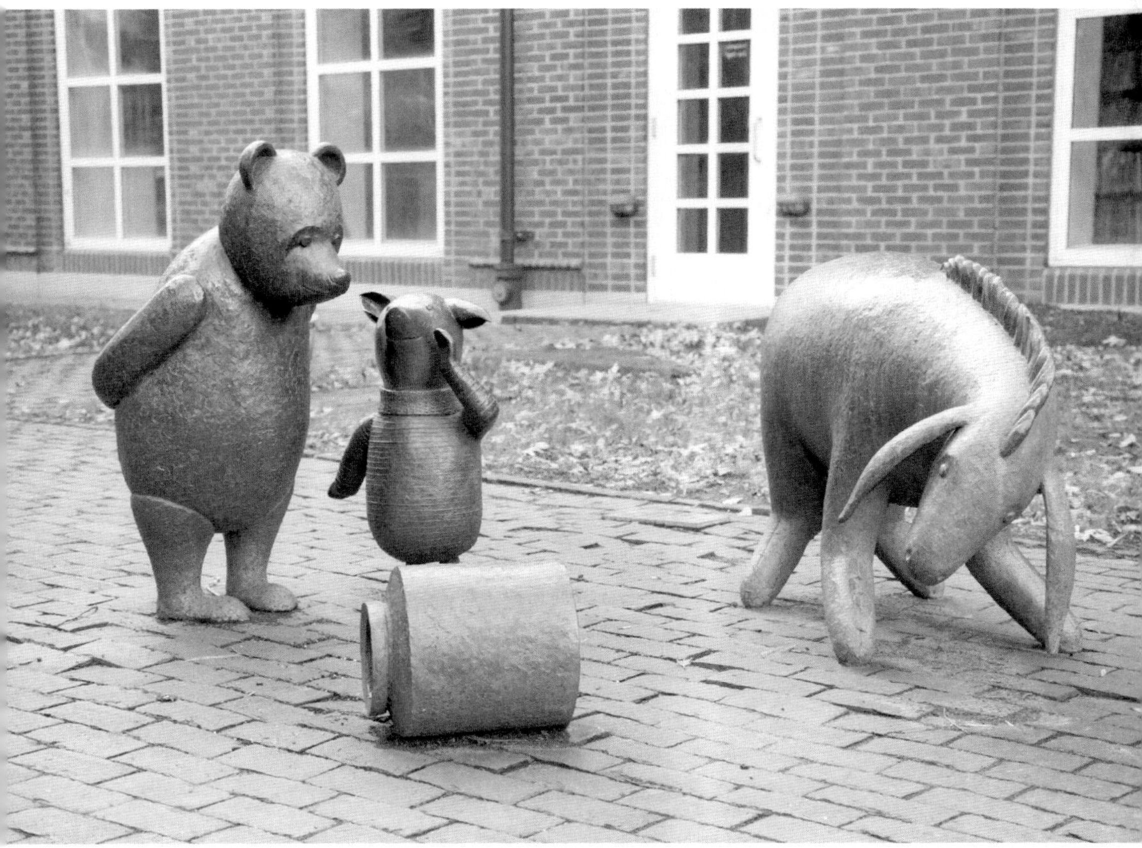

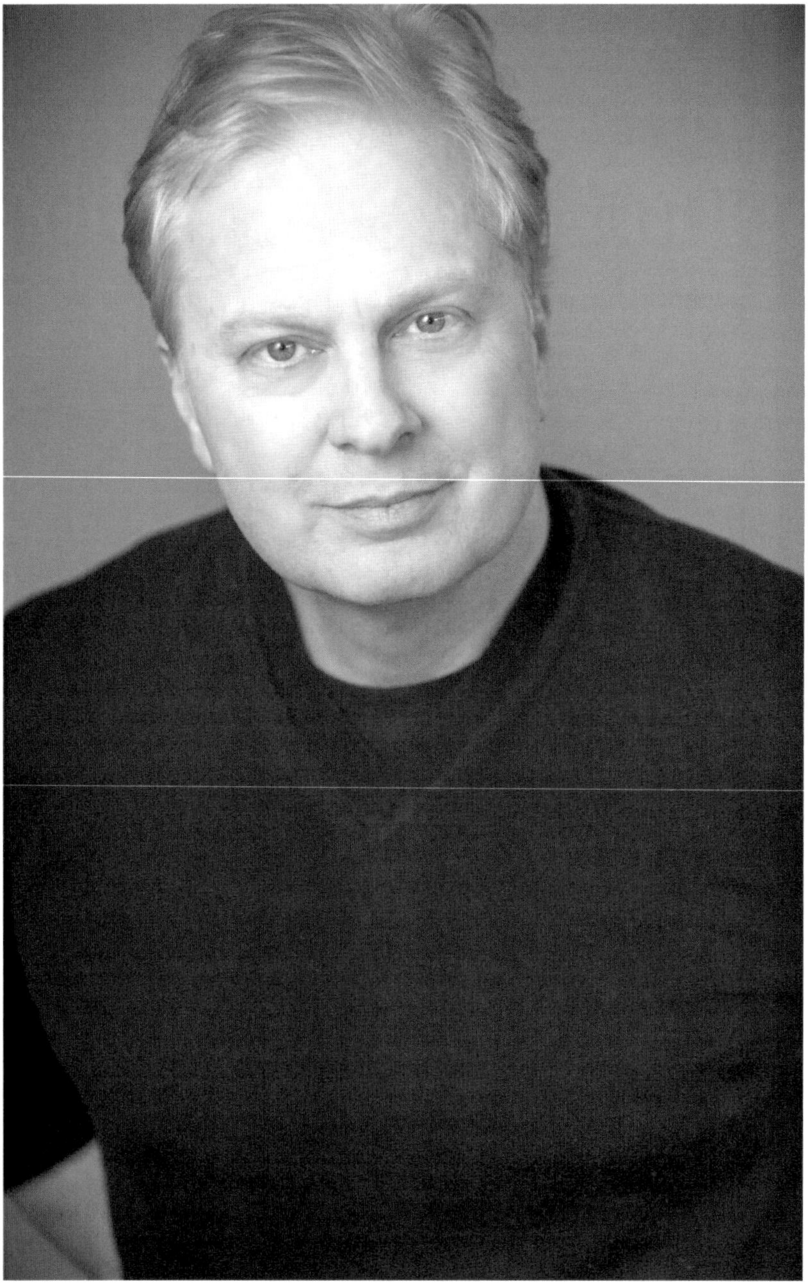

Tom Ashbrook, National Public Radio Journalist

Tom Ashbrook can talk about anything. In two one-hour segments, the award-winning journalist and host of National Public Radio's *On Point* conducts weekday conversations about everything from breaking news to the history of maps with assorted professionals and ordinary citizens from around the world. The show that the Newton resident began hosting after September 11, 2001, now runs on 286 stations nationwide, with a weekly audience of 1.5 million.

Ashbrook's career in journalism includes years as a foreign correspondent, newspaper editor, and author. He is the 1989 winner of the Livingston Award for National Reporting. (Photograph by Liz Linder.)

Anita Diamant, Author and Mikveh Visionary

After 15 years as a successful freelance journalist and nonfiction writer, Newton author Anita Diamant tried her hand at fiction, never expecting that her first novel, *The Red Tent*, would achieve the popularity and fame it received. Despite its lack of an advertising budget, the book became a word-of-mouth best seller. Book groups, independent bookstores, and readers spread the word about the novel that would become a *New York Times* bestseller. *The Red Tent*, a fictional story giving voice to a silent female rape victim in the Old Testament, won the Book Sense Best Fiction Award (since renamed the Indies Choice Book Award) from independent booksellers in 2001. It has been published in more than 25 countries worldwide with translations into 20 languages.

Diamant's contributions to the community go deeper than the several novels she has since published or the nonfiction guidebooks to Jewish life and lifecycle events she had previously written. In 2000, Diamant began a campaign to build a community *mikveh* (a bath for Jewish ritual immersion). Her vision—building a contemporary mikveh that met the needs of non-Orthodox Jews, both men and women—became reality in 2004 with the opening of Mayyim Hayyim: Living Waters Community Mikveh and Education Center, located in a renovated Victorian house on Washington Street in Auburndale.

Diamant's most recent novel, *The Boston Girl*, published at the end of 2014. (Photograph by Gretje Fergeson; courtesy of Anita Diamant.)

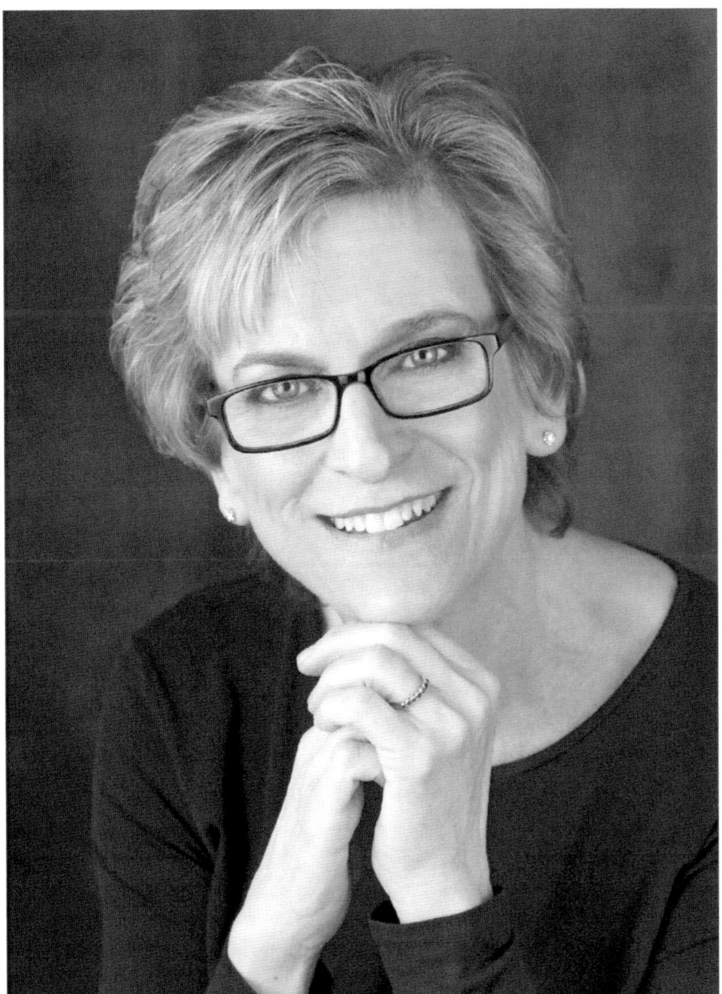

Dan Shaughnessy, Sports Columnist

Born in Groton, Massachusetts, in 1953, well-known *Boston Globe* sports columnist Dan Shaughnessy started his career covering the Baltimore Orioles for the *Baltimore Sun* in 1977. When he joined the *Boston Globe* in 1981, he moved to Newton and eventually settled in Newton Corner.

Shaughnessy popularized the term "Curse of the Bambino," describing the superstition Red Sox fans held about the sale of Babe Ruth to the Yankees in 1918 after the Red Sox' last World Series win prior to 2004. Fans of Boston sports teams love to slam, praise, and critique Shaughnessy's opinions.

Shaughnessy's peers have awarded him several times as one of the best in his profession. He has received the Massachusetts Sportswriter of the Year Award many times and has been named one of the top-10 sports columnists in America by the Associated Press Sports Editors multiple times.

He is the author of several best-selling sports books, including *Curse of the Bambino*, *Reversing the Curse*, and *Francona*. (Photograph by Stan Grossfeld; courtesy of Dan Shaughnessy.)

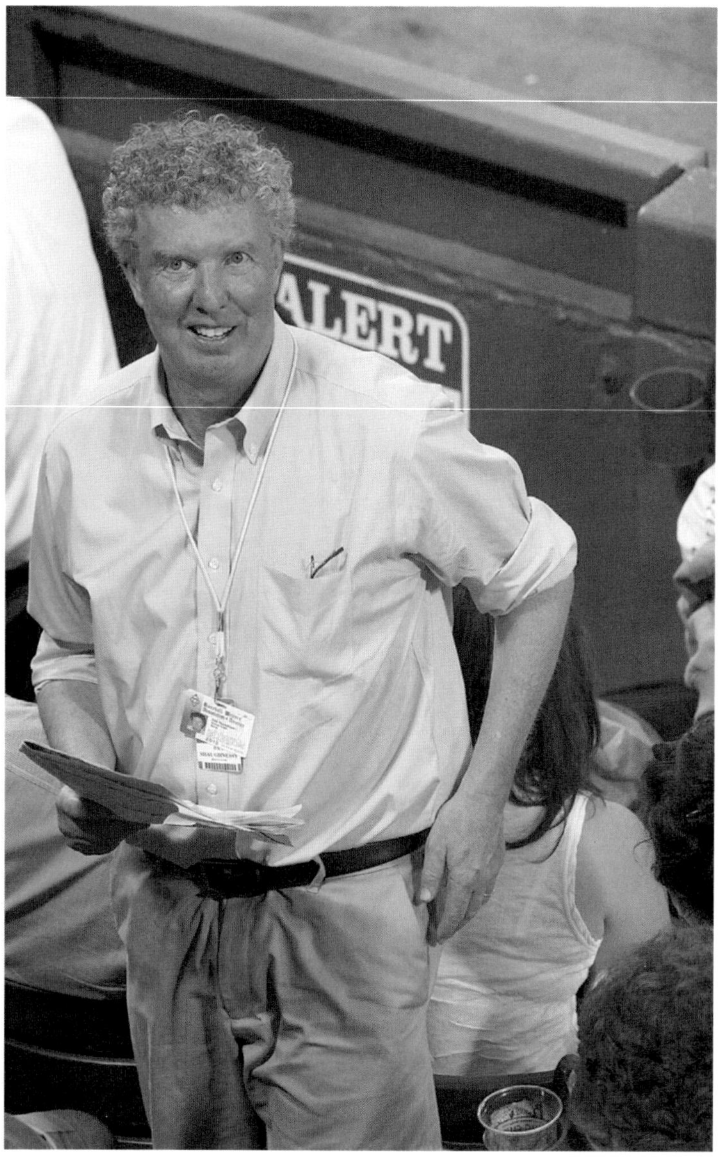

CHAPTER TEN

Educators and Students

Since the town built its first school in 1699, a one-room 16-by-14-foot structure, education has been a bedrock of the community. Newton's public schools have earned a reputation for excellence, and the city, in turn, is known for the priority it places on education. According to Newton's first mayor, James Hyde, in his bicentennial address to the city, "all through the two centuries that have passed since its incorporation Newton has made the most liberal appropriations for its public schools, thus standing in the front ranks among the many cities and towns of the Commonwealth."

Newton was an education leader in the mid-1800s due, in large part, to public education advocate and the state's first secretary of education, Horace Mann. Newton was also home to Nathaniel Allen in 1854, founder of the racially integrated West Newton English and Classical High School, which housed the country's first kindergarten.

With great schools come great educators, and countless legends exist among Newton's teachers. Residents tell stories of reading teachers like Larry Zuckerman, the deceased creator of *Zuckerman's Barn*, a website where fifth-graders posted and shared book reviews, creating for students a new approach to reading a book. People invariably mention Jim Marini's name when asked about those who have stood out in the Newton public schools, referring to the former Newton North High School teacher, middle school assistant principal, Newton North principal, assistant superintendent of schools, and finally, interim superintendent of schools for one year. And Mark Springer, long-standing principal of Mason-Rice Elementary School, likely made an unforgettable impression on his students when he appeared in 2009 on the PBS children's show *Arthur* to talk about his cancer diagnosis.

Little surpasses the grief and tragedy that struck the community on April 27, 2001. In this chapter, readers will learn—or revisit—the story about the four middle school children who died in a bus crash during a school band trip to Canada.

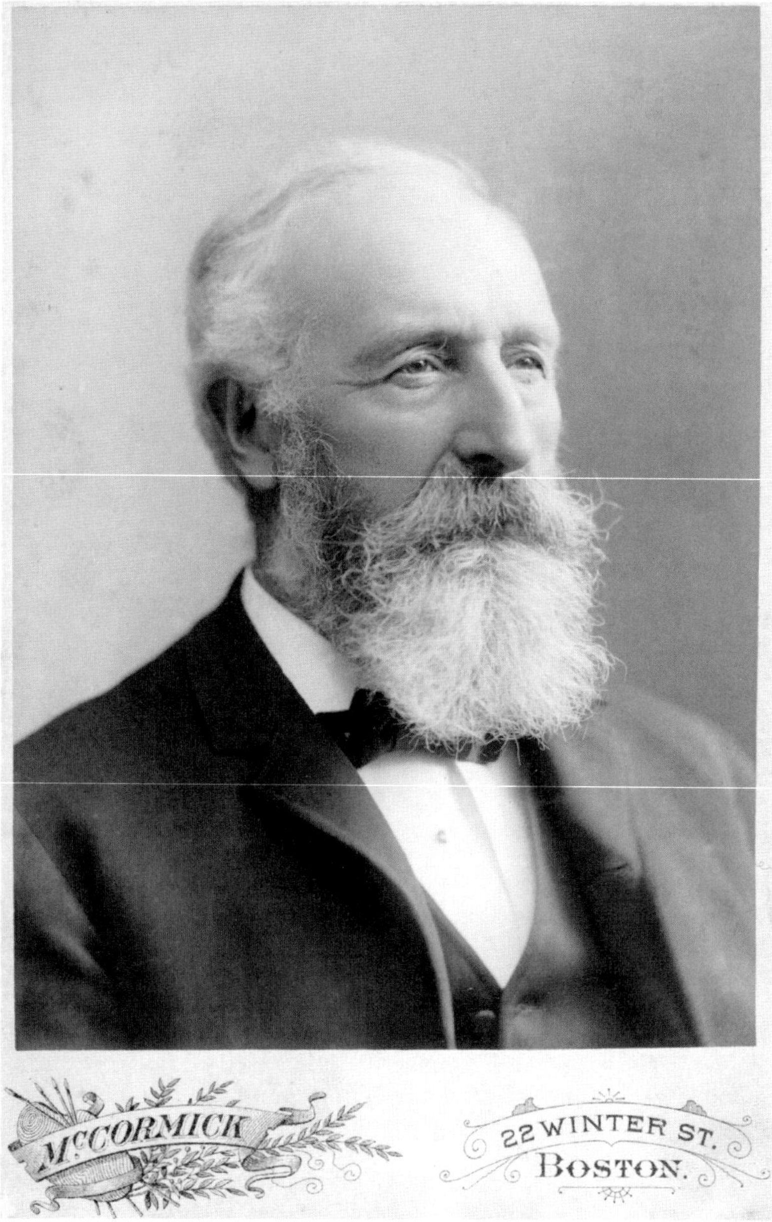

Nathaniel Topliff Allen, Educator
Nathaniel Allen was an educator and reformer who was equally passionate about progressive education, abolition, and women's suffrage. With the encouragement of Newton resident Horace Mann, Allen in 1854 founded the West Newton English and Classical High School, which housed the country's first kindergarten and, unique for its time, accepted students regardless of sex or race. His West Newton home, a stop on the Underground Railroad and where he lived for more than 50 years, was a frequent gathering place for stimulating conversations among politicians, dignitaries, and educators.

Along with the people who shared his passion for liberal causes, Allen was known as one of "the incendiaries and radicals of West Newton." President of the West Newton Anti-Slavery Society, he was also a strong supporter of the temperance and antitobacco movements. (Courtesy of Historic Newton.)

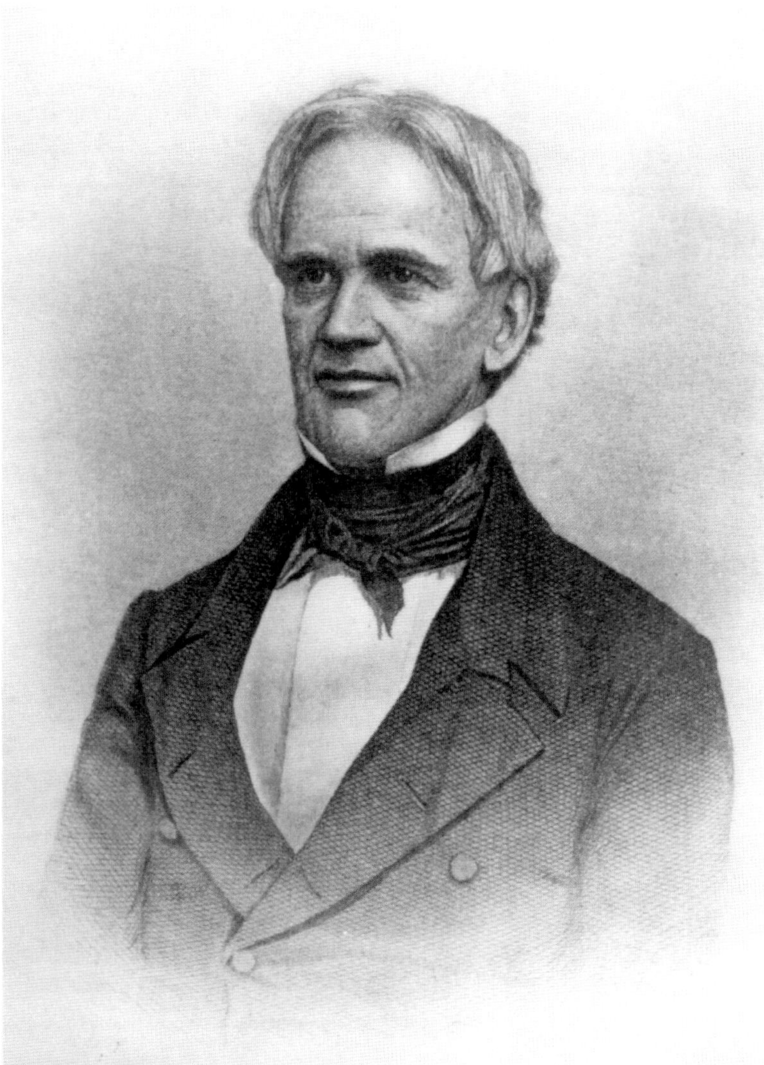

Horace Mann, Architect of Modern Public Education

Massachusetts's first secretary of education, Horace Mann, believed that every child deserved an education regardless of his or her ability to pay for it. Considered by many as "the father of American public education," Mann's influence extended beyond Massachusetts as other states began using taxpayer funds for education.

While running the first State Normal School for teachers in West Newton (after moving it from Lexington) in 1844, Mann built a house on West Newton Hill. The education reformer was one of the founders of the West Newton Athenaeum as a library in 1849. While the library was initially financed by subscriptions and donations, the goal was to turn it into a free library, and in 1894 the Athenaeum merged with the Free Library.

Mann was elected to the US House of Representatives in 1848. In 1851, Mann's brother-in-law Nathaniel Hawthorne and family moved into the Manns' Newton home, where they stayed through half of 1852. There, Hawthorne wrote *The Blithedale Romance*.

The house was demolished in 1854 when Mann moved to Ohio to serve as president of Antioch College. (Courtesy of Historic Newton.)

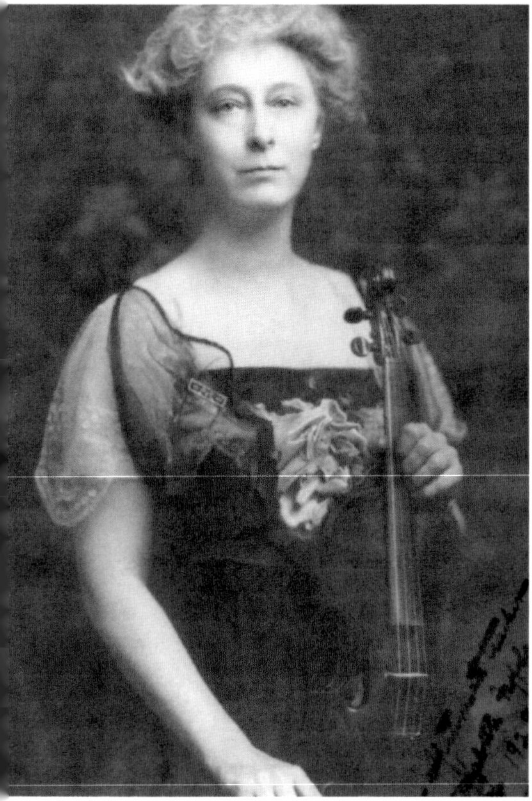

Elizabeth Fyffe, Bringing Music to Newton

Elizabeth Fyffe, founder of the All Newton Music School, moved to Newton from Boston where she had worked at a settlement house giving music lessons to children of poor families. Wanting to do the same for lower-income Newton families, the Cornell music major opened the West Newton Music School in April 1911.

Newton citizens donated generously so that scholarships and instruments could be offered to children who could not afford the fees. In 1920, the school opened a branch in Nonantum, leading to the name change: All Newton Music School. In 1965, it moved to its current home on Chestnut Street. Fyffe retired as director in 1932, though she stayed involved until her death in 1958. (Courtesy of All Newton Music School.)

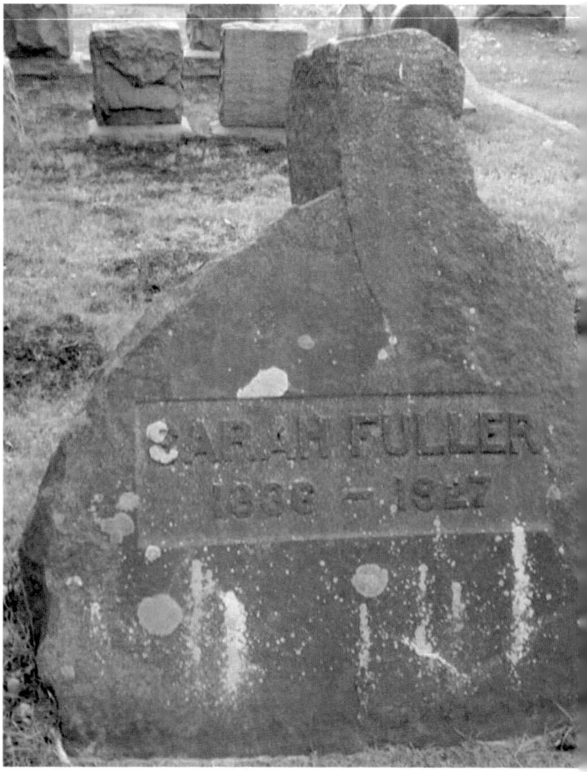

Sarah Fuller, Teacher of the Deaf

Sarah Fuller is credited with teaching Helen Keller to speak. Born in Weston but educated in both Weston and Newton, Fuller was the first principal of the first public school for the deaf, now named the Horace Mann School for the Deaf and Hard of Hearing in Boston. The founder of the Home for Little Deaf Children in 1902, Fuller is buried in St. Mary's Cemetery in Newton Lower Falls. (Photograph by Jan Franco.)

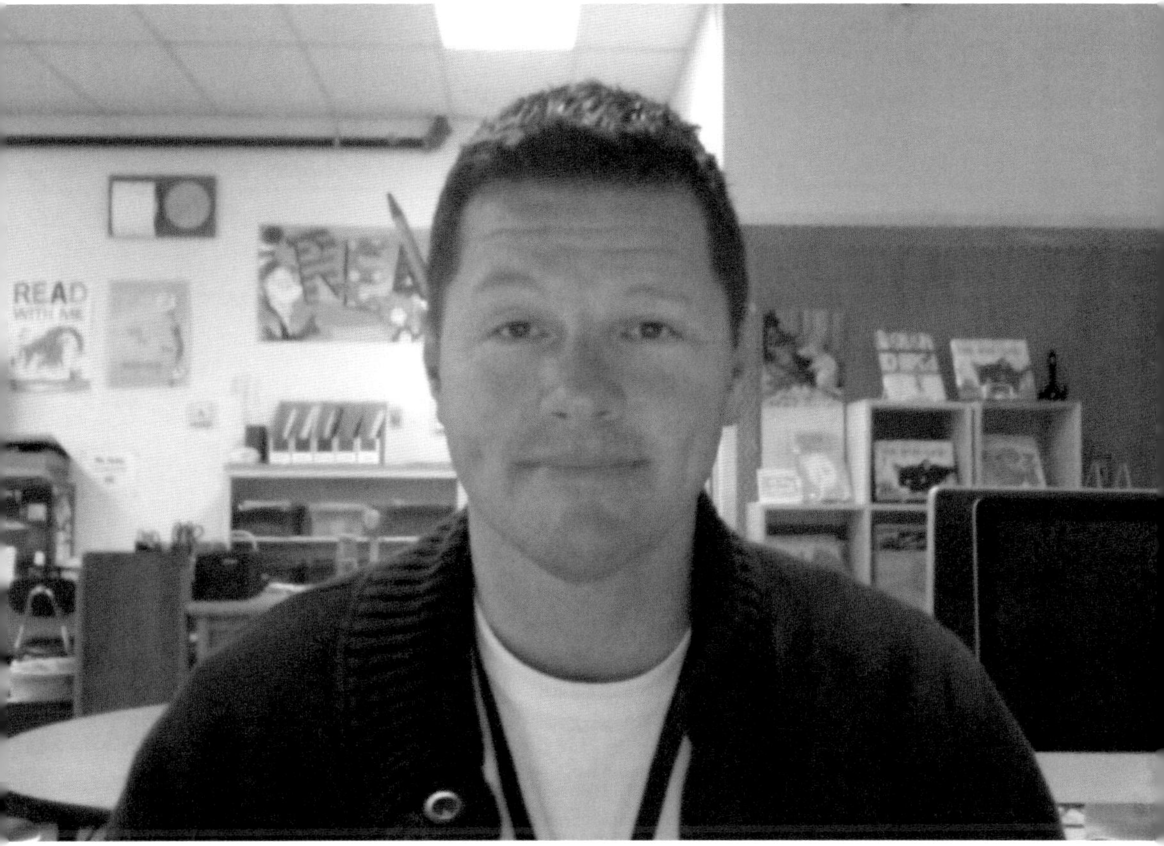

David Gaita, First Grade Teacher Came Out to Class

Before gay marriage was legal anywhere in the United States and before gay and lesbian characters were regulars on television sitcoms and dramas, Burr Elementary School teacher David Gaita came out to his first-grade class.

Gaita did not know that he was going to make national headlines when he walked into his classroom on May 17, 2000. While teaching a lesson on biographies, Gaita answered a student's question directly, telling the children that if he had a boyfriend, he would be a man. A conversation ensued, at the first-grade level, about what it meant to be gay.

Gaita sent a letter to parents advising them of the discussion, and Principal Cynthia Bencal informed the rest of the school families. Some parents were angry that they had not been warned beforehand in order to prepare for discussions with their children, but most supported Gaita.

The story hit the *Boston Globe*, and almost immediately, it made national headlines. Superintendent of schools Jeffrey Young spoke with the radio, television, and print media, always expressing support for Gaita. Mayor David Cohen was equally supportive.

The reaction was not all positive, though. One local radio station conducted a phone-in poll about whether Gaita should be fired. Gaita received death threats and hate letters from around the country, and, locally, vandals slashed the tires on his car.

The first-graders kept learning and stopped using the term "gay" offensively, according to Gaita, who continues to teach first grade at Burr. (Courtesy of David Gaita.)

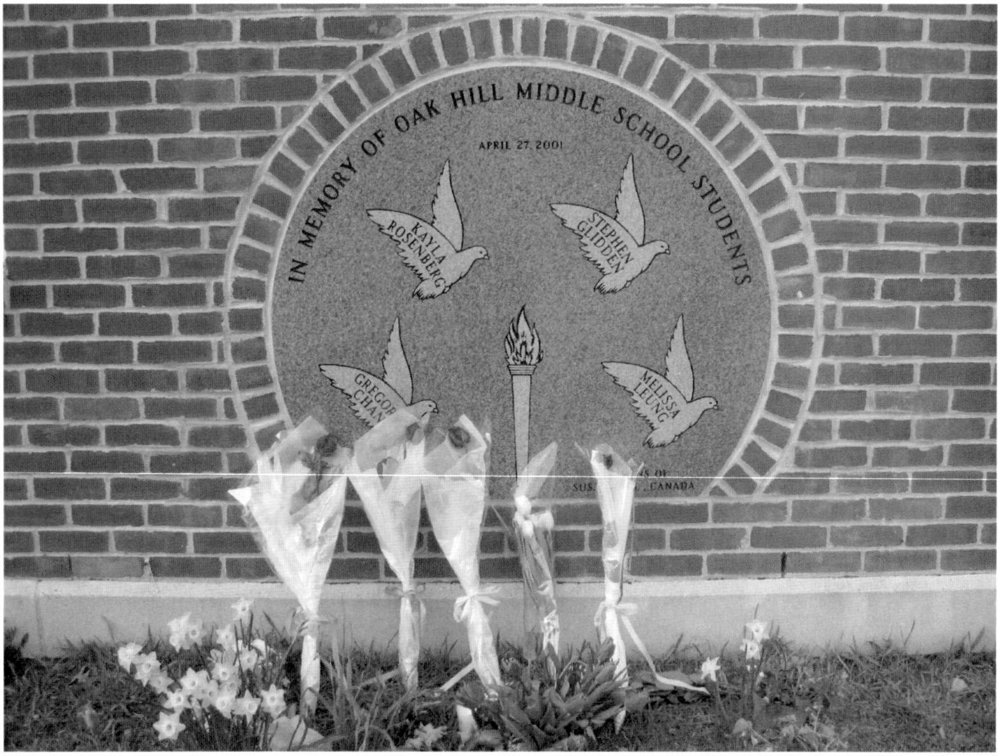

Stephen Glidden, Melissa Leung, Greg Chan, and Kayla Rosenberg
Seventh-grader Stephen Glidden (pictured on opposite page) was two weeks shy of his 13th birthday when he boarded the bus for the middle school band trip on the evening of Thursday, April 26, 2001. He and 41 other Oak Hill Middle School students, chaperoned by seven adults, were headed to Halifax, Nova Scotia, for a weekend of fun, excitement, and music. When Glidden returned, he would continue with his lessons for his June bar mitzvah.

The bus that left Newton at 7:00 p.m. never made it to its final destination. Nine hours of bus games, movies, and sleep later, there was an accident. The bus had flipped on a sharply curving highway exit outside Sussex, New Brunswick, killing four children who were in the back of the bus and injuring several others. Glidden, 12; eighth-grader Melissa Leung, 14; and seventh-graders Greg Chan, 13, and Kayla Rosenberg, 13, would not return to their Newton homes. The deaths of the four children at once shook and united the community.

April 27, 2001, and the days that followed are etched in the memories of most people living in Newton at the time. The city of 84,000 suddenly felt like a small town. Stories unfolded about parents hopping in their cars to drive to Sussex before knowing the extent of their children's injuries, children learning about the deaths of their best friends, and teachers putting aside their grief while comforting their students.

Residents of Newton and the Greater Boston area got to know the four children whose lives were cut short: Steve, a mischievous and sweet tenor saxophonist who loved the outdoors; Greg, a clarinetist and soccer player who loved to make people laugh; Melissa, a flutist with a caring heart who was never afraid to speak her mind; and Kayla, a trumpeter and lacrosse player known for her cheery disposition.

Each year on April 27, a Circle of Remembrance gathers outside Oak Hill Middle School to share stories, remember, cry, and laugh. Classmates who are now adults return and reflect on their appreciation now for what their teachers must have endured silently while comforting students.

From grief came some good, though, with Steve's family establishing the Steve Glidden Foundation to send disadvantaged children to camp and Kayla's family assisting in the development of an affordable housing project named the Kayla Rosenberg House. (Both courtesy of Elaine Alpert.)

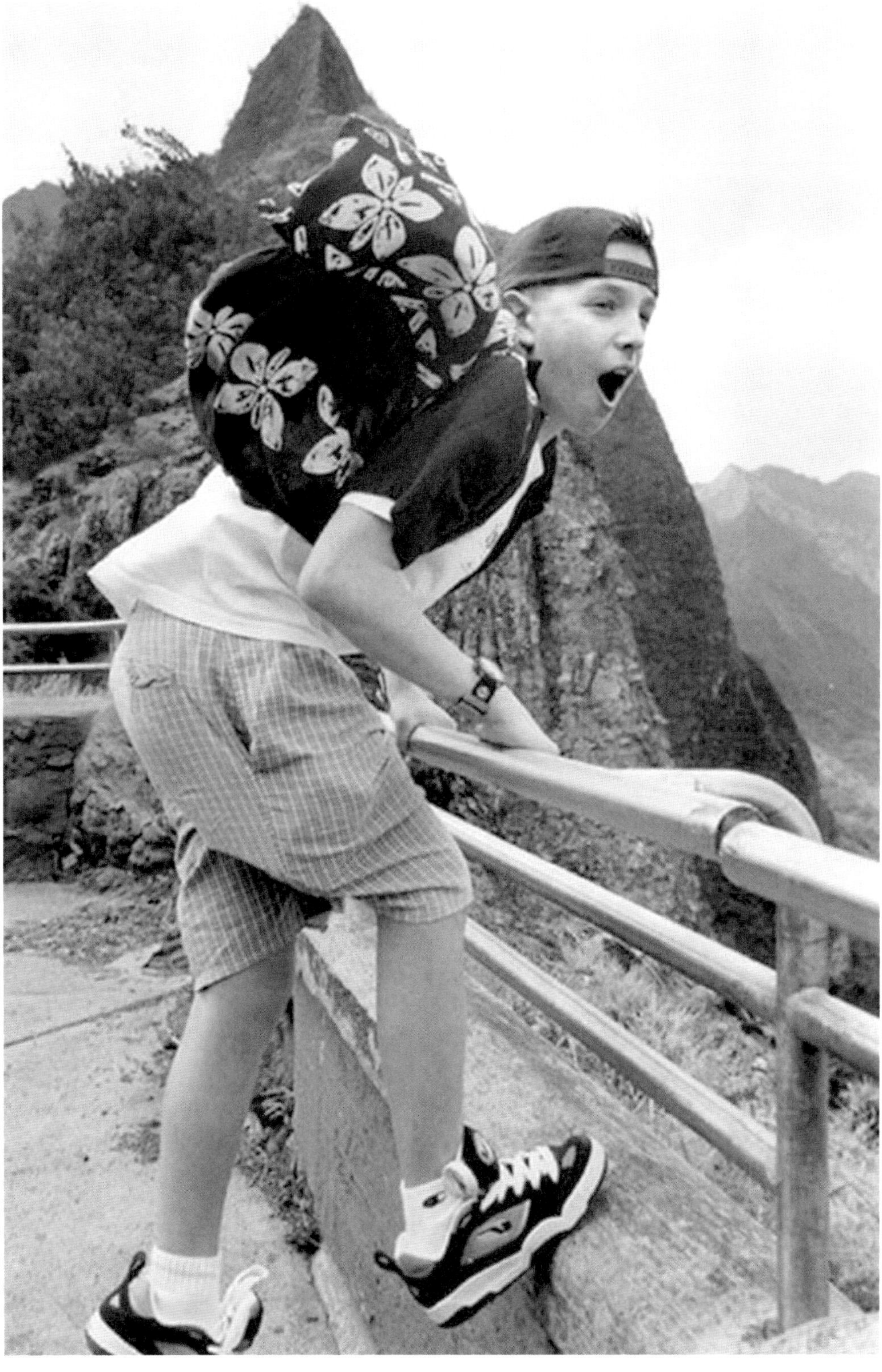

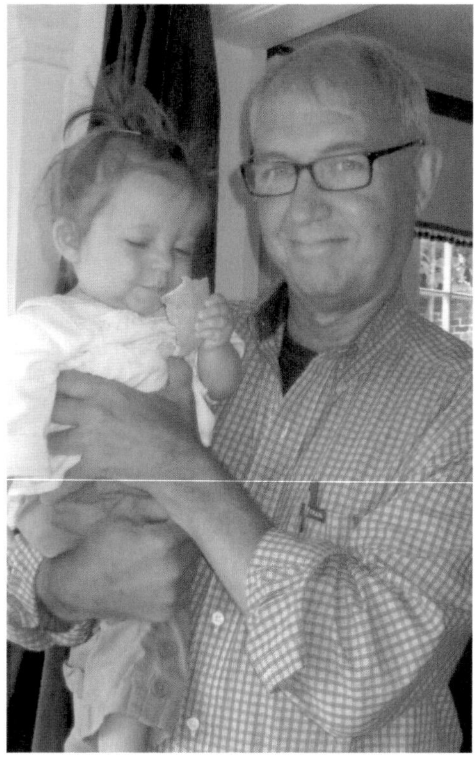

Thomas DePeter, English Teacher Earns an A

A lifetime scholar of literature, poetry, and philosophy, Tom DePeter taught English for 35 years at Newton North. A popular and unconventional teacher, he rejected standard learning techniques in favor of exposing students to the *New Yorker* and Woody Allen. They acted out works by the country's finest writers, and, one student said, he was such a good teacher that they forgot there was college credit at stake.

DePeter's true passion was drama, and he directed many challenging plays at Newton North, where he also coached the boys' lacrosse team to several successful seasons. (Courtesy of Sharon DePeter.)

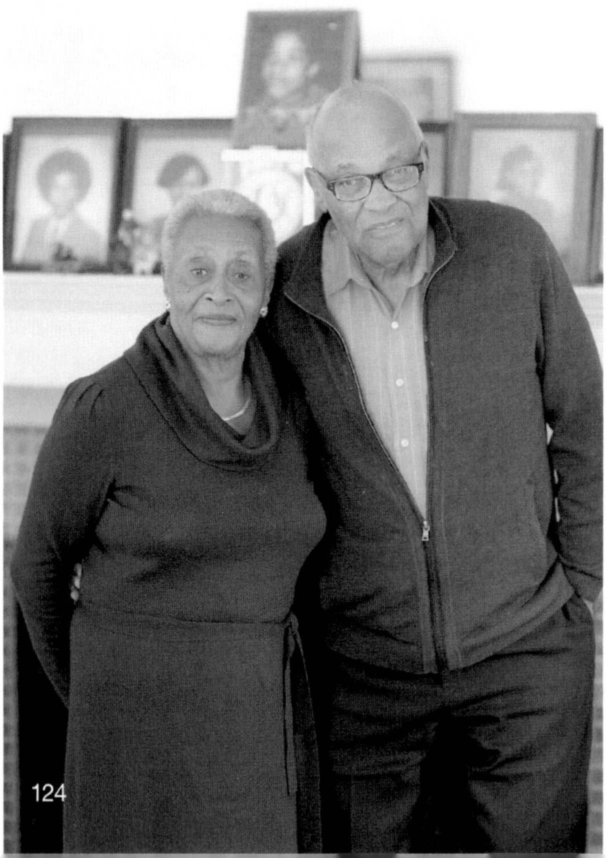

Katherine Butler Jones, First METCO Director

Katherine Butler Jones is a founding member of Metropolitan Council for Educational Opportunities (METCO) who was integral in building the program in Newton. After the state cut funding and the conservative Newton School Committee followed suit, Jones quit her 10-year job as the program's director and successfully ran for school committee, making her Newton's first African American school committee member. Jones, who is married to civic activist Hubie Jones (page 30), is an educator who cofounded and codirected the Roxbury-Newton Freedom School. She taught African American history at Boston University and urban education at Simmons and Wheelock Colleges. Jones has published several works on African American history. (Photograph by Brett Crawford; courtesy of Wicked Local Newton.)

BIBLIOGRAPHY

Anderson, Peter. "The Mann Behind the Mayor." *Boston Globe.* July 9, 1992.

Bernstein, Burton. *Family Matters.* New York: Summit Books, 1982.

bikesnobnyc.blogspot.com/2008/02/thanks-sheldon_05.html

Evans, Alison Ridley, ed. *Newton Centennial: 1873–1973.* Newton Centennial Commission, 1973.

Greene, Mary A. *Nathaniel T. Allen: Teacher, Reformer, Philanthropist.* Providence: 1906.

guides.newtonfreelibrary.net/newtonhistory

Hyde, James. "Address of Hon. James F.C. Hyde, First Mayor of Newton." Printed by Avery L. Rand, 1891.

Lucas, Peter. "Lowell's Always Been a Knockout to Joe DeNucci." *Lowell Sun.* January 28, 2010.

millercenter.org/president/harding/essays/cabinet/474

Nyhan, David. "The Mayor for All Seasons." *Boston Globe.* June 29, 1993.

Smith, S.F. *History of Newton, Massachusetts: Town and City From Its Earliest Settlement to the Present Time, 1630–1880.* Boston: The American Logotype Company, 1880.

Sweetser, M.F. *King's Handbook of Newton Massachusetts.* Boston: Moses King Corporation, 1889.

www.bostonglobe.com

www.emmytvlegends.org

www.govtrack.us

www.historicnewton.org

www.nobelprize.org

www.npr.org

www.odmp.org

www.wickedlocal.com/newton

INDEX

Albee, Edward Franklin II, 101
Albee, Edward Franklin III, 101
Albright, Tenley, 89, 93
Allen, Caroline Bassett, 17, 78
Allen, Nathaniel Topliff, 17, 78, 118
Allen, Woody, 124
Anderson, Judy, 33
Angier, Albert, 83
Ashbrook, Tom, 107, 114
Asimov, Isaac, 107
Avruch, Frank, 107, 112
Ball, Adelaide, 37
Bates, Katharine Lee, 9
Bauckman, Wendell, 36
Beard, Carol, 26
Beatrice, Jeffrey, 21
Bell, Frederick, 81
Bell, Henry, 80, 81
Bencal, Cynthia, 121
Bernstein, Leonard,100
Berrier, Senneth, 63
Bixby, Henry, 79
Boivin, Leo, 90
Bonnar, James King, 108
Bookbinder, Susan, 26
Brady, Lynne, 87
Brennan, Ken, 65
Brooke, Edward, 37
Brown, Sheldon, 57
Bruyn, Louise, 17, 25
Brzhnev, Leonid, 55
Bush, Barbara, 113
Carter, James P. Jr., 81
Chan, Greg, 122
Charles, Ray, 102
Chazov, Evgeni, 55
Chiel, Samuel, 78
C.K., Louis, 99
Clarke, Jaime, 61
Cohen, David, 33, 38, 41, 44, 49, 71, 121
Collins, Shano, 92
Coolidge, Calvin, 34, 35
Cooper, Audrey, 7, 24
Cotton, Mary, 45, 61
Cuenin, Walter, 69, 73, 76
Dall, Catherine Wells Healey, 78
Damon, Matt, 32, 99
Davis, Bette, 99
DeNucci, Joseph, 42
DePeter, Tom, 124
Diamant, Anita, 115
DiMaggio, Dominic, 89, 92
DiMaggio, Joe, 89, 92
Dinno, Raied and Saad, 45
Dodd, Christopher, 43
Drinan, Robert, 25
Dukakis, Michael, 27, 28, 29
Eddy, Mary Baker, 69
Emerson, Ralph Waldo, 107
Farlow, John, 11
Feeley, Charlie, 79
Fell, William, 82
Ferrera, Angelo, 61
Fig Newton, 39, 46
Fineberg, Gwendolyn, 26
First Unitarian Society in Newton, 69, 78
Ford, Gregory, 69
Fournier, Jeff, 68
Frank, Barney, 28, 43
Fuller, Sarah, 120
Fyffe, Elizabeth, 120
Gaherin, Seana, 46
Gaita, David, 7, 121
Gay, Ella Mae, 26
Gilfix, Benjamin, 72
Gilfix, Beri, 72
Glidden, Stephen, 122, 123
Gold, Gracie, 89
Gorbachev, Raisa, 113
Griffith, Emile, 42
Grossman, Steve, 28
Guillemin, Robert "Sidewalk Sam," 107
Hamilton, Pete, 89
Hannigan, Peg, 28, 29
Harding, Warren, 33, 34
Harwood, Paulette, 50
Haskell, Edwin, 107
Hawthorne, Nathaniel, 107, 119
Haywood, Howard, 71
Horvitz, H. Robert, 55
Huggins, Tim, 61
Hughes, Michael, 80
Hull, Josephine, 101
Hyde, James, 7, 10, 117
Jackson, John, 37
Jackson, William, 12, 13
Jacobson, Keith, 111
Jaynes, Julian, 69
Johnson, Thomas, 70
Jones, Hubert Eugene, 30, 124
Jones, Katherine, 124
Kaplan, Gerald, 87
Kaufer, Stephen, 45, 56
Keith, B.F., 101
Keller, Helen, 120
Kelley, Edmund, 70
Kennedy, Edward, 25, 33
Kennedy, Joseph III, 28
Kerry, John, 28, 29
Khachadourian, Rene, 60
King, B.B., 102
Koch, Jim, 45, 51
Kosa, Catherine, 26
Kourtis, Bill and Nick, 59
Kourtis, Toula, 58, 59
Krasinski, John, 99, 104
Kurzweil, Ray, 45, 48
Law, Bernard, 73
LeBlanc, Matt, 99, 105
Lemmon, Jack, 102
Leung, Melissa, 122
Levi, Leo, 20
Leviton, Michael, 56
Levy, Milt, 109
Levy, Paul, 49
Lewis, Robert, 87
Lewis, Virginia, 87
Lewis, Shirley, 102
Likely, Richard, 85
Lippin, Elmer, 69

Littlefield, Elliot, 82
Lodge, Henry Cabot, 40
Lown, Bernard, 55
Lucchino, Larry, 31
Lyons, Tom, 60
Mamet, David, 107
Mann, Horace, 17, 78, 117, 119
Mann, Mary Peabody, 17, 78
Mann, Ted, 24, 27, 33, 38, 39, 44, 46
Marini, Jim, 117
Mark, Bow Sim, 98, 106
Marrocco, Dominic, 79, 84
Marrocco, Roger, 23
Marsh, Linda, 26
McNamara, Ray, 79, 86, 87
Merrill, Carleton, 40
Miller, Toni, 26
Mitchell, James Henry, 46
Murphy, Lawrence, 79, 80
Myerson, Roger, 54
New England Mobile Book Fair, 45, 60
Newcomb, Ken, 111
Newton firefighters, 86, 87
Newton, Juice, 46
NewtonSERVES, 17
Newtonville Books, 7, 45, 61
Novak, B.J., 99, 104
Nyhan, David, 38
Obama, Barack, 44
O'Brien, Conan, 105
O'Hara, John, 46
O'Hara, Karl, 46
Ortiz, David, 89
Pappas, Mary Margaret, 26
Patrick, Deval, 44
Patton, George, 84
Pellegrini, Anthony "Fat," 22, 23, 28
Joanne Pellegrini, 23
Peltier, Ernie, 33
Pergament, Russel, 107, 111
Pettee, Otis, 16
Pickett, Wilson, 102
Plaut, Linda, 17
Pomroy, Rebecca, 9
Powell, Tyrone, 88
Prestejohn, Catherine, 52, 53
The Prestejohn family, 52, 53
Preston, Robert, 99
Radlo, Lillian Shapiro, 33
Reilly, Jerry, 111
Rice, James, 85
Rice, John, 85
Roberts, Richard, 54
Roosevelt, Theodore Jr., 35
Rosenberg, Jothy, 94, 95
Rosenberg, Kayla, 122
Roser, Charles, 46
Ross, Donald, 90
Rossi, Armando, 20
Ruth, George Herman "Babe," 116
Ryan, Holly, 31
Saltonstall, Leverett, 33, 40
Sandman, Mark, 106
Sangiolo, Amy, 41
Schickel, Trina, 26
Schon, Nancy, 107, 113
Sellers, David, 64
Sellers, David Jr., 64
Shanley, Paul, 69, 73
Sharp, Phillip, 54
Shaughnessy, Dan, 116
Sheehy, Rita, 26
Sherman, Roger, 11
Simpson, Edward, 80
Sloane, Barbara, 45
Sloane, Marshall, 45, 62
Smith, Samuel Francis, 16
Spear, Margaret, 36
Springer, Mark, 117
Springsteen, Bruce, 18
Stanley, F.E., 14, 15
Stanley, F.O., 14, 15
Starr, Billy, 17, 31
Stewart, Jimmy, 101
Stith, Charles, 18
Stives, Karen, 66
St. Mary of Carmen Society, 22, 23, 69, 74–77
Strymish, Louis, 60
Stulin, David, 87
Swartz, Michael, 63
Tatelman, Barry, 66, 67
Tatelman, Eliot, 66, 67
Totenberg, Nina, 103
Totenberg, Roman, 103
Twellman, Taylor, 89
Tsarnaev, Dzhokhar, 88
Turner, Ike and Tina, 102
Understanding Our Differences, 26
Varitek, Jason, 89, 96, 97
Warren, Joseph, 27, 29
Warren, Setti, 27, 28, 29, 38, 44
Weeks, John, 33, 34, 35
Weeks, Sinclair, 34
Wellman, William, 99
Wennbergh, Russell and Lillian, 66
White, Kevin, 43
Williams, Ted, 89, 91
Winslow, Sanford, 110
Yen, Donnie, 106
Youkilis, Kevin, 58, 89, 98
Young, Jeffrey, 121
Zakim, Leonard, 17, 18, 19
Zinn, Howard, 32
Zuckerman, Larry, 117